PAST TIMES

PAST TIMES

A daybook of Knoxville history

By Stephen V. Ash

The Knoxville News-Sentinel

A Scripps Howard Newspaper
Printed in the United States of America
First printing
ISBN 0-9615656-8-3

Foreword

Past Times is one of the most important contributions to Knoxville's Bicentennial celebration.

In college, I majored in history. This course of study gave me a deep appreciation for both the importance and the urgency of understanding our past.

In the crush of our daily lives, it is often difficult for us to have time to reflect on past events that have shaped our community and the course of our lives.

Stephen V. Ash has done an outstanding job of capsulizing important periods of our past. He presents the past in an interesting, informative way.

Most importantly, he transforms key periods from our history into relevant topics for us today.

I salute Stephen Ash and The Knoxville News-Sentinel for this much-needed and appreciated contribution to our Bicentennial.

—Victor Ashe
Mayor of Knoxville
July, 1991

Author's preface

Knoxville's 200 years of history have been crowded with fascinating events and colorful characters. This book, which is part of The Knoxville News-Sentinel's contribution to the Knoxville Bicentennial celebration, recounts an episode from the city's past for each day of the year. These 365 articles were originally published as a daily column that ran in The News-Sentinel during the bicentennial year, 1991, under the title, Past Times.

Historically-minded readers will find in this volume plenty of information on the major events and forces that shaped Knoxville's history and on the men and women who played prominent historical roles. And, for the trivia buffs, the book also brings to light many of the forgotten characters and less-than-earthshaking episodes that have enlivened the city's past.

Only a few of the numerous people who contributed in some way to this volume can be mentioned here. Harry Moskos, editor of The News-Sentinel, originated the idea of publishing a day-by-day bicentennial history of Knoxville. Susan Alexander, News-Sentinel public service director, oversaw the whole project and took responsibility for layout, design and illustrations. Martin Gehring of The News-Sentinel designed the book cover. Sam Venable, Georgiana Vines and Chrystal White proofread the text. Valuable assistance in obtaining historical information and illustrations was provided by Nick Wyman and other staff members at the Special Collections department of the University of Tennessee Library; by Steve Cotham and his staff at the McClung Collection of the Lawson McGhee Library; and by Robert J. Booker of the Beck Cultural Exchange Center. Susan Wessels of Knoxville rendered very helpful services as a research assistant.

Photo acknowledgments

The News-Sentinel acknowledges with thanks the individuals and organizations that loaned photographs or sketches to accompany this text. They are:

Nick Wyman and the Special Collections department of University of Tennessee Library for the illustrations on pages 7, 33, 34, 38, 45, 50, 53, 56, 57, 63, 77, 85, 108, 120, 135, 138, 142, 154, 176, 177, 180, 186, 187 and 205;

University of Tennessee Archives for the photos on pages 32, 51 and 156;

Steve Cotham and the East Tennessee Historical Society for illustrations on pages 1, 3, 8, 22, 23, 35, 49, 78, 116 and 133;

Bob Booker and the Beck Cultural Exchange Center for the photos on pages 17, 96, 139 and 161;

Retired Capt. Jack Lewis of the Knoxville Fire Department for the photo on page 44;

Sgt. Ida Webb and the Knoxville Police Department for the photo on page 195;

The University of Tennessee Athletic Department for the photo on page 43;

Frances Curtis Young for the illustrations on pages 20 and 28; and

Jonathan Utley for the photo on page 196.

All remaining photographs are from The News-Sentinel's library files.

On the cover: A view of Gay Street looking south from Vine Avenue.

Jan. 1, 1794

On Jan. 1, 1794, William Blount issued a proclamation ordering the first territorial legislature to assemble in Knoxville the following month. Blount, a prominent North Carolina politician and land speculator, was at that time governor of the Southwest Territory, which later became the state of Tennessee. He had received that appointment in 1790 from his friend and ally, President George Washington, after North Carolina ceded its western lands to the new federal government.

William Blount

When Blount issued his proclamation, Knoxville was hardly more than two years old. Blount had chosen it to be the capital of the territory in 1791.

Knoxville and the other trans-Appalachian settlements in those years were rough, raw frontier villages at the edge of civilization. Blount's biggest problem as territorial governor, besides overseeing the establishment of county governments and looking after his own speculative enterprises, was dealing with the often hostile Cherokee Indians. The influx of white settlers that eventually overwhelmed the Cherokees soon brought the territory's population to the level required by Congress for the establishment of a legislature. Elections for representatives were held in December 1793.

Jan. 2, 1895

A branch of the Woman's Christian Temperance Union was established in Knoxville on Jan. 2, 1895. Its president was Mrs. L. Lauritzen, and its initial membership was 15. Four years later its membership had increased to 44.

That growth reflected the swelling size and influence of the prohibition movement in America during those years, a movement in which women played an important role.

Organizations such as the WCTU and the Anti-Saloon League achieved many successes at the state level, particularly in the South (Tennessee went "dry" in 1909). Furthermore, with the ratification of the 18th Amendment in 1919, the prohibitionists achieved their dream of a nationwide ban on alcohol.

The WCTU was founded in 1874. Its first Knoxville branch was established in 1883, its second in 1895 and its third in 1898. The activities of the Knoxville branches exemplified the policy of the national WCTU president, Frances Willard, who desired to promote a broad range of reforms beyond prohibition. Knoxville WCTU members ran a free kindergarten, aided "fallen women," helped establish the office of police matron for the city of Knoxville and persuaded the state Legislature to raise the age of consent for girls from 10 to 16 1/2.

Jan. 3, 1850

The first issue of the Knoxville Whig, a weekly newspaper, appeared on Jan. 3, 1850. Its editor and proprietor was William G. "Parson" Brownlow, who would become one of the most colorful characters in Knoxville history.

Born in Virginia in 1805, Brownlow spent 10 years as a circuit-riding Methodist preacher before settling down in 1839 to publish a newspaper in Elizabethton. A year later he moved to Jonesborough, where he published until he moved to Knoxville in 1849.

Like most newspapers in those days, the Whig was a political organ that made no pretense of objective reporting. Among the mottos printed on its masthead were "Cry Aloud and Spare Not" and "Independent in All Things, Neutral in Nothing."

Brownlow used the Whig not only to promote the temperance cause and the economic development of East Tennessee but also to castigate his enemies, of whom there were many. Despite offending many people, he also won a national reputation with his scathing editorials, and the Whig gained a wide readership outside Tennessee. By the end of the 1850s, it boasted a circulation of 12,000 – a remarkable figure for a small-town weekly in those days.

Despite his vociferous defense of the institution of slavery, Brownlow took a strong stand in favor of the Union when the secession crisis began in 1860.

The Civil War years brought him even greater notoriety, and the postwar years saw him elevated to the governorship of Tennessee.

Jan. 4, 1957

On Jan. 4, 1957, the Knoxville Chamber of Commerce reported that industrial employment in the Knoxville area had reached an all-time high of 45,705. The news was cheering to many concerned about Knoxville's economic future.

After World War II, plant closings and layoffs in the textile industry – the city's traditional industrial base – plagued the local economy. In 1956, six new industries – including Dixie Manufacturing Co., Perry Organ Manufacturing Co. and Knoxville Tool & Dye Co. – came to the Knoxville area.

Forty-four existing industries expanded that year. These gains more than compensated for the losses in the textile industry that year.

In 1954, worried that Knoxville's economy was stagnating, the Chamber of Commerce had established a Committee of 100 to create a planned industrial and commercial area in the city and to recruit new industries. In 1957, Chamber manager T.L. Howard boasted that the committee was "operating now . . . the soundest industrial development program in the history of Knoxville."

But Knoxville did not fully share in the nation's post-War boom. Throughout the 1950s, the city's economy lagged. Much later it became apparent that service industries, not manufacturing, were the key to Knoxville's economic future.

Jan. 5, 1915

In the Knoxville newspapers of Jan. 5, 1915, a three-page advertisement appeared announcing the "Great January Sale" at Miller's department store.

Department stores, offering a wide array of merchandise and catering to affluent urbanites, had become a fixture in America's cities by the early 1900s. In a way, they epitomized the most important social and economic trends of that era: urbanization, industrialization, mass production of consumer goods, prosperity and the expansion of the middle class. The establishment of Miller's department store on the northwest corner of Gay Street and Union Avenue symbolized Knoxville's emergence as a modern city.

Miller's department store

Listed in the ad under "Notions" were a large-size box of Ino Magic Cleanser for 15 cents, a nickel-plated alarm clock for 45 cents and seven rolls of Big Deal Crepe Toilet Paper for 25 cents. Pond's Cold Cream was 18 cents a jar. In the jewelry department one could find cut-glass salt and pepper shakers with silver caps for 69 cents a pair. Ladies' silk hosiery was 59 cents a pair. Men's silk ties were 10 cents apiece. Men's button-and-lace shoes were less than $2 a pair. Bath towels cost seven cents, pillow cases 13 cents and wool blankets $1.89. For upscale customers, lynx-fur muffs were available for $5.

Jan. 6, 1947

On Jan. 6, 1947, the East Tennessee Automobile Club appointed a committee to devise a solution to Knoxville's worsening traffic problems.

The number of automobiles in Knoxville grew rapidly after World War II, jamming the city's streets and overwhelming the antiquated traffic control system. Automobile Club secretary-manager Luke Wright, citing a projection that Knoxville's population would grow to 600,000 by the 1970s, declared that "we must do something about our traffic situation before it breaks down completely."

The planning committee was headed by Oak Ridge safety engineer D.A. McWhirter and included Knoxville assistant police chief Herman Dukes, Knoxville Utilities Board sales manager Clyde Carpenter, city transportation coordinator Oscar Tate, and businessmen Gustave Handly and Dewitt Shepard.

In announcing the formation of the committee, Wright offered a few suggestions: the widening of some streets to four lanes, a crackdown on double parking, and stricter enforcement of rules against weaving in and out of traffic.

The replacement of the city's trolley cars by buses later in 1947 reduced the snarls. But, as Knoxvillians today are well aware, the city's traffic problems have never really been solved – they have just moved west with the city's population.

Jan. 7, 1942

By Jan. 7, 1942, one month after the Japanese attack on Pearl Harbor, Knoxvillians were actively involved in the great national effort to secure victory in the Second World War.

On that date the Knox County Red Cross War Fund drive – whose motto was “Fight for the American Way; Give a Day’s Pay to the Red Cross” – drew within $22,000 of its $80,000 goal. TVA employees alone contributed over $5,000.

A Knoxville News-Sentinel editorial urged citizens to put the fund drive over the top: “This is no time to lag in giving. . . . Let’s finish the job this week. . . . Giving to the Red Cross is patriotism in action.”

Enthusiasm for the war effort was accompanied by concern about shortages and rationing. Auto dealers received word that no more new cars would be delivered from Detroit. Grocers, facing a shortage of paper bags, asked customers to bring their own baskets.

Knox County’s two tire rationing boards, having decreed a January allowance of only 446 tires (the usual monthly consumption was 2,000), were deluged with calls from worried citizens, especially business owners and commuters. Dairymen announced a plan to make deliveries every other day rather than daily.

The first tire authorized under the new rationing system went to Jettie M. Cooper, Knoxville city nurse, for her nursing service car.

Jan. 8, 1817

On Jan. 8, 1817, Knoxville took a big stride toward respectability. On that day a group of leading citizens formed a public library company.

Knoxville, just emerging from its frontier period, was a rustic town of 1,000 inhabitants, but some of its residents were determined to smooth its rough edges by promoting cultural endeavors.

Forty-seven men and one woman subscribed $5 or more and signed the “Proposals for Forming a Library Company” on Jan. 8. Like dozens of others established in the United States in those years, it followed the pattern set by Benjamin Franklin’s subscription library of 1732. These were private voluntary organizations. Free public libraries were still some years in the future.

The document drawn up in 1817 by the 48 Knoxvillians reflected the Enlightenment ideals embodied by Benjamin Franklin. It described libraries as “eminently beneficial to a community, in greatly promoting the diffusion of knowledge . . . and creating a taste in the public mind for literary pursuits.”

With the proceeds from the subscriptions, the library members immediately began to procure books. Later that year the Tennessee Legislature bestowed official status by incorporating the Knoxville Library Company.

Jan. 9, 1923

On Jan. 9, 1923, America's most prominent evangelist gave Knoxvillians some of that old-time religion.

Billy Sunday had kicked off his six-week Knoxville revival two days earlier. Each day excited crowds filled the 7,000-seat tabernacle that had been erected on North Gay Street.

At the tabernacle on Jan. 9, he gave his audience a rousing sermon of the kind that had made him famous. He lambasted the selfishness and ingratitude of many professed Christians, and he decried the ethic of "church dignity" that discouraged emotional worship. "Many of you fold your arms in church and sit in your pews until you are mildewed," he declared. "Spiritual life is being killed by church dignity."

Sunday's stirring affirmation of faith and traditional values brought comfort to many who were troubled and bewildered by the rapid changes of the 20th century. Others, however, found his emotionalism and anti-intellectualism distasteful.

But Sunday scoffed at his detractors and boasted of his ignorance. "I don't know anything about theology," he told his Knoxville audience. "I know no more about theology than a jack rabbit does about ping-pong."

Jan. 10, 1934

A committee of city and county officials met on Jan. 10, 1934, to discuss the alarming increase in prostitution in Knoxville.

Like other cities all across America, Knoxville was in the grip of the Great Depression. Hard times, unemployment and hunger drove many people to desperation in those years. "Prostitutes on our streets have increased 100 percent in the last six months," announced Knoxville safety director Walter Anderson at the Jan. 10 meeting. "I am insisting that something be done now. These women stay in front of the churches, the YMCA, the YWCA; they are everywhere."

City police officer Mary Allen testified before the committee that "these women stand in doorways and snatch at the men. A minister was attacked. Traveling men say Knoxville is the worst place they ever saw."

The county welfare director declared that the worst public health problem was not tuberculosis but another disease, one that "walks the streets in silks and satins, making goo-goo eyes at the boys."

Knoxville was ill-prepared to deal with the problem. The city had no facilities for the detention of women. The best the committee could do was to resolve to look into the possibility of federal funding for a female prison and to recommend, as a temporary solution, the establishment of a female workhouse or detention center.

Jan. 11, 1796

In Knoxville on Jan. 11, 1796, Tennessee took a major step toward statehood. On that day delegates assembled in response to Territorial Gov. William Blount's proclamation calling for a constitutional convention.

Inhabitants of the Southwest Territory, as Tennessee was then designated, had affirmed in a referendum the previous year their desire for statehood. In December they had elected convention delegates (five from each of the territory's 11 counties).

The convention delegates worked swiftly. On Feb. 6, they unanimously approved Tennessee's first constitution.

Fearful of tyrannical executive power, the delegates limited the authority of the governor and vested most power in a bicameral legislature.

The convention delegates sent the document to President George Washington, who transmitted it to Congress with a recommendation for statehood. After some delay – occasioned by the fear of Federalists that Tennessee would align itself with the Jeffersonian Party in the upcoming national elections – Congress approved a bill granting statehood to Tennessee. President Washington signed it into law on June 1, 1796. Knoxville, which had been the territorial capital since 1790, became the state capital and remained so until 1811.

Jan. 12, 1905

On Jan. 12, 1905, the University of Tennessee Alumni Association issued a public appeal for state funds for the struggling university. The appeal, which would be echoed by every succeeding generation of UT supporters, decried the stinginess of the state government in supporting the university and called on the General Assembly then meeting in Nashville to be generous. And it contrasted Tennessee unfavorably with other states in an attempt to shame the Legislature into action.

"The time has come," the appeal proclaimed, "when we must begin in earnest to build a university which shall offer to the young men and women of Tennessee as good an opportunity for education . . . as the young men and women of other states have." An accompanying chart showed Tennessee dead last among Southern states in funding for higher education.

State funding for the university was a relatively new idea at that time. It was opposed by traditionalists who argued that the state had no obligation to educate its citizens beyond grade school.

Now, however, the Alumni Association called for $100,000. "If the state will help its university liberally, there is no doubt that the university will repay it tenfold in greater wealth and in nobler citizenship."

The appeal was not wholly successful. Only $25,000 was forthcoming from the General Assembly.

Jan. 13, 1816

Jan. 13, 1816, marked an important step in Knoxville's evolution. On that day the town's board of aldermen held its first meeting under the new town charter.

During the territorial period of the 1790s, Knoxville (which was then just a frontier village) was governed by five commissioners appointed by the governor. In 1797, a year after statehood was achieved, the General Assembly decreed that Knoxville's commissioners should be popularly elected.

By 1815, Knoxville had grown into a town of about 1,000 inhabitants, which necessitated a more elaborate form of government. That year, on Oct. 27, the General Assembly formally incorporated the town of Knoxville and created an annually elected board of aldermen to govern it.

The board was authorized to select a mayor from among its seven members. An election was held on Jan. 6, 1816, and one week later Knoxville's first aldermen met at the courthouse.

Thomas Emmerson

They appointed Thomas Emmerson mayor, parceled out other duties among themselves, and then proceeded to levy taxes. Other matters that fell within the purview of the aldermen included establishing a fire company and night watch, drawing up health regulations, regulating businesses, and setting punishments for lawbreakers.

Jan. 14, 1964

University of Tennessee students raised a cry of protest on Jan. 14, 1964, as the ABC television network prepared to bring the popular musical show "Hootenanny" to UT.

The students were objecting not to the show, but to what they described as ABC's attempt to promote a "hillbilly" image of UT. According to stories circulating around campus, representatives of the network had asked students to wear blue jeans, calico skirts, and checked shirts and to sit on hay bales during the show. ("Hootenanny" featured live folk music performances and offered frequent camera shots of the crowd watching and singing along.)

As petitions of protest went around the campus, the university's official spokesman hastened to assure students that ABC had no such patronizing intentions.

Tempers were soothed by the time the show was filmed Jan. 21 on the agriculture campus. The Knoxville News-Sentinel reported that an audience of 3,000 – wearing their customary attire – "sat dazzled, enraptured and entertained" by the Serendipity Singers, Homer and Jethro, and other popular groups.

Presiding over it all was the genial master of ceremonies, Jack Linkletter, who told the crowd that "you are as much a part of this show as the performers. We want you to clap and sing along."

The show was broadcast on national television four nights later.

Jan. 15, 1843

A small group of believers gathered in the upper room of the Knox County Courthouse on Jan. 15, 1843, and founded a church, which eventually became the First Baptist Church of Knoxville.

The first Knoxville Baptist Church was completed in 1850 and cost $8,000.

The little assemblage consisted of 46 persons. Twenty of them were black, probably slaves. (It was customary in the South in those days for slaves to be members in their owner's church.) By August the church had grown to 85 members, thanks to two stirring revivals in Knoxville that spring and summer.

This was an era of immense religious enthusiasm and church growth in America. Christian evangelicals, promising redemption and salvation to the faithful, influenced Knoxville, the South and the nation.

After the Civil War, Knoxville's black Baptists, like freed blacks all over the South, withdrew from the white-dominated church to form their own congregation.

Nevertheless, the First Baptist Church experienced a great growth in membership. By the 1880s, 650 men and women were on its rolls, even though two other white Baptist churches had been established in Knoxville by then. By 1925, First Baptist was Knoxville's biggest church, with more than 1,800 members.

Jan. 16, 1925

Twenty-one East Tennesseans dedicated to preserving their heritage met at the Lawson McGhee Library on Jan. 16, 1925, to establish the East Tennessee Historical Society. At that time, it was the only active historical society in the state.

Among its founders were Mary Utopia Rothrock, head librarian of Lawson McGhee; J.D. Hoskins, dean (and later president) of the University of Tennessee; and historian Philip M. Hamer. In its early years the society's activities were limited to monthly meetings, which featured a talk on a historical topic.

In 1929, the society expanded its mission with the establishment of an annual journal, the ETHS "Publications." Today it is regarded as one of the most successful regional historical societies in the nation. The society publishes books and a genealogy magazine, assists local historical societies throughout East Tennessee, and carries out projects designed to let interested amateur historians research and write history under the guidance of professionals.

The society has over 1,600 members. Its new accommodations in the refurbished Custom House, a Knoxville landmark, will be enhanced during the city's Bicentennial year by the addition of a museum of East Tennessee history.

Jan. 17, 1902

Those who were there no doubt always remembered Jan. 17, 1902, as the day of the "big bang" at the Knoxville Post Office.

Just after 7 o'clock that morning, The Knoxville Sentinel reported, "the post office was thrown into excitement and almost pandemonium." J. W. Martin, postal clerk, had been stamping envelopes as usual when he came to a thick one addressed to George Brown's hardware store. As he hit it with his cancellation stamp, the envelope blew up in his face, knocking him several feet across the room and leaving him dazed. Chief clerk T. M. Shipley, standing nearby, was nearly knocked down himself. Other letters lying near the suspect envelope were blown to bits.

Rumors went around town that some kind of "infernal machine" (i.e., a bomb) had been planted in the mail with criminal intent. But investigation revealed that the likely culprit was a small tin of Wolsrodes' Smokeless Gunpowder being mailed out as a free sample by a firm in New York.

The effectiveness of Wolsrodes' Gunpowder had thus been demonstrated most dramatically, but the authorities were not amused. As The Sentinel pointed out, sending dangerous materials through the mail was a "gross infraction of the postal laws" subject to a $5,000 fine.

Jan. 18, 1982

Monday, Jan. 18, 1982, will be forever remembered in Knoxville as the day of the great ice storm. The National Weather Service had predicted freezing rain for that evening, but no one thought it would bring the city to a halt.

It was the worst storm of its kind in Knoxville history. Streets became treacherous soon after the rain began falling at 6 p.m. Everything was coated with a slick layer of ice. More than 150 accident reports were called in before the police gave up trying to record them. Abandoned cars littered the streets. Police finally declared all roads impassable and grounded their own cruisers. Only five officers reported for the 10 p.m. shift.

Thousands of people spent the night in their cars or in restaurants or bars. The next morning found one business open downtown – Henry's Restaurant on South Gay Street, where a few customers managed to slide in for breakfast.

City salting trucks could not get out until 9 a.m., and then had to turn back due to the icy roads. Buses did not run, schools and the airport were closed, and an eerie quiet blanketed the city.

Temperatures soon warmed up and things were back to normal by Tuesday evening. Some time later, The Knoxville News-Sentinel ran a series on the great ice storm.

A deserted Gay Street the morning after Knoxville's ice storm

Jan. 19, 1838

Representative government in Knoxville took a big step forward on Jan. 19, 1838. On that day the General Assembly amended Knoxville's charter to make the town's government more responsive to the will of the people.

Since 1815, when the original charter was granted, the town had been run by seven aldermen, elected at large, who selected the mayor from among their own members. The amendment of 1838 provided for the popular election of the mayor and for the aldermen's election by ward.

The first mayoral election was held a year later in January 1839. W.B.A. Ramsey beat James Park by 49 votes to 48.

Later that year an ordinance was passed dividing the town into three wards, each to be represented by two aldermen. Knoxville was thus touched by the spirit of democratic reform that swept America during what is now called the Jacksonian era.

But the democracy that Knoxvillians and other Americans created was limited. Women could not vote, nor could slaves, nor could anyone under the age of 21. The fact that fewer than 100 voters took part in the first mayoral election, at a time when Knoxville had about 1,800 residents, reflected not just voter apathy but restricted suffrage.

Jan. 20, 1890

On Jan. 20, 1890, The Knoxville Sentinel published the results of its investigation of a new election law mandating the use of secret ballots.

Two days earlier the city had held its first election under Tennessee's Dortch law, which required that in the state's big cities the Australian ballot system be used. Under that system the voter marked a special ballot in secret.

The practice before that time was for the voter to turn in a printed ticket bearing the name of the candidate of his choice. This facilitated corruption, many believed, because big-city machine politicians had tickets printed up by the thousands for distribution to poor, ignorant voters whose votes they had bought. Under the Australian system, however, the political bosses had no way of knowing if the votes they paid for were actually cast the way they wanted.

After thoroughly investigating the matter, The Sentinel concluded that the Australian ballot was "the best system yet devised for rescuing our elections from the debauching influences of the briber." On election day "the professional (ward) heelers and dispensers of boodle found their occupation well nigh gone. They could stand aloof and give their instructions, but . . . there was no assurance that the votes were delivered as bargained for. . . . It was the most orderly city election we have had in 25 years."

Jan. 21, 1840

The great presidential election race of 1840 was in full swing by Jan. 21 of that year, and on that day Knoxville's Democratic newspaper leveled a broadside at the Whig candidate.

E. G. Eastman, editor of the Knoxville Argus and Commercial Herald, was enthusiastic and unrestrained in denouncing Gen. William Henry Harrison, whom he called "the old lady." He reviled Harrison as an abolitionist – an absurd charge, but one sure to win votes among the strongly proslavery citizens of Knoxville.

Furthermore, Eastman claimed that Harrison favored a law allowing creditors to require debtors to work off their debts through personal servitude. "This might do for the 12th century, for the days of feudalism," the editor remarked sarcastically, "but it should stamp into indelible disgrace the name of that man, who had dared such an insult" to American liberty and justice.

Such exaggerated rhetoric was a hallmark of the presidential race of 1840, the famous "log cabin and hard cider" campaign. Unfortunately for Eastman and his fellow Democrats, the Whigs also understood the game of political hype. By portraying the Democratic candidate, Martin Van Buren, as an effete, wine-sipping aristocrat – in contrast to Harrison, whom they idealized as a simple and unpretentious man who lived in a log cabin and drank hard cider – the Whigs rode to victory in the election.

Jan. 22, 1916

An editorial in The Knoxville Sentinel on Jan. 22, 1916, took the nation's colleges to task for failing to teach their students about current events.

What sparked The Sentinel editor's indignation was an article in The New York Times discussing the results of a current events test given to students at two Northeastern colleges.

The test, according to The Sentinel, showed the students to be "densely ignorant or oblivious of all the tremendous events that are shaking the world."

World War I was then raging in Europe and every day the newspapers were filled with stories about it. Yet many of the students were unable to answer such basic questions as: Who is in command of the French army? Who is the prime minister of England? Who is von Hindenburg? Where is Gallipoli?

"Would it not be a good idea," The Sentinel editor opined, "to substitute a course of current newspaper reading for the history course in our colleges and universities for the time being? There is more history in the making at the present time than ever before since the beginning of recorded time."

A current events course, he concluded, would be "vastly more profitable and productive than studies of the past."

Jan. 23, 1958

Jan. 23, 1958, marked the end of an era in Knoxville. On that day the postmaster of Knoxville announced that all spittoons would be removed from the post office.

Spittoons had long been a fixture in Knoxville's public buildings. They had survived even after the tobacco habits of the public changed. To some, they seemed as indispensable as the American flag and the president's portrait, even if few men still chewed.

In 1958, however, postal officials in Washington declared that for reason of health and economy the spittoons had to go. They cited the case of New York City, where a special platoon of cuspidor cleaners had to be employed by the post office at a cost of $80,000 a year.

Knoxville Postmaster C. Edwin Graves supported the new policy, and he expressed regret that his jurisdiction extended only to the first floor of the federal building, where the post office was located. In the federal court offices on the floors above, spittoons would remain. U.S. District Court Judge Robert L. Taylor and U.S. Attorney John C. Crawford Jr. were both known to take an occasional chew while mulling over matters of law.

Likewise, the two battered spittoons that flanked the lawyers' tables in the federal courtroom would remain. Great traditions die hard.

Jan. 24, 1971

In a newspaper article published on Jan. 24, 1971, Knoxvillians voiced many of the discontents that plagued the nation in that era.

Tormented by the Vietnam War, political extremism, and economic woes, Americans were an anguished people in the early 1970s.

In an effort to understand the public mood, The Knoxville News-Sentinel sent out a reporter to ask a cross-section of citizens what was on their minds. "I think the country's going downhill," a TVA employee remarked. "Unemployment, for one thing, and the high cost of living. . . . I don't know what it will take to change it."

A retiree agreed that the country has "gone to the dogs. . . . There's a whole lot of things I'd like to see changed. The Vietnam War is one of them. I don't think our boys should be over there."

A young activist feared that "control is being taken away from the people" and that America was becoming a "fascist-type state." At the other end of the political spectrum, a policeman declared that the "police can't do anything (to fight crime) any more. . . . We really need the judges and the courts on our side." A salesman expressed the sentiments of many older Americans when he spoke wistfully of the days "when I was a boy. It was a much slower, easier life. . . . Everything changes (today) – nothing stays the same."

Jan. 25, 1938

There was good news and bad news for Knoxville at a community forum held in the Knoxville High School auditorium on Jan. 25, 1938. The forum – one of a series sponsored by the local Adult Education Council to address the question, "What kind of a community have we, and where are we going?" – brought out some sobering facts.

Unemployment was lower in Knoxville than in Memphis, Nashville, or Chattanooga – good news in those years of the Great Depression – but the percentage of citizens requiring emergency relief was higher. Wages paid by manufacturers averaged only $900 a year in Knoxville; in the other cities the figure was $1000.

Approximately 40 percent of Knoxvillians lacked tubs or showers, 26 percent were without electricity. In education, Knoxville spent only about half as much per pupil as other American cities of its size. Of those Knoxville and Knox County students who entered first grade, only 44 percent later entered high school and only 15 percent eventually graduated. Knoxville spent less on public health than did Tennessee's other cities.

Knoxville was growing in population and spreading physically but lacked any systematic way of planning for the future.

Jan. 26, 1793

Knoxvillians who read the town's newspaper on Jan. 26, 1793, found vivid reminders of just how precarious frontier life could be.

The pages of the Gazette were filled with news of Indian troubles. Residents of the little outpost that was Knoxville in those years lived with the constant threat of annihilation by native Americans determined to resist the westward migration of the whites.

There was news of Capt. Samuel Hanley, recently released from captivity by Cherokees and Creeks who had decided to spare his life. There was a story about the capture of a woman and her three children, carried off to the Cherokee towns beyond the reach of rescuers. A government interpreter brought in news that the Cherokee chiefs were trying "to induce the young warriors to desist from the commission of depredations on the citizens of the United States."

Given the critical Indian situation, two advertisements in the Gazette took on special significance. Capt. Robert King offered an $8 reward for the capture of William Percifeld, who had deserted from his militia company. And William Cochran, member of another militia company, offered a $10 reward for information leading to the recovery of his stolen rifle, "or fifteen dollars for the gun and thief."

Jan. 27, 1864

On Jan. 27, 1864, two local citizens wrote a letter begging the Union army commander in Knoxville to protect them and others from the Northern troops' plundering and impressment.

Knoxville had been occupied by a large Union force since the previous September. The troops, short on supplies, were forced to scout around the countryside and seize what they could find.

Citizens suffered severely, as the letter from George W. Mabry and H.S. Heiskell made painfully clear. "Their existence is threatened by the destruction of their fencing and the taking of their family supplies of provisions. . . . The soldiers . . . are robbing smokehouses and taking the corn and seed oats.

"If the army needs all we have," the two men concluded, "let us know and we will leave the country. . . . Deal with us as you please, but let us know the worst."

The Union commander on that same day issued orders reminding his troops that many of the local citizens were Unionists who deserved protection. He ordered officers to "take prompt measures" to prevent pillaging.

Furthermore, he said, "officers impressing forage and subsistence must see that enough is left (for) the citizens to prevent their suffering during the coming winter."

Jan. 28, 1888

A letter to the editor in the Jan. 28, 1888, issue of The Knoxville Sentinel called attention to a problem that has plagued the city ever since: inadequate teachers' salaries.

The letter-writer, who signed himself or herself "Observer," set forth facts and figures showing that "many of our best teachers have been driven from the field by low wages." School principals in Knoxville received only $55 to $75 per month. In Chattanooga, by contrast, they received $90 to $115.

"Our public schools are the pride of the city," Observer insisted, "and the corps of teachers will compare favorably in efficiency with any Southern city." But "meager salaries" imposed a hardship on the teachers, who were "expected to keep up with the times in methods and improvements in teaching, wear respectable clothing, (and) pay for something to eat."

Furthermore, many teachers were paying out of their own pockets for students' pens and other materials.

The letter concluded with a demand for a 25 percent increase in the city's appropriation for schools. The education budget should be at least as large as that for the police force, Observer asserted, because teachers were no less important than policemen "in pushing forward the interests and progress of the city."

Jan. 29, 1844

On Jan. 29, 1844, the Tennessee General Assembly passed an act creating a state school for the deaf, to be established in Knoxville. Later that year the school's trustees met in Knoxville, acquired a school building, and hired teachers and a principal.

The first principal was the Rev. Thomas McIntire, an Ohioan who was an experienced teacher of the deaf. McIntire and his dedicated band of teachers reflected the new attitude toward caring for society's unfortunates that was taking shape in those decades before the Civil War, an era that historians have identified as one of the great reform periods of American history.

Knoxville's School for the Deaf and Dumb, 1848

Inspired by the work of Thomas Gallaudet in Connecticut, a number of states established schools for the training of the deaf. Similar reform efforts brought great changes in the treatment of the blind, the insane, and prisoners.

The first session of the deaf school at Knoxville had an enrollment of nine. By 1857 it had reached 70, making it one of the largest of its kind in the country. Despite interruptions during the Civil War, when the school was closed and the building used as a military hospital, the school continued to grow. By 1898 it had 197 pupils, not counting those in the separate school for blacks that had been established in 1881.

Jan. 30, 1917

On Jan. 30, 1917, the Knoxville school superintendent gave a pep talk to the city's black high school students. Speaking on the opening day of the second term at Knoxville Colored High School, superintendent W.E. Miller urged the students to concentrate on gaining knowledge rather than simply making good grades.

Too many students, he said, focus narrowly on getting a good report card when they should be more broadly interested in acquiring a real foundation of education. Many parents, he pointed out, were guilty of encouraging such misplaced priorities. The question that should be asked of graduates, he insisted, was not "what grades have you made?" but "what can you do?"

Miller's speech was somewhat remarkable for that day and age, for it lacked the racist or patronizing tone that characterized many white pronouncements to black audiences.

The early decades of the 20th century were the most difficult years Southern blacks endured after the abolition of slavery. Lynchings, rigid segregation enforced by Jim Crow laws, and vehement racism kept blacks frightened and oppressed. For the most part, Southern blacks in those years followed the conservative precepts of Booker T. Washington and quietly accepted their subordinate status. There was no other choice.

Knoxville Colored High School, 1916-1928

Jan. 31, 1925

A census of Knoxville's churches taken on Jan. 31, 1925, indicated how big and diversified the city was becoming.

A survey in 1868 had found 13 congregations in the city: four Presbyterian (three white and one black), three Methodist (two white and one black), two Baptist (one white and one black), two Episcopalian, one Roman Catholic and one Jewish. The city's population at that time was more than 8,000.

By 1925 the population had grown to about 90,000 and the number of churches to 134. Moreover, Knoxville's religious diversity had been enriched by the formation of a second Catholic and a second Jewish congregation and by the addition of many previously unrepresented denominations, including Christian, United Brethren, Lutheran, Mennonite, Unitarian, Friends, Christian Science, Seventh-day Adventist and Church of God, as well as several interdenominational churches.

Knoxville's largest church in 1925 was First Baptist, with a membership of 1,812. The fastest growing church in town was University Avenue Methodist, with 112 members – up 433 percent in four years.

Though the Baptists had fewer churches than the Methodists, they had more members than any other denomination.

Feb. 1, 1792

After an arduous journey by wagon from Philadelphia, Hugh Dunlap arrived in Knoxville with a load of goods on Feb. 1, 1792. Dunlap, one of Knoxville's first merchants, had been on the road since December.

Travel between the little frontier town of Knoxville and the main centers of civilization to the east was extremely difficult in those days, and imported goods were therefore scarce and expensive. Nevertheless, for those who could afford such goods, Dunlap and other merchants imported fine cloth, sugar and coffee, books and paper, and even slaves.

Because hard currency was in short supply, barter was common. A pound of gunpowder, for instance, could be had for $1 or three bushels of corn.

Exporting from Knoxville was easier than importing in that era, for flatboats could float down the Tennessee, Ohio, and Mississippi rivers all the way to New Orleans. Thus, very early in its history, Knoxville became an export center for the surplus produce of East Tennessee, which included corn (often in the form of whiskey), bacon, cotton, and furs. It was not until the advent of the steamboat and the railroad some decades later, however, that Knoxville and East Tennessee could truly begin to shed their isolation and enter the national economy.

Feb. 2, 1977

One of the most destructive fires in Knoxville's history broke out on the afternoon of Feb. 2, 1977. It destroyed three clothing manufacturing plants and a retail firm housed in an old building complex on Dale Avenue.

Greenbrier Industries, Jandi Classics, Normak International, and Wynn Retail Center, together employing 1,500 workers, were wiped out in the multi-million dollar blaze. Fortunately, none of the employees was killed or injured.

It required four companies to contain the fire. The huge blaze and smoke column were visible as far away as Loudon County. A witness reported that children smoking cigarettes by the railroad tracks had started a small grass fire behind the building. Firefighters were called immediately, but a wall hindered access to the area. The fire quickly spread to the building, which had housed the Appalachian Spinning Mill and was still filled with highly flammable cotton lint.

An even worse disaster was averted when fire crews managed to prevent the spread of the fire to some fuel tanks at the west end of the building, only a few hundred feet from the Rohm and Haas plant.

This fire was one of several disastrous ones that struck Knoxville in the 1970s, including the Gay Street Terminal Building fire of 1974 and the Silver Manufacturing fire of 1976.

Firefighters battle the blaze at the Wynn Retail Center.

Feb. 3, 1899

On Feb. 3, 1899, Knoxville welcomed home 200 veterans of the Spanish-American War.

Nearly a year earlier, in April 1898, when the war had broken out and a wave of patriotic enthusiasm had swept Tennessee and the nation, these 200 men of Knoxville and Knox County had volunteered to serve their country.

Members of Co. D, Third Tennessee Volunteer Infantry

The regiment of which they were a part – the Third Tennessee Infantry – was the first volunteer regiment in the South to be mustered into U.S. service for the war. The regiment was sent to Chickamauga Park, Ga., for training. Like most other American volunteers in that brief war, the men of the Third Tennessee saw no combat.

Upon learning that the regiment was being mustered out in January 1899, the people of Knoxville decided to honor the returning Knoxville area men with a grand reception and banquet at Market Hall.

Among the local luminaries appointed to the reception committee were Mayor Samuel G. Heiskell and Judge Oliver P. Temple.

At the reception on Feb. 3, a military band played, speeches were made and each soldier was presented with a medal. "All in all," one participant wrote, "few if any happier events have occurred in Knoxville."

Feb. 4, 1883

On Feb. 4, 1883, the Knoxville Daily Chronicle added its voice to the chorus of local boosters who were determined to make Knoxville a great city of the "New South."

Like every other Southern city in the decades after the Civil War, Knoxville had a contingent of forward-looking citizens – mostly businessmen – whose dream was to drag the South away from traditionalism, agrarianism, and complacency and into the mainstream of modern industrial society.

The Chronicle of Feb. 4 contained a half-page feature promoting Knoxville. It was aimed at energetic and progressive outsiders who might be looking for an attractive city in which to settle and do business. Hundreds of copies were sent out across the country.

"Knoxville is noted for her quietness, her sobriety, her institutions of learning and charity," the Chronicle boasted. "The climate is the golden mean between the heat of the extreme South and the cold of the extreme North. . . . Capital can be invested in Knoxville. . . with the certainty of success."

And, just in case any of those up North thought Knoxville was a nest of Yankee-hating, unreconstructed rebels, the Chronicle added that "the feeling here among all parties is liberal and national. We judge men by their conduct, and not by their birthplace."

Feb. 5, 1968

A News-Sentinel editorial on Feb. 5, 1968, reflected the shock and dismay of many Knoxvillians at the latest bad news about the Vietnam War.

Five days earlier communist forces had launched a huge offensive (the Tet offensive) that caught American forces off guard. Dozens of bases and cities were overrun.

Americans were aghast. President Lyndon Johnson had previously assured the public that the war was being won. And now, even as the Tet offensive wreaked havoc across South Vietnam, Johnson insisted that it was a major defeat for the communists.

"President Johnson may have convinced himself the Viet Cong suffered a staggering military defeat," the News-Sentinel editorial said. "But it is highly doubtful he can convince the American people. . . . (There is a) gaping hole now blown in the administration's rosy picture of our 'steady progress' in Vietnam."

The News-Sentinel stopped short of demanding an end to the war, however. Like most Americans, the editor believed the lesson of Tet was that "we were getting cocky and we got socked for it," and that the solution was to knuckle down and "stop treating this as a part-time, easy war."

For some, however, the real lesson of Tet was that the war was unwinnable.

Feb. 6, 1796

In Knoxville on Feb. 6, 1796, Tennessee's first constitutional convention unanimously approved the state constitution drawn up by a committee headed by Charles McClung.

McClung, born in Pennsylvania in 1761, learned agricultural and mechanical skills on his family's Lancaster County farm and penmanship and clerical skills in the office of a Philadelphia merchant. He set out at the age of 27 with a horse and $100 in cash to seek his fortune on the frontier. He arrived at James White's home, the future site of Knoxville, in 1788. Two years later he married White's daughter, Margaret. In 1791 he surveyed the town site for his father-in-law, laying it off in square lots that were then raffled off — the event that is regarded as the founding of Knoxville.

Charles McClung

In addition to his important role in the 1796 constitutional convention, he served as a militia officer, a U.S. commissioner to survey the Holston treaty boundary line, a Knox County trustee, a Blount College trustee and a presidential elector. He died in 1835.

Not the least of McClung's contributions to Knoxville was his long line of distinguished descendants, including his grandson, the financier Charles McClung McGhee.

Feb. 7, 1917

On Feb. 7, 1917, the Knoxville chapter of the American Red Cross was established. This was at a time when the United States was being drawn closer and closer to participation in the First World War.

Two months later, when America entered the war, the Knoxville Red Cross was ready to do its part. Over the next two years the Knoxville chapter and its 60 local auxiliaries carried out an energetic and wide-ranging program of war work. Staffed and directed primarily by women, the Red Cross was at that time one of the few public institutions in Knoxville in which women were permitted to put their talents to use.

Under the leadership of Mrs. N.E. Logan, Mrs. J. Stewart French, and others, the Knoxville Red Cross raised over $200,000 in donations and organized the work of more than 6,000 volunteers in the city and county. These volunteers made surgical dressings and hospital garments, knitted socks and sweaters and mittens for soldiers, operated a canteen at the Southern Railroad depot to serve the hundreds of thousands of troops who passed through Knoxville during the war, and provided medical, financial, and legal aid to the families of soldiers. A Junior Red Cross, with 31 auxiliaries in the city and county schools, gave Knoxville children an opportunity to participate in the war effort.

Feb. 8, 1907

A public meeting was held at Knoxville's Market Hall on Feb. 8, 1907, to debate the liquor question.

Prohibition sentiment was growing in Knoxville at that time, as it was across the nation. Convinced that saloons were nests of vice, many wanted to put them out of business.

Everybody who was anybody in the city showed up at the meeting to speak their piece. The first was Mayor Samuel G. Heiskell, who denied using alcohol himself but argued that banning saloons would cost the city $33,500 in whiskey-tax revenue and thus require a property-tax hike. He urged instead that they be confined to one section of town and regulated.

Samuel G. Heiskell

Businessman Daniel M. Rose, on the other hand, spoke up for prohibition. He insisted that the cost of poor houses, insane asylums, and crime control made necessary by the existence of saloons outweighed the whiskey-tax revenue.

The meeting was rowdy. Cheers and catcalls greeted every speaker. In the end, the majority rejected prohibition in favor of stricter control of saloons. Nevertheless, prohibitionists won in a referendum the next month. Later that year, Knoxville became "dry."

Feb. 9, 1866

On Feb. 9, 1866, George Washington LeVere, a black Presbyterian minister, arrived in Knoxville to assume the leadership of Shiloh Presbyterian Church.

Shiloh Presbyterian was one of several black churches founded in Knoxville in the immediate post-Civil War years, a time when many of the South's newly emancipated blacks sought to enlarge their freedom by withdrawing from the white-dominated churches they had belonged to as slaves. Shiloh – originally called the First Colored Presbyterian Church of Knoxville – was organized in September 1865 with the help of two white ministers sent by the northern Presbyterian Church. The founding members of Shiloh included 11 blacks from Second Presbyterian Church and one from First Presbyterian.

LeVere, who had served as chaplain of the 20th U.S. Colored Infantry during the Civil War, had trouble finding a building to house his congregation because in Knoxville at that time there was much white prejudice against black churches. He and his parishioners were forced to meet in private homes until they had raised the money to buy a lot on Clinch Avenue and erect a church building on it. By the turn of the century it had 120 members. By 1925, it had 227 members and was one of 30 black churches in Knoxville.

Feb. 10, 1842

Knoxvillians celebrated their city's semicentennial on Feb. 10, 1842. Even though the date was wrong (subsequent research established Oct. 3, 1791, as the date of Knoxville's founding), the event was a grand one.

Just about everyone in and around Knoxville turned out for the occasion, the centerpiece of which was a magnificent oration in the 19th-century style by Thomas W. Humes, a prominent clergyman and later president of the University of Tennessee. Humes' lengthy speech reviewed the early years of Knoxville's history, lavishly praised the town's founding fathers, and expressed the hope that the next half-century would bring even greater glory. "Let us enter upon the Future," he said, with "noble conceptions" that would lead to "worthy deeds."

Following the speech, Knoxville's elite ladies and gentlemen attended a banquet at the City Hotel. Among the formal toasts offered was one to the early settlers of Knoxville: "Honored be their memories, and gratified our recollections of their perseverance, their courage, and their fortitude."

The organizers of the event were temperance advocates and no alcohol was served at the banquet. The Rev.William Mack was no doubt expressing his approval of that policy when he offered this toast: "Sparkling and free, cold water, pure water, bright water for me."

Feb. 11, 1871

An editorial in The Knoxville Chronicle of Feb. 11, 1871, expressed concern about the growing influence of money in politics.

This was during the era that Mark Twain dubbed the Gilded Age. It was a time of tremendous national optimism, economic growth and westward expansion but also a time in which the spirit of reform and self-sacrifice that had marked the antebellum and Civil War years was abandoned in favor of materialism, self-interest and ruthless exploitation.

In the Gilded Age vast fortunes were made, the great robber barons of the business world arose, and greed and corruption flourished. Most Americans paid little attention to the state of the nation's morals.

A few, however, raised a cry of alarm. One of them was The Chronicle's editor, who warned that "men of wealth and ambition are grasping and scheming for power, while the unsuspecting masses are . . . robbed of their rights." Politicians were being bought and sold. "In a great many instances, lobbyists have had complete control of legislative bodies."

The solution, the editor insisted, was for the public to become more aware and less indifferent. Any legislator who "votes away (the people's) money and their privileges . . . because someone pays him to do so" should be treated as a "common thief."

Feb. 12, 1802

On Feb. 12, 1802, Knoxville's commissioners met to draw up a set of ordinances.

Knoxville was a mere village of 400 inhabitants at that time. The state legislature had not yet seen fit to incorporate it officially as a town, but had provided a form of government for it.

Under an act of 1797, the voters of Knoxville were permitted to elect five commissioners who served two-year terms.

The commissioners who gathered on Feb. 12, 1802, did not feel obliged to pass detailed regulations or provide extensive services. Knoxville was simply too small and its citizens too self-sufficient to require much in the way of local government.

The ordinances enacted that day dealt with health and safety, public order and morals. Streets were to be kept free of filth, wells were to be securely enclosed, and slaughterhouses, wooden chimneys and privy holes less than six feet deep were banned.

Horses and carriages were not to be ridden at excessive speeds on town streets, and horses were not to run at large. Firing guns was prohibited. Gatherings of slaves were strictly regulated. Stores had to close on Sundays. Violations were punishable by a fine of 50 cents or, for slaves, 10 lashes.

To enforce the ordinances the commissioners hired a "town sergeant" and ordered him to patrol the streets.

Feb. 13, 1929

On Feb. 13, 1929, a modern-day "Pied Piper" came to Knoxville.

The "Pied Piper" was A.F. Amann, professional rat exterminator. He carried a briefcase instead of a flute and wore a derby instead of a peaked cap.

He had been hired by city authorities to wage war on Knoxville's rat population, estimated at 200,000 – two rats for every Knoxvillian. Amann planned an eight-week campaign in which he and his three assistants would go block by block through the city and would place poisoned food for the rats to find. Amann assured the public that his "Seven Course Banquet of Death" – which included fish, meat, vegetables, salad and fruit – would wipe out 80 percent of the rats but pose no threat to pets or children.

He employed a special tasteless and odorless poison. It took effect when the victim drank water, producing a chemical reaction causing paralysis and death.

Amann's briefcase contained numerous letters testifying to the effectiveness of his method. A self-professed expert in rat psychology, Amann explained that part of his strategy was to place the poisoned food in out-of- the-way places so that the rats would think they were stealing it. Rats are "natural thieves," he said, and they prefer groceries over garbage.

Feb. 14, 1983

On Feb. 14, 1983, the Butcher banking empire began to collapse.

On that day state and federal banking officials declared the United American Bank of Knoxville insolvent and closed it. Simultaneously, Jake Butcher resigned as the bank's chairman. Police were stationed at the bank's headquarters at United American Plaza to bar Butcher and other board members from the bank offices.

The closing of UAB-Knoxville – East Tennessee's largest bank, with over a billion dollars in assets and deposits – came as a shock to its employees and many other Knoxvillians. It was the fourth-largest commercial bank failure in U.S. history at that time.

Although another bank quickly took over UAB-Knoxville and depositors were not harmed, the closing triggered a train of events that eventually toppled the whole Butcher empire.

Jake Butcher and his brother, C.H. Butcher Jr., had achieved a spectacular rise to power during the preceding decade. Jake had twice run for Tennessee governor and had served as chairman of the 1982 Knoxville World's Fair. Following the failure of UAB-Knoxville, widespread illegal banking practices in the Butcher empire were brought to light, eventually leading to prison terms for both Butcher brothers and a number of their associates.

Two examiners for the Federal Deposit Insurance Corp. lock the doors at the West Haven branch of United American Bank of Knoxville.

Feb. 15, 1905

On Feb. 15, 1905, Knoxville played host to visiting members of the Tennessee Legislature. Legislative junkets to inspect state institutions in Knoxville were a regular feature of each biennial General Assembly in those days.

On this occasion, a number of the legislators toured the University of Tennessee's agricultural experiment station and scientific laboratories, and then attended chapel with the students. Asked to say a few words after the services, several of the legislators complimented the work of the university and encouraged the students in their studies. Then the students sang the university song, "Tennessee."

Meanwhile, other legislators toured the Tennessee Deaf and Dumb School, where they were treated to a demonstration of the students' reading, writing and gymnastic skills. Later, in the school chapel, one legislator addressed the student body while an interpreter translated the remarks into sign language.

Knoxville's leaders always went out of their way to wine and dine the legislators on these visits. A banquet was held at the Imperial Hotel that night to welcome the visitors. Beer and punch enlivened the occasion, cigars were handed out all around, and visitors and hosts alike agreed that the event was a grand success.

Feb. 16, 1942

Knoxville men lined up all over the city on Feb. 16, 1942, to register for the draft.

America had entered the Second World War just 10 weeks earlier, and the government had recently decreed that all men between the ages of 20 and 45 who had not previously registered must do so on Feb. 16.

At the courthouse, where county clerks supervised the registration, and at various schools around the city, where teachers and principals carried out the task, registrants queued up and signed their names. The specified age range was so wide that in numerous instances fathers and sons signed up together.

Some of the older registrants were veterans of the First World War. Among the younger registrants were 20 University of Tennessee football players.

Every effort was made to ensure that no one was missed. Registrars went to the homes of those men who were bedridden. Jailers and hospital superintendents saw to it that the men under their supervision were enrolled.

By the time the registration ended at 9 o'clock that night, about 12,000 men in Knoxville and Knox County had signed up. They had become a part of the greatest mobilization in the nation's history, a vast mustering of American manpower that eventually put 15 million men and women into uniform.

Feb. 17, 1956

On Feb. 17, 1956, the Knoxville Fraternal Order of Police proposed a novel solution to the problem of hot rodding.

The American people had become deeply troubled about juvenile delinquency in the early 1950s. To some it seemed that the whole teenage generation was alienated and rebellious, as exemplified by James Dean in the movie "Rebel Without a Cause."

Hot rodding and drag racing had emerged as popular forms of youthful self-expression. Knoxville, like many other American cities, experienced an epidemic of dangerous, late-night auto races on city streets. The FOP's idea, set forth by police captain Elmer Dyke, was to set up a police-supervised drag strip for Knoxville area teenagers. It would carry out time trials for single cars, but no competitive racing would be permitted. Cars would have to pass a safety inspection.

"Such a track will attract teenagers who need a place to blow off steam," Dyke said. "Hot rodding exists now on the highways at irregular night hours. Our purpose will be to bring it under the closest supervision and at reasonable hours. If we save one life, the whole thing will be worthwhile."

Teenagers who joined the FOP drag club would have to pledge to drive safely and to report illegal hot rodding. Any member cited for traffic violations could be fined or dropped from the club.

Feb. 18, 1894

Feb. 18, 1894, was long remembered by many Knoxvillians as the day of the great cable car disaster.

A Knoxville entrepreneur had conceived the idea of building a cable car system across the Tennessee River. By early 1894 it was in operation. A 15-foot-long cable car, suspended on two cables and powered by steam, crossed the river from a point on the north side near Third Creek to a point at the top of Longstreet's Heights, nearly 300 feet above the south side of the river.

The cable car, as drawn in Scientific American

But on Sunday, Feb. 18, tragedy struck. As the car neared the top of the heights, one cable snapped, whipped back and crushed one end of the car. The car rolled back to a point above the middle of the river, where it hung.

A dramatic rescue of the eight passengers, one of whom was critically injured, was carried out as hundreds of spectators watched from the shore. One by one, the passengers were lowered by rope to a barge in the river below. The injured passenger, a young lawyer named Oliver Ledgerwood, died later that day. A coroner's jury charged the cable car operators with carelessness.

The cable car never reopened.

Feb. 19, 1928

On Sunday, Feb. 19, 1928, a Knoxville minister spoke to his congregation about the contrast between "modern girls" and "old-fashioned girls."

The 1920s were a time of great change for American women. Many took jobs outside the home. Liberalized divorce laws and birth control permitted some to escape traditional bonds to husband and children. Freer clothing styles for women and more public tolerance of female smoking and drinking were hallmarks of the age epitomized by the "flapper."

Americans of a conservative bent were disturbed by these liberal trends. Among them was the Rev. Stanley Hayne of Central Methodist Church, who on Feb. 19 extolled the virtues of the "old-fashioned girl." Modesty was one of her charms, Hayne said, "in sharp contrast with the brazenly frank behavior which is all too common today." Furthermore, "the old-fashioned girl could wash dishes, sweep, make beds, feed chickens. . . . It is a good thing for women to learn the art of homemaking; it is a dangerous thing for them to undertake home-breaking."

"But," the minister concluded on a conciliatory note, "I do not believe that any former generation deserves more praise than the present. On the whole, the modern girl is as good as history knows."

Feb. 20, 1852

On Feb. 20, 1852, the Knoxville Board of Aldermen passed an ordinance prohibiting slaves from emptying kitchen slops into the street. Whites were also prohibited from doing so, but any white person who violated the ordinance was merely fined. Slaves, on the other hand, were punished with a whipping – five to 15 lashes from the town constable.

The authorities in Knoxville, like those in other Southern towns in the antebellum years, carefully monitored and restricted the activities of the slave population. Fearful of an insurrection by "bad" slaves and convinced that even "good" slaves were childlike creatures who needed white guidance and strict discipline, white Southerners forbade slaves to gather without white supervision or to travel without a pass from their master, and slaves were punished for any undeferential behavior toward whites.

Some free blacks, who also faced restrictions, successfully carved out niches for themselves in antebellum Knoxville. Among them were John Dogan, a blacksmith, and Alfred Anderson, who ran a saloon and ice cream parlor on Main Street.

Of the 598 blacks in Knoxville in the early 1850s, 136 were free. Together, slaves and free blacks made up almost 30 percent of Knoxville's population at that time.

Feb. 21, 1949

On Feb. 21, 1949, a group of Knoxville women voiced their opinions on one of the developments that was transforming American society in the post-World War II years: the proliferation of labor-saving home appliances.

The widespread prosperity of that era enabled many families to purchase appliances and also encouraged American industry to develop new appliances. Automatic washing machines, dishwashers, and a host of other products relieved housewives of much drudgery. But they also raised troubling questions.

A News-Sentinel reporter at a meeting of the Knoxville Home Economics Association on Feb. 21 posed this question to its members: Do modern appliances leave the housewife with too little to do? "Definitely no!," replied one, "because these modern gadgets give the housewife time to study, be with her family, and to keep abreast of the times. They help her husband and children become proud of her."

The consensus among the members was that labor-saving devices allowed women to better fulfull their traditional roles as wives, mothers, housekeepers, and community volunteers. As the years went by, however, more and more women turned their sights on careers outside the home.

Feb. 22, 1876

In 1876, Knoxvillians celebrated Washington's birthday with a grand military parade and ball. Because that year also marked the centennial of American independence, the events took on special significance.

Four companies of smartly uniformed men marched through the streets of Knoxville that afternoon. The sidewalks were crowded with excited spectators and the stirring music of military bands filled the air. One by one, the McGhee Guards, the O'Conner Zouaves, the Dickinson Light Guards, and the University Cadets passed down Gay Street, around the Custom House, and then back to their respective armories.

Such volunteer military companies could be found in every American town in that era. They were the descendants of the frontier militia.

That night the O'Conner Zouaves hosted a ball at Spiro's Hall, where music and dancing went on until the early hours of the morning. Meanwhile, the Dickinson Light Guards attended the wedding of one of their members. The University Cadets trooped off to the Opera House to attend the annual presentation of the University's two literary societies. There they listened to a speech on "The Effect of Machinery" and a debate on the question, "Is Europe Tending to Republicanism?"

Feb. 23, 1869

On Feb. 23, 1869, one of Knoxville's most distinguished citizens gave a long and learned speech on his favorite topic – the great natural and human resources of Knoxville and East Tennessee.

Oliver P. Temple was a prominent lawyer, judge, and Republican politician. From the time he moved to Knoxville in 1848 until his death in 1907 he was also a zealous promoter of the region's industrial development.

In his speech, delivered at a meeting of the East Tennessee Industrial Association in Knoxville, Temple was in fact preaching to the converted. His real purpose was to convince outsiders that Knoxville and East Tennessee were a land of opportunity. The speech was later printed up in pamphlet form for national distribution.

Temple boasted of the state's recently created public school system, "which opens the doors of knowledge to every child in the State – black or white, rich or poor."

To northerners who hesitated to come south because of the unrest and violence that marked the era of Reconstruction, Temple offered the assurance that "the people of East Tennessee are at peace. The outrages of which strangers may read are in Middle and West Tennessee. . . . The immigrant will be as safe here as in New York or Pennsylvania."

Feb. 24, 1910

A prominent woman speaker offered some thoughts to the people of Knoxville on Feb. 24, 1910.

Elizabeth Hiller had come to Knoxville to present her lecture course on cooking. An expert on nutrition, she traveled throughout the country, speaking and gathering information on the commodity marketing system. In her lectures, she tried to help her audience of housewives become skilled, scientific homemakers.

She was also regarded as something of an oracle on women's issues. To an inquiring Knoxville reporter she voiced the opinion that "handsome and extravagant window displays" in stores created "unrest and jealousy" among poor women unable to afford expensive goods.

Furthermore, although she thought many women were "superior in intellect to men" and quite capable of voting intelligently, she believed women did not need the right to vote. And she was skeptical of women in the business world. A woman's "first duty," she said, "is to her home."

In some ways Hiller was the embodiment of that period historians call the Progressive Era. It was a time when many leading thinkers emphasized the need for scientific solutions to the nation's problems, expressed fears about the influence of capitalism, and held deeply ambivalent beliefs about the role of women.

Feb. 25, 1885

On Feb. 25, 1885, Knoxville was in the midst of a heated political controversy. The issue was a new form of city government.

On Feb. 24, a number of Knoxville's prominent leaders, calling themselves the Committee of Fifty-Two, met to debate the matter. Among the provisions recommended by some were registration and poll tax requirements for voting and property qualifications for holding office.

These provisions angered some poorer citizens, and the issue quickly assumed an aspect of class conflict. The next day, Feb. 25, the Knoxville Daily Chronicle printed a vehement letter from an anonymous spokesman for the city's poor men.

"Why should a committee of real estate owners, a majority of whom are wealthy, attempt to deprive the . . . poor men of all participation in the government?" asked the letter writer. "The common people never hesitate to do their duty in suppressing fires. . . . The poor men of this city have contributed largely to the wealth of some of the very men who are now . . . attempting to disfranchise them. . . . There was a time when some of these men (of the Committee) were as 'poor as church mice,' but now that fortune has smiled upon them they are terribly opposed to the 'poor white trash and negroes' holding office and voting."

Feb. 26, 1969

On Feb. 26, 1969, the University of Tennessee erupted in controversy over the issue of dormitory hours for women.

The university had followed a paternalistic policy toward female students, imposing strict curfews on women while treating male students as adults. In 1969, UT students protested.

Following a walkout by some students, the UT-Knoxville administration agreed to an experimental no-curfew policy for women. On Feb. 26, however, a dispute arose over the number of women covered by the new policy. UTK administrators announced that about one-third would be covered.

The Student Government Association and its president, Chris Whittle, claiming the figure agreed upon was 85 percent, accused the UT statewide administrators of high-handedly overruling the UTK administrators. The SGA passed a resolution censuring UT President Andy Holt, Vice President Ed Boling and others. The resolution claimed that these men had "shown disdain for academic freedom . . . and in so doing, can no longer rightfully call (themselves) educators."

Chris Whittle

Feb. 27, 1931

The city of Knoxville imposed a new set of traffic regulations on Feb. 27, 1931.

Knoxville's automobile traffic had mushroomed since the first car appeared on the city's streets in 1899. The 1920s in particular were boom years for the automobile. In 1920, there were about 5,400 in the city, or one for every 16 residents. By 1930, there were 24,000, or one for every six residents. As the city streets grew more congested, stricter traffic regulations were needed.

The new traffic code of 1931 prohibited parking on Gay Street during the evening rush hour and limited it to one hour at other times. All-night parking was banned on all city streets. No right turn on a red light was permitted at any intersection except at the south end of the Gay Street bridge.

The downtown speed limit was reduced from 30 to 20 miles per hour. The penalty for running a red light or stop sign was set at $5. Anyone caught cutting into a funeral procession could be fined up to $50. Drivers living outside the city but regularly using city streets were required to purchase a city license tag at an annual cost of $1. All accidents had to be reported to the police. Garage operators were required to report cars with accident damage or bullet holes.

Gay Street in the late 1920's

Feb. 28, 1857

On Feb. 28, 1857, the irrepressible William G. Brownlow lambasted Knoxville's greedy property owners and shady businessmen.

Brownlow, editor of the Knoxville Whig, was always alert to any problem that threatened the growth and prosperity of the city. In an editorial on Feb. 28, he declared that "outrageously high rents" and inflated land prices were hindering the city's development.

A store on Gay Street, he pointed out, could not be rented for less than $1,000 a year. Family residences averaged $200 to $500. Should a man decide to build his own store on one of the business streets, he would have to pay up to $150 per linear foot for the property.

"Lots are cheaper on Broadway in New York, or Market Street in Philadelphia," Brownlow insisted. These high prices "are injuring the city," he continued, "keeping merchants, manufacturers, and mechanics away – and will, if they persist . . . (bring) progress to a dead halt."

Furthermore, he said, Knoxville "has been cursed . . . with the bogus operations of designing men . . . men splurging in this, that and the other enterprise, and finally caving in, as

William G. "Parson" Brownlow

hopeless bankrupts – ruining innocent men" who loaned them money. Such practices, Brownlow concluded, were nothing but a "refined species of roguery."

March 1, 1897

March 1, 1897, was the day of the great Depot Street riot in Knoxville.

The riot had its origins in a rivalry between the Knoxville Electric Street Railway, headed by C.C. Howell, and the Citizens Street Railway, headed by William Gibbs McAdoo. McAdoo planned to build a trolley line on Depot that would compete with Howell's.

A city ordinance prohibited street work before April, but McAdoo got an injunction from the Knox County Court to allow him to work. McAdoo gathered his workers, and Howell called police.

Policemen arrived to enforce the ordinance. McAdoo called deputies to enforce the injunction. A crowd sympathetic to McAdoo gathered. Mayor Samuel Heiskell sent in police reinforcements, and later, firemen.

The workmen and sympathizers pelted police and firemen with bricks and stones. The police opened fire with shotguns and killed one laborer – a black man named Will Arnold.

A newspaper artist's rendering of the riot

March 2, 1918

On Saturday, March 2, 1918, the people of Knoxville were patriotically doing their part in World War I.

On that day 41 downtown merchants voluntarily closed their stores at 6 p.m., thereby conserving fuel as the government had requested. Early Saturday closings would remain in effect for the duration of the war, the merchants promised.

Knoxvillians were also donating books and magazines to the army as part of a campaign to provide reading material for the soldiers. So far 500 books had been collected by Boy Scouts or dropped off at the Lawson McGhee Library.

The local chairman of the Council of National Defense announced on March 2 that a big campaign was in the offing to enlist boys under draft age to work on farms. There was a critical labor shortage on the farms because so many farm workers had gone into military service.

That same day, an official of the federal Food Administration reminded Knoxvillians to follow the government's rules on food and energy conservation and especially to observe "heatless and meatless" days. Anyone who failed to do so "is not true to Old Glory," he said. "He is not a genuine American." Furthermore, he advised, "fire the cook if she is not patriotic."

March 3, 1923

On March 3, 1923, the people of Knoxville voted themselves a new form of government.

The city had had a commission form of government since 1911, but it had become increasingly unpopular. Fiscal shortages, inadequate city services, mismanagement and several instances of fraud and graft had marked the years of commission rule.

A debate ensued over the best type of government to adopt. A referendum was scheduled to let the voters decide. The Legislature then would alter the city charter according to the voters' wishes. The March 3 referendum gave a solid victory to a city-manager form of government.

The city-manager system received 3,765 votes, as opposed to 1,851 for an aldermanic system and 295 for a revised commission system.

The city-manager system was a favorite of many urban reformers throughout the nation. It put executive authority in the hands of a professional who was not elected directly but appointed by the city council. Under this system, it was presumed, the city would be run by an honest, efficient, nonpartisan administrator.

In announcing the referendum totals, The Knoxville Sentinel – a supporter of the city-manager system – declared that "Knoxville has redeemed herself" and applauded the "patriotic citizens" who "threw off the yoke of commission rule."

March 4, 1828

The first steamboat to visit Knoxville arrived on March 4, 1828.

When the Atlas steamed up the Tennessee River that morning, its cannon booming, Knoxvillians turned out en masse to welcome it.

Capt. S.D. Conner had brought the boat all the way from Alabama, which required negotiating the treacherous Muscle Shoals. Conner presented a flag to the city officials, who replied with speeches of congratulation.

To many Knoxvillians the event seemed to be the dawn of a new era. Until the development of the steamboat, traffic on the Tennessee River could only go one way – downstream. The voyage of the Atlas held out the promise that Knoxville could establish a two-way trade with cities as far away as New Orleans.

On March 5 the Atlas, carrying a number of prominent Knoxvillians, steamed upriver to the home of J.G.M. Ramsey, a leading promoter of East Tennessee's development. But Ramsey threw cold water on the dreams of the steamboat enthusiasts by telling them that Knoxville's future lay with the railroads.

Ramsey was right. Although a regular steamboat service was soon established, the Muscle Shoals remained a serious hindrance to through traffic. Knoxville's real integration into the national economy did not come until the city's first railroad connection was completed in the 1850s.

March 5, 1845

On March 5, 1845, East Tennessee University (later the University of Tennessee) announced its recently revised rules and policies.

The announcement was mainly intended to assure parents of prospective students that their sons (there were no women students at that time) would be as strictly disciplined at school as they were at home. The university "is remarkable for the moral and studious habits of its inmates," the announcement read.

No physical punishment was ever used, "moral suasion only being relied upon." The faculty not only undertook to educate the students, but also "to inculcate the principles of the Christian religion . . . to encourage polite and gentlemanly bearing, and to establish habits of neatness, order, propriety and industry."

All students were expected to be in bed, with lights out, at 10 p.m. and were required to get up at 6 a.m. Rooms were inspected every morning before breakfast. Every student who came from a distance was assigned a local guardian who received and disbursed all the student's funds. Parents who might be trying to rid themselves of troublesome sons were warned that "this institution is designed for the benefit of those who desire to learn, and not as a place of resort for the idle and vicious."

March 6, 1933

Knoxville and the nation began a "bank holiday" on Monday, March 6, 1933, as part of President Franklin D. Roosevelt's "New Deal."

Roosevelt had taken office just two days earlier, at a time when the Great Depression had reached its nadir and a banking panic was sweeping the nation.

The bank holiday was one of his first executive orders. It closed all banks for four days, to give Congress time to begin working on emergency banking measures to restore public confidence.

The bank holiday created some temporary inconveniences for Knoxvillians. Payrolls were delayed, and stores, restaurants, and offices faced a scarcity of small change. O'Neil's Cafe on Market Street ran out of coins and small bills by noon that day. City manager Neil Bass sent his employees around to churches to see if they could change large bills from their Sunday collections.

Despite the inconveniences, most Knoxvillians applauded the president's decisive actions and were inspired by his rhetoric. A News-Sentinel editorial on March 6, reflecting this mood, commended Roosevelt's "courage and vision" and declared that "there is more hope in the country today than at any time in recent months."

March 7, 1909

On March 7, 1909, the finishing touches were put on the new Bijou Theater on Gay Street.

The years around the turn of the century were the golden age of vaudeville, and the Bijou was built specifically for vaudeville shows. It reflected the latest in theater design with excellent acoustics, Classical Revival interior architecture, a seating capacity of 1,500, two balconies, box seats, a 70-foot-wide stage, a large orchestra pit, a dozen spacious dressing rooms, electric lights onstage and throughout the house, hot and cold running water, a big ventilation fan, and an Otis elevator.

Opening night at the Bijou Theater

The theater cost $50,000 to build.

Opening night was March 8, 1909. A packed house enjoyed George M. Cohan's "Little Johnny Jones," a musical that had recently been a big hit in New York and had introduced the song "Give My Regards to Broadway."

About 1915 a screen and projectors were installed in the Bijou so that movies could be featured as well as stage shows.

In those years of strict segregation, the Bijou was the only Knoxville theater that admitted blacks along with whites. However, blacks had to enter by a separate entrance on Cumberland Avenue and were restricted to seats in one of the balconies.

March 8, 1867

The great flood of 1867 reached its high-water mark in Knoxville on March 8 of that year.

It was the most disastrous flood to hit the Tennessee Valley in recorded history. It began with a much heavier than usual snow accumulation in the East Tennessee mountains that winter, followed by a week-long thaw in late February and then a heavy rain in early March.

Flooding began in upper East Tennessee before the rain ceased. As the flood moved south along the Holston and French Broad rivers (which meet above Knoxville to form the Tennessee River) it gathered intensity.

It hit Knoxville with tremendous force, washing 100 people out of their homes. The bridge across the river, built by Union troops during the Civil War, was carried away, and a number of smaller bridges around town were damaged or destroyed. A sash and blind factory, a lumber mill, and numerous warehouses along the river were also wiped out.

The flood crested in Knoxville at 4:30 p.m. on March 8.

In the 1940s a construction crew working on the river bank near the Gay Street Bridge found the words "H.W.M. 1867" chiseled in rock. They represented the high-water mark of the great flood — 33 feet above the river's normal level.

March 9, 1808

A provocative letter in the Knoxville Gazette of March 9, 1808, asked the crucial question, "Shall we have peace or war?"

The issue had arisen over Great Britain's high-handed treatment of the United States. Engaged in a desperate war against Napoleon, the British were interdicting trade between France and neutral countries, including the United States.

The letter-writer, who signed himself "Tennessean," called for a declaration of war. In the first place, he said, war would preserve the nation's honor. "War is a calamity," he admitted, but it is better than "peace with disgrace." Furthermore, war would stimulate the economy by reducing foreign imports and thus forcing Americans to develop their own manufacturing. And third, war would make Americans a purer, tougher people by cutting off their supply of European-made luxury items. Luxury, said "Tennessean," induces laziness, weakens the mind and body, and leads to "vice and a total corruption of manners."

Four years later the U.S. went to war against Britain. Though it is doubtful that Americans were morally improved as a result, they could at least claim to have preserved the nation's honor. And, as "Tennessean" had predicted, the war proved to be a great stimulus to manufacturing.

March 10,1940

On March 10, 1940, Knoxvillians got a chance to voice their opinions on "Gone With the Wind."

On that day The News-Sentinel published the winning entries of the weekly You-Tell-Us letter writing contest. That week the topic was "Gone With the Wind," which had just won the Academy Award for Best Picture of 1939.

Three out of four contestants agreed that the award was well deserved. One described the film as "a living, breathing reality of such magnificent pictorial beauty, as to be positively breath-taking." Another praised it as "a celluloid landmark." A third called it "not only the best picture of last year but of all movie years."

Among the dissenters was one who cast her vote for "Goodbye, Mr. Chips." Unlike most women, she said, she did not idolize Clark Gable: "I am not one of those who would stand all day in the hot sun for a glimpse or a wink" from him.

Another critic thought Vivien Leigh "was Scarlett only on the surface. There was no depth to her performance. It was shallow and superficial."

Another declared that "GWTW" glorified Scarlett's cruelty; by praising such a movie, she said, "we are forsaking the one moral that God put among the first, the purity and sweetness of woman."

March 11, 1954

Mayor George Dempster, under attack by his political foes, came out fighting on March 11, 1954.

Renowned for his flamboyant political style, Dempster responded characteristically that day to an attempt to oust him from office. Recall petitions had secured 6,000 signatures.

Dempster blamed the recall movement on a "cabal of racketeers" and "two disgruntled would-be politicians." The racketeers, he claimed, opposed him because he had run all the bootleggers and slot-machine operators out of the city. The two politicians, he said, were unhappy about their defeat in the mayoral election.

George Dempster

Dempster survived the recall attempt and went on to complete his term as mayor, which ended in 1955.

Born in Knoxville in 1887, Dempster was the inventor of the famous Dempster Dumpster, an ingenious trash-removal system now familiar worldwide.

His public service included humanitarian work and terms as Knoxville city manager and councilman. Landmarks for which he could claim credit are the Henley Bridge, Bill Meyer Stadium and McGhee Tyson Airport.

March 12, 1879

On March 12, 1879, the editor of the Knoxville Chronicle offered some thoughts on one of the differences between northerners and southerners: their distinctive inclinations regarding violence and crime.

The bloody Civil War had ended only 14 years earlier, and the traumatic Reconstruction period had been over for just two years. Americans were still keenly aware of their sectional identification and heritage.

The Chronicle editorial reflected the South's peculiar combination of guilt and pride. Southerners, the editor noted, had a reputation for violence which was "not altogether without foundation." Dueling had been common until recent years, he pointed out, and even now many southerners considered a difference of opinion "sufficient provocation for putting a bullet hole through the man who refuses to think and talk as we do." This "propensity to shoot or stab or break each others' heads . . . may have been exaggerated," he concluded, "but it must be admitted that the southern people are of a somewhat pugnacious temperament."

But, he continued, "at least we have not had the reputation of being cold-blooded criminals. Crimes which are committed with deliberation, such as arson, burglary, robbery, etc.," he suggested, "have been more common among northern people."

March 13, 1947

The Cold War was well under way by March 13, 1947, and on that day Knoxvillians spoke out on the world-wide communist threat.

President Harry Truman had just asked Congress for $400 million to aid Greece and Turkey in their fight against communist insurgents. The United States, said the president, must stand ready to support any nation struggling against internal or external communist aggression.

A majority of Knoxvillians polled by The News-Sentinel on March 13 supported the president.

A man surveyed confessed that he did not thoroughly understand the situation and therefore could only "trust (Secretary of State George) Marshall and President Truman and their advisors to do the wise thing."

An editorial in The News-Sentinel that day also endorsed Truman's policy. "Germany and Japan were defeated," it said, "but the conflict between freedom and totalitarianism goes on." The failure to stop communism in Greece and Turkey, the editor continued, would lead to further communist aggression.

Such sentiments became widely accepted in America in the ensuing years, and they were a crucial part of the ideology that led the nation into war in Korea and Vietnam.

March 14, 1893

The Knoxville Chamber of Commerce met on March 14, 1893, to hear the latest developments concerning the proposed Panama Canal.

Judge Henry R. Gibson, who spoke to the chamber, enthusiastically endorsed the idea of building such a canal and making it a U.S. possession.

His speech reflected the thinking of many. The United States had by that time completed the settlement of its western frontier and had become a wealthy, populous, industrial giant. Many believed that it was time for America to stake a claim to world power.

"The United States is now practically settled," Judge Gibson declared, "and there now must be a new door sought for adventure." The Panama Canal, providing a shortcut to the Orient, would be strategically crucial in the coming international struggle. If the United States did not acquire it, Gibson said, "some foreign power will." The canal would be a boon to East Tennessee in particular, he pointed out, for coal was needed in the Orient.

The expansionist, competitive national mood personified by Judge Gibson found dramatic expression in the ensuing years. In 1898, America wrested an empire from Spain. And in 1903, the United States took possession of the Panama Canal Zone.

March 15, 1902

On March 15, 1902, the Census Bureau released the latest figures on Knoxville's industrial growth.

The statistics, based on the 1900 census, were in some respects good news for the city. They showed that during the preceding decade Knoxville had surpassed all other Tennessee cities in the growth rate of capital investment and industrial workforce. Nevertheless, as an industrial center Knoxville still ranked fourth behind Nashville, Memphis and Chattanooga.

The census confirmed that textile production had surpassed iron manufacturing as Knoxville's most important industry. Brookside Cotton Mills, with 1,200 employees, and Knoxville Woolen Mills, with 900, were the city's two largest employers. Knoxville Iron Co., with 850 employees, was third.

Altogether, industry employed over 30 percent of all Knoxville workers – a higher proportion than in Nashville, Memphis, and even Atlanta and Birmingham.

Knoxville industry continued to grow over the next two decades but, much to the disappointment of its boosters, the city never became an industrial center of real significance.

March 16, 1921

In a rousing demonstration of the "volunteer spirit," University of Tennessee students and faculty turned out with picks and shovels on March 16, 1921, to build an athletic field.

Up to that time UT sports teams had had to use various small, inadequate fields around the campus. But in 1919, W.S. Shields, a Knoxville banker and UT trustee, had donated money to acquire land south of the campus for a new field. UT came up with matching funds, and Shields-Watkins Field (named in honor of Shields and his wife, Alice Watkins Shields) was born.

Stands were built at the site (17 rows, seating 3,200 spectators) and some dirt was moved, but the field remained rough, uneven, and unusable.

On March 16, 1921, however, the university canceled classes, and students and faculty – volunteers all – assembled on the field. Armed with tools loaned by ALCOA, and nourished by a picnic lunch prepared by the UT home economics department, the volunteers proceeded to level and fix the field and lay out the gridiron, baseball diamond and track.

The christening came on March 19 when the UT baseball team played Cincinnati, losing 7-6. The first football game on the new field was played on Sept. 24, when UT shut out Emory & Henry, 27-0.

Volunteer workers toil toward the completion of Shields-Watkins Field.

March 17, 1885

On March 17, 1885, Knoxville got a professional fire department.

In the city's earliest days, all citizens were required to turn out with buckets in case of a fire. Soon, however, volunteer fire companies were organized, with the city providing hand-operated pumping engines.

The inadequacy of the volunteer system and the primitive equipment were underscored by a series of disastrous fires in the 19th century, including one in 1867 that damaged the Franklin Hotel and another in 1869 that burned down the Masonic Temple.

Gradually the city improved its fire-fighting capability. An 1867 ordinance set apart the downtown area as a special fire zone where construction of wooden buildings was prohibited. That same year, the city bought its first steam-operated fire engine.

Herman Schenk, first paid fire chief

In 1870, the office of city fire chief was created. The chief, who served without compensation, commanded the work of the volunteer companies. In 1885, the city formed a fully professional, paid fire department. Three years later, following the introduction of electricity to Knoxville, the city's first fire alarm system was installed.

March 18, 1903

On March 18, 1903, Knoxville was in the midst of a serious smallpox epidemic.

In those days, when mass inoculation was not routine, smallpox was a deadly and much-feared disease. Dozens of cases appeared in the city beginning in January 1903, and by March the health authorities were worried.

Health officer James T. Kennedy and city physician J.F. Scott quarantined every smallpox victim who came to their attention, but the disease still spread out of control. Kennedy and Scott also set up a detention center outside town for those who had contracted or been exposed to the disease. The center was ready by March 18, and that day 50 persons were taken there.

The next day the city health board met in special session and passed a resolution urging all citizens to be vaccinated, ordered Dr. Scott to vaccinate everyone living within 100 yards of a smallpox victim, ordered the closing and fumigation of two stores whose employees had come down with the disease, and ordered the prosecution of any physician or head of family who failed to report a case of the disease.

The Knoxville Sentinel warned that "the situation for the city is somewhat grave, and those who have not been vaccinated should . . . do so at once."

March 19, 1864

At a special meeting of East Tennessee University's trustees on March 19, 1864, Thomas W. Humes was appointed temporary president of the university.

At that time Knoxville and the nation were in the midst of the Civil War. The university (later the University of Tennessee) had been closed since early 1862, when its buildings were taken over by Confederate troops and its president, J.J. Ridley, resigned.

The war years were extremely hard on the struggling little school, which later became the state university. No sooner did the Confederate troops pull out in 1863 than Union troops arrived and occupied College Hill. The Yankees posted a battery of artillery and a brigade of infantry on the Hill, cut down trees, tore down fences, dug mountains of fortifications, and occupied all the university buildings except two.

By the time the war ended in 1865 the university's physical plant was a wreck. The grounds were mutilated, the buildings damaged inside and out, the library and scientific equipment destroyed. When classes resumed in March 1866 they had to be held in the Deaf and Dumb School in another part of town. By September the university buildings were ready for use, but as late as 1869 a visitor reported that they were still quite dilapidated.

College Hill in 1865, stripped of its trees by Union troops

March 20, 1957

Early in the morning of March 20, 1957, Fulton High School was ransacked by vandals.

When teachers and students arrived later they found an indescribable scene.

The corridors, as The News-Sentinel reported, looked as if they "had been hit by a dynamite blast." At least half of the student lockers had been opened and their contents strewn about.

A ransacked corridor inside Fulton High School

The floors were littered with paper and books. Obscenities had been scrawled on the walls, and windows smashed.

Damage totaled about $1,500. It was one of the worst incidents of school vandalism in Knoxville history.

The next day city detectives entered Fulton High classrooms and arrested four 16-year-old male students, all of them members of the "B-team" football squad. Under questioning, the four admitted vandalizing the school. "The devil just got in me, I guess," one of the boys explained.

The arrests brought up the issue of how to treat juvenile delinquents. Fulton's principal, when interviewed by The News-Sentinel, insisted that they "should be dealt with as criminals. We should quit mollycoddling them."

Chief of police Joe Kimsey, citing no less an authority than FBI director J. Edgar Hoover, approved making public the names of young offenders, as a deterrent.

March 21, 1872

Knoxvillians were warned March 21, 1872, to be on the lookout for a con man.

The Knoxville Chronicle reported that day that a man calling himself Wilson Carter had turned up in town the previous week. He was pleasant and well-spoken and said that he had been a Confederate officer during the Civil War.

He went on to relate a sad story about losing his business in the great Chicago fire of 1871. Now, he said, he needed work.

His tale touched the heart of a Knoxville Iron Co. employee, a young man who was the sole support of his widowed mother and younger brothers. This man brought Carter to his home and put him up for a few days while Carter supposedly looked for work.

When Carter claimed to have found a job at the Virginia and Georgia Railroad depot, the young Knoxville man lent him his best suit, shirt, and shoes for his first day on the job.

Alas, it developed that Carter was a fraud. He had no job. When confronted with the truth he fled, clothes and all.

"He is about five feet ten inches high," the Chronicle advised, "very much sunburned, wears his hair parted in the middle, is rather dignified, (has a) light moustache and goatee. . . . Unsuspecting people should be on their guard."

March 22, 1938

A public forum in Knoxville on March 22, 1938, sparked a lively discussion of the question, "What is ahead for youth in our community?"

Comments from the panelists and audience focused on two issues that were on the minds of young people: sex education and jobs.

As one young man pointed out, students were graduated from high school without any kind of education in "the most vital thing in our lives" – meaning sex, marriage and the family. An older man noted in response that few teachers were qualified to teach such a course and, furthermore, some conservative communities "would rise up against it."

However, another young man insisted it was needed. "Youth is going to get its knowledge somewhere," he said. Wouldn't it be better to get it in school "than from the gutter?"

The unemployment problem provoked even more heat. These were the years of the Great Depression, and the young were particularly hard-hit. One young man said, "We're beating around the bush (in talking about sex education). Our trouble is economic. We have been told for nine years that this situation is only temporary. . . . How much longer (do) they expect youth to be patient and loyal to a system that hasn't worked since 1929?"

March 23, 1961

On March 23, 1961, Knoxville Mayor John J. Duncan declared war on litter.

"I think this is one of the dirtiest cities you can find anywhere in the country," Duncan said. Anti-litter educational programs were needed for children and adults alike, he declared.

He promised a one-week grace period during which Knoxvillians must rid themselves of their long-established littering habits. After one week, litterbugs would be arrested.

John Duncan

The mayor's ally in this campaign was the Knox Beautiful Commission, whose chairman, Charles Callis, vowed to "get our county cleaned up and get it looking right." The Dogwood Arts Festival was less than a month away, and in preparation for it the Commission had adoped the slogan "Let's Clean Up – Company's Coming."

Littering was actually one of the simplest and least controversial problems Duncan faced as Knoxville's mayor. Annexation battles, a dwindling population and industrial base, and a major confrontation over racial integration complicated Duncan's five-and-a-half year term, which ended in 1964 when he won election to the U.S. House of Representatives – an office he held until his death in 1988.

March 24, 1892

Two dozen young men gathered in Knoxville on the evening of March 24, 1892, to form a chapter of the Sons of Confederate Veterans.

Twenty-seven years had passed since the Civil War, and now the children of the wartime generation were ready to join their parents in honoring the patriots of the Confederacy. Across the South in those years, young and old alike manifested an almost religious devotion to the "Cult of the Lost Cause."

The men who met voted to name the chapter after the great Confederate cavalryman J.E.B. Stuart. They also set forth the aims of their organization, which included caring for poor and disabled veterans, tending Confederate cemeteries and erecting monuments honoring "the unparalleled bravery and fortitude of the soldiers of the Confederacy."

Another aim, based on the belief that the South had not gotten a fair shake in the history books, was to collect documentation for "an impartial history" of the war.

The ambivalence of that generation – who wanted to be both good Southerners and good Americans – was reflected in the remarks of the chapter chairman, the Rev. Carter Helm Jones. "Let it be understood," he said after delivering a paean to the martyrs of the South, "that there is not a more loyal person in the United States than I."

March 25, 1906

The pews were crowded on Sunday, March 25, 1906, when the Rev. W.T. Rodgers preached at the Knoxville Cumberland Presbyterian Church.

Rodgers delivered a jeremiad that morning that held his listeners spellbound. America was heading for destruction, he said, for the Bible says we reap what we sow. "Our nation has been sowing saloons, theaters, dance halls, gambling dens, brothels and lawlessness," he declared, "and now we are reaping an awful harvest of crime and insanity and disrespect for courts and law.''

Among the sources of all this corruption, said Rodgers, the theater ranked high. Adultery and murder were the prominent themes of the stage, and the theaters "even thrust these criminal scenes into the eyes of the whole community with their vulgar billboards." Newspapers were also to blame, for their lurid crime stories appealed to "morbid and ill-balanced minds." The legal profession shared the responsibility, too, for its "willingness to prostitute itself to the protection of criminals." But above all was the saloon, "the chief cause of crime, murder, insanity and lawlessness in our country."

What must America do to save itself from perdition? Outlaw liquor, first of all, Rodgers said, and then reform the educational system, redistribute wealth and reinvigorate the churches.

March 26, 1886

On March 26, 1886, the East Tennessee Insane Asylum (now known as Lakeshore Mental Health Institute) opened its doors to new patients.

Built between 1884 and 1886, the asylum represented the state of the art in the treatment of the mentally ill. The facilities were among the most modern in the nation. Experienced doctors and attendants were hired.

The first patients were a group of 47 men transferred by rail on March 17 from the old, overcrowded Nashville asylum. A large crowd of curious Knoxvillians showed up at the railroad station that day to see the "lunatics," as they were commonly called.

Though he had thus failed to keep the arrival of the first patients from becoming a public spectacle, the director of the asylum did promise to build a fence around it to keep out sightseers.

New patients were accepted beginning on March 26, and the asylum quickly became a bustling institution with its own farm and dairy. By 1898 it had 332 patients – including some blacks, who, according to law, were housed in a separate building.

East Tennessee Insane Asylum

March 27, 1914

On March 27, 1914, Knoxville Mayor Samuel G. Heiskell took a stand on the issue of prostitution. It had recently become a big issue in Knoxville and across the nation.

Traditionally, prostitution had been tolerated in America's cities. But in the early 20th century urban reformers declared that it must go.

Some years earlier, Heiskell had responded not by abolishing prostitution but by segregating it. He created a quasi-official red light district where prostitutes could live and work. By 1914, however, a group of concerned citizens had taken it upon themselves to run the prostitutes out.

On March 27, Mayor Heiskell spoke before the city commissioners and defended the red light district. Prostitution could be controlled, he said, but never stamped out. Knoxville's red light district had been a sensible solution to the problem. Running the prostitutes off had only scattered them throughout the city. The result, he insisted, would be even more illicit sex and venereal disease because many men who feared being seen at a "public bawdy house" would gladly patronize a prostitute in a secluded neighborhood.

The commissioners, siding with the mayor, passed a resolution condemning the closing of the red light district. The reformers, however, had their way. The red light district was gone for good.

March 28, 1925

Knoxville lost one of its preeminent citizens on March 28, 1925, when William J. Oliver died.

A sort of latter-day "carpetbagger" – he was born in Indiana – Oliver had come to Knoxville about 1902 to seek his fortune. Unlike the stereotypical carpetbagger of Reconstruction days, however, he came with a solid record of business success and he was welcomed by progressive Knoxvillians as just the sort of ambitious outsider Knoxville needed to shake off its lethargy.

William J. Oliver

Over the next two decades Oliver created a vast business empire and brought wealth and publicity to Knoxville. He built the L&N Railroad from Knoxville to Georgia, another railroad to the Smoky Mountains, and a huge manufacturing plant on Dale Avenue.

Oliver was also instrumental in bringing the Appalachian Exposition of 1910 to Knoxville. Its purpose was to highlight the region's resources in order to promote not only their exploitation, but also their conservation.

But Oliver also embodied some of the darker aspects of that age, an era which produced the "robber barons." For example, his financial manipulations led the Smoky Mountains railroad into bankruptcy.

March 29, 1980

On March 29, 1980, Knoxville and the nation were suffering through one of the worst periods of inflation in U.S. history.

The cost of living was rising at an annual rate of 18 percent. Major banks had just hiked their prime rate to 19 1/2 percent. Home mortgage rates had climbed to 17 percent, effectively ending mortgage lending in most of the nation. A Gallup poll showed that the median amount spent by families for food each week had increased to $59.

Knoxvillians, like other Americans, were angry and fearful. A News-Sentinel editorial on March 29 lambasted President Jimmy Carter, who claimed that relief was in sight. "That is what we've heard since the administration arrived: Patience, inflation will be brought down. . . . They are right – inflation will abate someday since it cannot soar forever. But before that point comes runaway prices that may well ruin working people, savers, investors and pensioners."

A letter to the editor in that same issue declared that "our country started sliding downhill after Jimmy Carter took office . . . and we're headed for rock-bottom. He doesn't know what to do and never has."

Such sentiments were widespread, and they contributed greatly to Carter's overwhelming defeat by Ronald Reagan in the November 1980 election.

March 30, 1911

On March 30, 1911, Brooklyn's big league baseball team arrived in Knoxville for a two-game series with the University of Tennessee Volunteers.

The Brooklyn team – then known as the Trolley Dodgers – was on a preseason tour, playing exhibition games against minor league and college teams and picking up recruits. No one expected the Volunteers to beat the great Brooklyn nine (actually about 30 strong, including nine pitchers), but the games were enthusiastically anticipated in Knoxville. In those days, UT baseball was at least as popular as football.

Unfortunately, cold weather on March 31 forced the cancellation of the first game. Some of the Trolley Dodgers took advantage of the day off to go riding around town. One of these parties came to grief when the Hudson they were riding in skidded off the pavement at Fifth Avenue and Morgan Street, sending one player to Knoxville General Hospital with cuts and bruises.

A game was played on April 1 and, to no one's surprise, the Volunteers got trounced, 17-3.

The UT Volunteers of 1911

March 31, 1976

By March 31, 1976, Knoxville's downtown parking situation had reached crisis proportions.

Parking downtown had been a problem, of course, ever since automobiles had become popular early in the 20th century. Some relief had come in the 1960s when many offices and retail stores abandoned downtown Knoxville. But a host of construction projects in the 1970s created headaches. The downtown fire hall preempted 100 parking spaces, the Summit Hill Project 150 spaces, the United American Bank 250, and the City-County Building 350.

On March 31, Knoxville's Community Development Corp. executive director declared that the city was in a "deficit short-term parking situation" and singled out the United American Bank as "the sledgehammer that broke the camel's back." A study showed 5,885 parking spaces were available in the central business district, but that demand reached 7,400 at peak hours.

Some observers insisted, however, that the real problem was that downtown parkers were spoiled. Peripheral lots were available, but it seemed that parkers preferred to pay the high rates for prime spaces. It was pointed out that many of the same people who complained about walking a few blocks to work downtown would walk even farther, without complaint, when shopping at West Town Mall.

April 1, 1887

On April 1, 1887, the East Tennessee Telephone Co. bought out the small telephone exchange then serving Knoxville and proceeded to expand and modernize the city's phone service.

Knoxville's first telephone system – a private line connecting a coal company's office on Gay Street with its yard on Jacksboro Street – had been installed in 1879. The next year a New York company established a commercial telephone exchange in Knoxville with 33 subscribers.

After the East Tennessee Telephone Co. bought the exchange in 1887, it replaced the old equipment with a state-of-the-art magneto system. By 1890, Knoxville could boast 350 subscribers, although that was considerably fewer than in Memphis, Nashville, or Chattanooga. Even as late as 1920, when the city's population had reached 78,000, only 7,100 phones were in use.

Long distance service began in 1884, when the telephone company extended a connection to Maryville. Knoxville secured connections outside East Tennessee in 1903, when AT&T's long-distance lines arrived.

A second company, the People's Telephone Co., began operating in Knoxville in 1894. For the next 34 years the city had two separate telephone exchanges, and to be able to reach all the phones in Knoxville one had to subscribe to both exchanges and own two phones. This awkward situation ended in 1928 when Southern Bell consolidated the two exchanges.

April 2, 1970

On April 2, 1970, an official of the Greater Knoxville Bowling Association denounced the city's recent crackdown on clubs illegally selling liquor by the drink.

The crackdown had come just as Knoxville was playing host to the big American Bowling Congress tournament. Police raids on various clubs had put a damper on the post-game celebrations of the visiting bowlers.

"We spent thousands of dollars, a lot of time and effort to land the ABC" tournament, said John Eaton of the GKBA. "We bring in thousands of visitors to our city, then we do things like this (the raids) to make them not ever want to come back."

Eaton was not alone in his criticism of the crackdown. City Councilmen Theotis Robinson Jr. and Kyle Testerman, who had been present at the Sundowner Lounge when it was raided two nights earlier, also condemned the action. Testerman charged that the raids were selective, picking on the less exclusive clubs while avoiding the country clubs. Robinson pointed out that prohibiting liquor by the drink drove convention business away from Knoxville and left a big source of tax revenue untapped.

Testerman used the liquor issue in his successful 1971 mayoral campaign against Mayor Leonard Rogers. In 1972, a city referendum legalized liquor by the drink.

April 3, 1869

Former President Andrew Johnson came to Knoxville on April 3, 1869, and received a rousing welcome.

Johnson's term as president had ended only a month before. His four years in office, one of the most turbulent periods in American political history, had been marked by bitter battles between Johnson and Radical Republicans over reconstructing the former Confederate states and assisting the freed slaves.

Andrew Johnson

The Radical-dominated Congress impeached Johnson and almost succeeded in removing him from office. He left Washington in 1869 despised by his political enemies but adored by conservative white Southerners.

On April 3, a special train brought Johnson from his hometown of Greeneville to the Knoxville depot, where he was met by a huge crowd. He then rode up Gay Street in an open carriage while a brass band played and thousands cheered from sidewalks and windows.

At the Lamar House, prominent Knoxville politician T.A.R. Nelson praised Johnson as "fearless and uncompromising." Johnson then delivered a two-hour speech in which he defended his actions as president.

April 4, 1919

On April 4, 1919, Knoxvillians turned out to welcome back some of the "doughboys."

World War I had ended five months earlier, and the 115th Field Artillery was coming home at last. The regiment was part of the American Expeditionary Force that had helped turn the tide on the battlefields of France and defeat the German enemy. Like all the other returning American heroes of the Great War, the men of the 115th were met by a huge outpouring of patriotic enthusiasm wherever they passed.

Knoxville had planned a big celebration. When the troops arrived at the Southern Railroad depot on the morning of April 4, they were told that the city was theirs for the day. Movie houses were opened to them free of charge, streetcar transportation was likewise free and hundreds of automobiles were put at their disposal. A vaudeville show was given for their benefit at the Bijou Theater. Free food and cigarettes were on hand everywhere for the boys in khaki.

In return the soldiers showed off their war souvenirs, including German equipment, French coins and the regimental mascot, a fox terrier named Lady taken from a captured German officer.

The big event culminated that afternoon with a parade of the whole regiment down Gay Street.

April 5, 1912

One of the most impressive public funerals in Knoxville history took place on April 5, 1912, when the mortal remains of Robert Love Taylor were laid to rest.

A Carter County native and three-term Democratic governor of Tennessee, Bob Taylor was one of the most beloved figures in the state's history. He is perhaps best remembered now for his 1886 gubernatorial election campaign, dubbed the "War of the Roses," in which the opposing Republican candidate was Bob's own brother, Alf.

The whole state mourned Bob Taylor's death in 1912. After lying in state in Nashville, his body was carried by train to Knoxville on April 5. There followed a two-hour funeral service before a standing-room-only crowd of 5,000. One speaker praised Taylor as a man whose "soul was full of music," a man of "great heart – a heart that overflowed all bounds."

After the eulogies, a formal processional – which included the University of Tennessee cadet battalion and military band, the Elks, the Knights Templar, and a host of public officials – accompanied the casket to Old Gray Cemetery, where a veritable mountain of wreaths and flowers stood by the gravesite.

Church bells tolled and businesses were closed during the processional. City, county, and federal offices were closed.

April 6, 1831

On April 6, 1831, the Knoxville Register reported the results of the recent final exams at the Knoxville Female Academy.

The Female Academy, founded in 1827, was one of many such schools in America at that time. Academies were private schools offering instruction at what we today would consider the high school level – a relatively advanced level in that era when few boys or girls went beyond grade school. Female academies such as Knoxville's charged tuition and catered to elite families.

Such education was not intended, of course, to prepare girls for careers, for women were barred from nearly all occupations outside the home in those days. It was intended to create refined and cultured young ladies who would be suitable wives and mothers in elite society.

Thus, the curriculum at the Knoxville Female Academy, while including literature, history, philosophy, math and science, put strong emphasis on the "ornamental" studies, such as piano, painting, drawing, lace-making and sewing.

The Register described the Female Academy's April 1831 exams, which were conducted before an audience of parents and others, as "an exhibition of industry and skill . . . rarely equalled," adding that "it is truly a matter of congratulation that the community is awake to the importance of female education."

April 7, 1968

Sunday, April 7, 1968, was a day of mourning and of trepidation in Knoxville.

Martin Luther King Jr., the nation's most prominent black leader, had been assassinated in Memphis three days earlier. Memorial services were held all over Knoxville on the 7th, and many stores usually open on Sunday were closed.

At the Civic Coliseum, religious leaders of several faiths led a service of remembrance. At the University of Tennessee, a ceremony was held in the auditorium of the student center. At each service, speakers echoed President Lyndon Johnson's call for an end to racial hatred as a fitting tribute to King.

A Knoxville News-Sentinel editorial that day deplored King's murder and noted regretfully that "ours is not the land of brotherhood and equal opportunity we like to think."

But mixed with the city's sorrow was fear – fear that black rage over the assassination might explode into riots in Knoxville as it already had in other cities across the country. Mayor Leonard Rogers publicly discouraged marches or other outdoor gatherings because they might, he said, "provide a setting for trouble."

The News-Sentinel's editorial castigated the rioters: "These are not the disciples of Dr. King, angered and saddened by his senseless murder. . . . They are hooligan opportunists."

April 8, 1897

Knoxville's terrible "Million-Dollar Fire" struck on April 8, 1897.

The fire began in the Hotel Knox on Gay Street. Before it was extinguished it consumed every building on the east side of Gay between Commerce and Union avenues. Besides the hotel, at least 10 buildings were destroyed, including Sterchi Brothers Furniture store, the W.W. Woodruff Wholesale Hardware Co., and the S.B. Newman Printing Co.

Two people were confirmed dead in the blaze, both of them guests at the hotel. One was a lightning rod salesman from Pulaski, the other an elderly Massachusetts man traveling south for his health. A third man later died of injuries received jumping out a window of the hotel.

The damage totaled well over $1 million. While Knoxville had suffered serious fires previously, none had caused a loss greater than $60,000.

Mayor Samuel G. Heiskell issued a statement the day of the fire assuring the public that "new business houses will be built on the sites of the old ones and business will be resumed. The loss, while serious to Knoxville, will prove only a temporary setback."

The mayor was right. Within three days, most of the businesses had found new quarters and were back in operation. Within a year, all of the destroyed buildings but one had been rebuilt.

The results of the "Million-Dollar Fire," as seen from the southwest corner of Gay and Union

April 9, 1962

A former missionary to Cuba visited Knoxville on April 9, 1962, and spoke on the Cuban situation.

Cuba was on everybody's mind in those years. In 1959, Fidel Castro had led a revolution there and then had established close ties with the Soviet Union.

Fearful of a communist enclave so close to our shores, President John F. Kennedy had in 1961 authorized a U.S. government-supported invasion of the island by anti-Castro exiles. It failed, and Castro remained firmly in power.

When the Rev. Thomas H. Willey spoke in Knoxville on April 9, 1962, he offered judgments based on 23 years as a Baptist missionary in Cuba. First of all, he blamed the U.S. government for failing to provide aid to Cuba in years past and thus permitting conditions to develop that allowed Castro to seize power.

The State Department is "full of dupes," Willey said, and "it burns me up." Churches shared the blame, he insisted, for "they didn't send technicians and the right kind of help while there was yet time."

Many Americans had come to similar conclusions in the wake of the Cuban fiasco. One of them was President Kennedy, who created the Peace Corps as part of a broad U.S. program to help developing nations and thus prevent their becoming breeding grounds for communism.

April 10, 1933

On April 10, 1933, one month after taking office, President Franklin Roosevelt outlined for Congress a huge development project for the Tennessee River valley. Thus was the Tennessee Valley Authority born.

Roosevelt and his planners envisioned TVA as a multifaceted program to modernize one of America's most backward regions and to tap its enormous natural resources. TVA would carry out flood control, river navigation, power generation, soil conservation and a host of other projects.

"This in a true sense is a return to the spirit and vision of the pioneer," Roosevelt's message said. "If we are successful here we can march on, step by step, in a like development of other great natural territorial units within our borders."

Congress responded enthusiastically, as it did to most of Roosevelt's suggestions in those first months of his administration. On May 18, the president signed the TVA bill into law.

TVA established its headquarters in Knoxville, and it immediately became an influential institution.

TVA hiring for Norris Dam construction

April 11, 1951

Knoxvillians, like all Americans, were shocked to learn on April 11, 1951, that President Harry Truman had fired Gen. Douglas MacArthur, the supreme commander of American and allied forces in Korea.

Truman and MacArthur had clashed over strategy in the war that was then raging in Korea. MacArthur wanted to expand the conflict by moving against the Chinese communists, who were aiding North Korea. Truman insisted on a limited war. When MacArthur publicly criticized the president, Truman fired him.

Public sentiment in Knoxville and across the nation was strongly supportive of MacArthur. Frustrated by the idea of limited war, Americans rallied around MacArthur.

Local reaction was exemplified by Ruth Stephens, University of Tennessee history professor and international affairs pundit, who told The News-Sentinel that "Gen. MacArthur's program was designed to defeat communism in the Far East. I am afraid his dismissal means that we're willing to stop short of victory." The real issue, she said, was not MacArthur's actions. "The issue is: Is it safe to surrender to communism any place?"

A News-Sentinel editorial commented that "MacArthur's crime is that he saw no sense in fighting a losing or a futile war."

April 12, 1911

April 12, 1911, was the day of the great airplane show in Knoxville.

Since its beginnings with the Wright brothers just eight years earlier, aviation had progressed rapidly and aviators were fast becoming the new American heroes. Two of the best – J.A.D. McCurdy and Lincoln Beachey – came to Knoxville in their Curtiss biplanes on April 12 and put on an exhibition.

Over 2,500 people went out to Johnson's racetrack that day to see the show. Thousands more watched for free from distant hills. For many it was their very first glimpse of the marvelous new flying machines.

As the crowd gawked, cheered and applauded, McCurdy and Beachey raced their planes over the track, climbed thousands of feet in the air, and dropped make-believe bombs on a model of a battleship.

That night, McCurdy, who was not only a dashing flyboy but a serious student of the science of aviation, lectured at the University of Tennessee engineering department. He spoke on the history of flight, explained his preference for biplanes over monoplanes, and predicted that aviation would eventually cease to be just a sport and would "become part of the commercial means of transportation," just like the automobile.

April 13, 1945

On April 13, 1945, all of Knoxville was in mourning for the president of the United States.

Franklin D. Roosevelt, who had led the nation through the Great Depression and the Second World War, had died suddenly the day before. His successor, Harry S. Truman, immediately took up the task of completing the victory over Germany and Japan.

In Knoxville on April 13, special memorial services were held in every school. Many offices and businesses were closed. Flags flew at half-staff all around the city. Grief was plainly visible on every face. At the USO center, GIs were seen openly weeping as they listened to the radio reports.

The News-Sentinel that day omitted the comics and other features to devote full coverage to the news. "Save this paper as a record for the future," the paper advised.

The News-Sentinel's editorial that day spoke movingly about the nation's loss. "In every home and on all the seas and in the foxholes of every fighting front, his fellow citizens pay homage to their fallen commander-in-chief. Their grief is personal. People felt they knew him. As no other man of his generation, and few of any age, he inspired a highly individual regard. . . . History will rate him high. . . . He led this nation through perils in which it might have perished."

April 14, 1981

An important court case involving school drug searches was decided in Knoxville on April 14, 1981.

Suit had been brought in federal court against school officials by the mother of a female student at Karns High School who had been suspended in 1980 following a search of her purse, clothing and car. The plaintiff contended that the search was a violation of civil rights.

The girl had been searched after another student claimed he had bought pills from her. In court, school officials testified that they found marijuana residue in her purse and, later, in her car. It was revealed, however, that at an earlier school board hearing on the matter, officials had said nothing illegal was found in the purse.

The pills turned out to be over-the-counter caffeine pills. The girl testified that she knew nothing about the marijuana in the car. Her stepfather swore that the car was his and that he had smoked marijuana in it. The judge instructed the jury that the girl could not be held responsible for illegal substances in her car of which she was unaware.

After two hours of deliberation, the jury found that the girl's civil rights had not been violated. The case cleared the way for sterner measures in the public schools to deal with possible drug problems.

April 15, 1959

On April 15, 1959, following the sudden death of Mayor Jack Dance, the City Council elected Councilman Cas Walker interim mayor.

The election was not without controversy. One dissenting councilman protested that Walker, who was also vice mayor and chairman of the Beer Board, was being given too much power. Walker assured the public that he would serve to the best of his ability, but acknowledged that "everybody don't agree with me all the time."

That was an understatement. During the more than 30 years he was active in politics, Cas Walker raised the hackles of a good many people. But he also won the loyalty of many others, particularly poor and working-class citizens, black as well as white, whose interests he represented against what he termed the "silk-stocking crowd."

Cas Walker

His numerous political controversies – which included engaging in a fistfight at a City Council meeting – helped make Walker a legend in his own time.

So did his business activities. As the owner of a chain of grocery stores and a master of publicity, Walker made millions of dollars. Throwing live chickens off the roof of his stores and offering free dog dips with every $10 grocery purchase were only two of his crowd-pleasing stunts.

April 16, 1912

"Monster Ship Titanic Founders," read The Knoxville Sentinel's headlines on April 16, 1912. That day Knoxvillians learned of the "wholesale loss of life" on the huge liner, which had hit an iceberg and sunk in the icy Atlantic Ocean.

The tragedy was brought home to the people of Knoxville when it was learned that a former resident, the Rev. R.J. Bateman, whose daughter still lived here, was among those lost. He had resided in the city until 1902 and had won esteem for his work among the poor.

Also among those lost was a former Washington correspondent for The Sentinel, Archibald W. Butte, who was at the time an aide to President Taft.

Moreover, it was learned that prominent Knoxville businessman M.B. Arnstein had intended to make a return trip from Europe on the Titanic the next summer. He had now booked passage on another ship, The Sentinel reported, remarking that "while he felt a little squeamish since he heard the news . . . yet he was not a fatalist and would make his ocean voyage just the same."

A Sentinel editorial pointed out that "in the long annals of the sea there is no record of a single disaster as great as this," and urged that ships "be required to carry lifeboats enough to carry every passenger, officer and seaman aboard."

April 17, 1840

A group of newspaper editors and printers gathered at the Mansion House Hotel in Knoxville on the evening of April 17, 1840, to celebrate the founding of the East Tennessee Typographical Society.

They hailed the formation of their society as a great event, for it brought together all the members of the printing craft in Knoxville. In the society, the business and political rivalries of Knoxville's three newspapers were put aside, and the members worked for their common interests.

There were toasts to the press; to Benjamin Franklin, patron saint of American printers; to "the editor who loves truth better than party"; and to "the memory of the veterans of the craft who have passed away."

Frederick S. Heiskell, Knoxville's foremost newspaper editor and president of the society, spoke in praise of the invention of printing. "By this noble art," he said, "every man may acquire knowledge and may become enlightened. Printing removed the veil which obscured the reason of man – it broke the chain that bound him in ignorance and shed a halo of light, dispelling the darkness that overhung the world."

The Knoxville Times reported that the members "dispersed in great good humor" – which was undoubtedly true, as they had drunk at least 25 toasts.

April 18, 1901

The Knoxville city health officer got a shock on April 18, 1901, when he went to investigate a report of a foul odor on the grounds of the Tennessee Medical College.

With the help of a policeman, health officer James Kennedy located a spot in the ground from which the stench seemed to emanate. After digging down about two feet, the men uncovered a rotting human corpse.

The discovery was reported to Dr. W.S. Nash of the Medical College, whereupon a dispute arose. Nash claimed that it was merely a partial skeleton, with no flesh attached and no odor, and that it must have been buried years earlier, before the Medical College was built. He denied any prior knowledge of it.

But Kennedy was insistent. It was a relatively recent burial, he said, and the corpse was quite putrid. He went on to state his opinion that the body had been "pickled" and used in the Medical College before burial.

The dispute ended quietly. Kennedy agreed to take no action if the nuisance was removed. Nash agreed to have it reburied in the county cemetery.

Presumably, however, the incident was a lesson to Medical College students and faculty inclined to take the easy approach to disposing of their used corpses.

April 19, 1946

On April 19, 1946, the Tennessee Supreme Court upheld Knoxville's decision to switch to Eastern Standard Time.

The city had held a referendum the previous November that mandated the change from Central Standard to Eastern Standard. But a citizens' group had challenged the legality of the referendum. The Supreme Court's decision overruled that challenge. Mayor Cas Walker then issued a proclamation setting April 28 as the date for the switch to Eastern Standard Time.

While the majority of Knoxvillians favored the switch, there was a good deal of confusion accompanying it. For one thing, Knoxville declined to go along with daylight-saving time. Thus, when other cities in the Eastern Time Zone went on daylight-saving time, Knoxville's clocks remained an hour behind.

Furthermore, while 16 other East Tennessee towns (including Oak Ridge, Maryville, Gatlinburg, Sevierville, and Morristown) joined Knoxville in making the switch to Eastern Standard Time on April 28, others did not – thus rendering East Tennessee a crazy-quilt patchwork of different time zones.

Moreover, Knoxville's railroads continued to print their schedules in Central Time.

Not until some years later, when Knoxville accepted daylight-saving time and all of East Tennessee went on Eastern Time, was the confusion eliminated.

April 20, 1935

On April 20, 1935, many of Knoxville's leading citizens rallied in behalf of the Tennessee Valley Authority.

TVA, then only two years old, had broad support in Knoxville. When a bill to expand TVA's powers appeared stalled in Congress in April 1935, Knoxvillians rallied.

On April 20 Mayor John T. O'Connor sent a telegram to Congress and urged mayors and citizens all up and down the Valley to do the same. Furthermore, he and other Knoxville leaders announced plans for a TVA Appreciation Week to be held in May.

The announcement was accompanied by strong statements of support from Knoxville's business leaders. Southern Bell district manager Frank Garratt said, "TVA has done more for Knoxville than anything that has come this way since I have been here, and that is 30 years." Weston Fulton of Fulton Sylphon praised TVA for bringing money and jobs into Knoxville.

The News-Sentinel added its endorsement in an editorial: "These past two years have been crowded with new and rich experiences for East Tennesseans. . . . Nothing could be more fitting than the proposed TVA Appreciation Week. . . . Such a demonstration will give reassurance to President Roosevelt of our faith in his leadership."

April 21, 1898

On April 21, 1898, Knoxvillians were caught up in the excitement of the outbreak of the Spanish-American War.

The day before, Congress had authorized the use of troops to free Cuba from Spanish rule. For years, Americans had been disturbed by stories of Spanish atrocities in the rebellious Cuban colony. The crisis came to a head early in 1898 when the U.S. battleship Maine was blown up in Havana harbor, a disaster Americans blamed on the Spanish.

"The Drums Beat to Arms: War With Spain Now Begins" read The Knoxville Sentinel's headline on April 21. Early that day, when it was learned that a troop train carrying the men of Battery D, Fifth U.S. Artillery was passing through town, Knoxvillians turned out to cheer the troops.

At the courthouse that night, what began as a Democratic political rally turned into a patriotic rally.

The Sentinel's editorial that evening reflected the enthusiasm and brash confidence of most Americans as the war began: "The supremacy of the high civilization of North America over the effete and decaying culture of Spain ought not to leave the contest long in doubt. . . . Spain will be wiped from our hemisphere. Cuba will enjoy the air of liberty. The world will applaud our act."

Spanish-American War troops parade down Gay Street.

April 22, 1926

A revival in Knoxville had some unusual visitors on April 22, 1926.

The revival had been in progress for two weeks. Hundreds of people crowded into a big tent each night to hear the Rev. Mel Leaman preach.

On April 22, the crowd was augmented by a group of 250 Ku Klux Klansmen in white robes. They sat together in a special section, listened solemnly to the entire sermon, and afterward praised Leaman's work and presented him with a large cash donation.

The Ku Klux Klan enjoyed great popularity in the 1920s, not just in Knoxville but throughout the nation. It resembled the earlier Klan of Reconstruction days in that it was a racist organization devoted to white supremacy. The Klan of the 1920s, however, included on its hate-list Catholics and foreigners along with blacks. The newer Klan was also less secret and (with some notable exceptions) less violent than the earlier one. The Knoxville Klan of the 1920s was typical of many local Klan groups in that it was mostly a social club whose members enjoyed participating in parades and other public events.

The next night, April 23, the Klansmen again attended Leaman's revival. This was surely one of the most anomalous gatherings in Knoxville history, for the featured entertainment that evening was a 250-member black choir.

April 23, 1838

On April 23, 1838, the Knoxville Board of Aldermen passed an ordinance prohibiting the desecration of the Sabbath.

The ordinance was typical of those passed by many towns in the early decades of the 19th century. In those years a great wave of Protestant evangelicalism swept the nation, and many Americans became convinced that society was godless and corrupt and must be reformed.

Knoxville's 1838 ordinance forbade any business to remain open on Sunday, especially saloons. Furthermore, boats could not be loaded or unloaded at the wharf on Sundays, nor could wagons load or unload merchandise on the streets. In fact, no laborers or merchants could do any work on Sunday, nor could any citizen even chop wood.

In the latter part of the 19th century there arose a new attitude toward Sabbath observance that looked upon Sundays as a day for recreation as well as worship. Reflecting this trend, the aldermen in 1870 modified Knoxville's Sabbath ordinance to allow ice-cream shops and soda fountains to remain open on Sundays. Furthermore, the law was relaxed to allow milkmen and icemen to make home deliveries, and also to permit butchers to stock their shops on Sunday for Monday morning's market – provided this was done in a quiet way.

April 24, 1908

An article in The Knoxville Sentinel on April 24, 1908, encouraged women to look into alternative careers.

The turn of the century was an era of dizzying change. America was rapidly being transformed from a traditional agrarian nation into a modern urban one.

More young women were living on their own, and divorce was becoming more common. Thus, more and more women needed to become self-supporting.

Carrie Callaway, the author of The Sentinel article, went through the short list of occupations open to women. The fields of schoolteaching and stenography were "already over-crowded," she said. Nursing was too taxing physically for many women. Clerking in retail stores "is too wearing and harassing."

Callaway then suggested three areas in which women might consider carving out a niche. Why not be a florist, she said. Women are "inseparably connected with flowers" and "love to work with plants," and there was no reason to exclude them. Or why not be a tailor catering to women? Women who needed quality clothes would no doubt prefer to go to a female tailor. Likewise, there was a need for laundries specializing in cleaning and mending women's clothes. "Why does not some enterprising woman fill this need for her own sex?"

April 25, 1821

The East Tennessee Bible Society held its annual meeting in Knoxville on April 25, 1821.

The ETBS was an auxiliary of the American Bible Society, founded in 1816 to disseminate the Christian Testament throughout America and the world.

At the April 25 meeting, the members of the ETBS heard a gloomy report from the directors. The people of East Tennessee, it seemed, were generally indifferent to the work of the society. In many counties few volunteers could be found to act as the society's agents. The result was that "a very large proportion of the population do not possess the Bible."

There were a few bright spots in the report. Baptists had been active as agents in some areas. In one county where no man volunteered, women had stepped forward to help. The society had achieved success in its work among the Cherokee Indians who had been "without the word of God."

The report concluded with the wish that volunteers could be found in each East Tennessee county. And even more important, the report pointed out, was the work of the national society among the "heathen nations" whose inhabitants "are sitting in darkness and the shadow of death, without any acquaintance with the true God."

April 26, 1888

On April 26, 1888, Knoxville's black community was up in arms over the slaying of a black man by a white police officer.

The episode had begun on April 14, when officer Sam Torbett tried to arrest a suspect on Market Square. When the man resisted, Torbett pulled his pistol and used it as a club. The pistol discharged and hit a bystander, a black man named George Wilson.

Badly wounded in the abdomen, Wilson succumbed to blood poisoning on April 26. A coroner's jury consisting of four blacks and three whites was assembled immediately. The jury heard testimony from several witnesses, including a black policeman who swore officer Torbett had overreacted and had no cause to draw his pistol.

The jury concluded that "Wilson came to his death indirectly by a pistol ball fired from a pistol in the hands of Samuel Torbett."

Fearful that Torbett might get off scot-free, members of Knoxville's black community quickly went into action. They demanded that Torbett be tried for murder, raised money to assist in the prosecution and hired their own lawyer.

Their work was not in vain. Torbett was arrested that very day and later charged with first-degree murder.

April 27, 1926

By April 27, 1926, the condition of the county workhouse in Knoxville had become a public scandal.

The workhouse housed minor offenders, such as vagrants and public drunks, who could not pay their fines. In 1926, The Knoxville News and The Knoxville Sentinel (which later merged to form The News-Sentinel) both launched investigations of workhouse conditions, complete with photos. The reports were shocking, revealing unspeakable filth and overcrowding. In one cell, seven men slept side-by-side in an eight-foot-wide bunk. In another cell, stacked bunks had only 22 inches of headroom.

"The workhouse system is fundamentally bad," The News announced in an editorial on April 27. "To pen men up in crowded bunks, where they do not have room to sit upright, foul-smelling because of the complete absence of plumbing, would be too cruel a punishment even for murder and highway robbery."

A county official who supervised the workhouse admitted that it constituted a "monstrous injustice" and blamed inadequate funding by the penny-pinching County Court.

Eventually the public outrage stirred up by the newspapers' revelations forced the court to clean up the workhouse.

April 28, 1973

Knoxvillians gathered solemnly on April 28, 1973, to pay tribute to Knox Countians who had lost their lives in the Vietnam War.

America's participation in the war had ended only a short time before. At Knoxville's City Hall, a monument – the "Memorial Eagle" – had been erected to honor the county's dead. The dedication ceremonies on April 28 were attended by public officials, relatives of those lost in the war and many other citizens. All listened with tears in their eyes as patriotic songs were sung and the names of the 98 dead were read aloud. Then Mayor Kyle Testerman spoke, noting that "the memory of their service is indelibly fixed in our hearts and minds."

Col. Norman Gaddis, foreground, views the "Memorial Eagle."

The guest of honor at the ceremony was Air Force Col. and former Knoxvillian Norman C. Gaddis, recently released from six years of confinement in a North Vietnamese prisoner of war camp. Gaddis told the crowd of his deep gratitude for being asked to help "pay homage to the sons of Tennessee who gave their lives so others might live in freedom."

That evening a banquet was held at the Hyatt Regency to honor Col. Gaddis. In his remarks there, he spoke about his wartime experiences and praised the American people who would not let the prisoners be forgotten during the long war.

April 29, 1877

Knoxville lost one of its most prominent and colorful citizens on April 29, 1877, when William G. "Parson" Brownlow died.

Since his arrival in Knoxville in 1849, Brownlow had never ceased to make waves. As editor of the Knoxville Whig, he became famous for his uncompromising opinions. A staunch supporter of the Union during the Civil War, he made himself so obnoxious to Confederate authorities that they banished him to the North in 1862.

When Union troops captured Knoxville in 1863, the irrepressible Brownlow returned, re-established the Whig (adding "and Rebel Ventilator" to its name) and resumed his anti-Confederate tirades. His stature as a Unionist led to his election as governor in 1865. The ensuing four years of his governorship brought more controversy, as Brownlow battled ex-rebels, Democrats and the Ku Klux Klan, and – ironically, considering his longtime pro-slavery beliefs – successfully fought to enfranchise blacks.

Elected to the U.S. Senate in 1869, Brownlow served one term, then returned to Knoxville and resumed his newspaper work until his death in 1877.

Even in his later years he seems never to have mellowed. Always outspoken and opinionated, he adhered to the mottoes he had announced in the Whig from the beginning: "Cry Aloud and Spare Not," and "Independent in All Things, Neutral in Nothing."

April 30, 1875

The Opera House was packed on April 30, 1875, as Knoxvillians gathered to see Tom Thumb.

One of the most celebrated entertainers of the 19th century, Tom Thumb (a 40-inch-tall midget, born Charles S. Stratton) had become famous before the Civil War as one of the stars of P.T. Barnum's Museum in New York, which featured oddities such as bearded ladies, trained fleas, and the original "Siamese twins." Tom's marriage to Miss Minnie Warren – a dwarf even smaller than himself – was one of the most publicized show-business events of the 1860s.

By 1875, "General" Tom Thumb had assembled a troupe of midgets and dwarfs and was touring on his own. His four shows in Knoxville on April 30 and May 1 featured performances by Miss Minnie, who sang and then compared heights with children in the audience (she was about the same size as a four-year-old girl). Also appearing were "Commodore" Nutt, who did his impersonation of an Irishman and sang "My Mother Says I Musn't"; and "Major" Newell, who demonstrated his agility on roller skates.

The highlight of the show was the duet by Mr. and Mrs. Tom Thumb. "The general presents a commanding appearance on the stage," wrote one member of the audience, who concluded that the show was "one of the finest our citizens have ever had the pleasure of witnessing."

May 1, 1982

"World Comes to Knoxville" announced The News-Sentinel's top headline on May 1, 1982. On that day the World's Fair opened.

It was the culmination of years of planning and controversy. The idea of a World's Fair in Knoxville was conceived in the 1970s during the administration of Mayor Kyle Testerman and carried to fruition under Mayor Randy Tyree. Supporters of the fair touted it as the propulsive force for a "quantum jump" that would revitalize the whole city.

President Ronald Reagan and Jake Butcher at opening ceremonies

Banker Jake Butcher headed a committee to study the feasibility of the project. Federal, state and city funds were secured, a 72-acre site was prepared in the Second Creek valley, official sanction was granted by the Bureau of International Expositions, and one by one foreign nations committed to the Knoxville fair. Opposition was voiced from the beginning by some who warned that the project was merely a private developers' scheme financed by public money and who cast doubt on the rosy promises of the fair boosters.

By May 1, 22 foreign nations had joined in. President Ronald Reagan was on hand that day to officially open the Knoxville World's Fair, whose theme — symbolized by the Sunsphere — was "Energy Turns the World." Millions of visitors came to the city over the next six months, but the debate over how much Knoxville benefitted by the fair continues to this day.

Tour buses jam the North Gate to the fair site.

May 2, 1855

Knoxville photographer J. R. Brockelbank informed the public on May 2, 1855, that he had just installed a skylight in his studio on the corner of Gay and Main and that he was now "prepared to take daguerreotypes, singly or in groups of from two to twelve, upon strict artistic principles."

The art of photography was born in France in 1839 with the development of the daguerreotype camera, which produced images on a copper plate coated with light-sensitive silver nitrate. The technique spread quickly to the United States, and soon every town had its daguerreotype studio where inexpensive photographs could be made. Dubbed "the mirror with a memory," the daguerreotype was an apt expression of American democracy and egalitarianism in the Jacksonian era, for it allowed the common people for the first time to have their portraits made. Before that time, hand-painted likenesses were the only portraits available, and only the well-to-do could afford them.

Poor indoor lighting in that era – plus`the slow photographic process that required the subject to sit perfectly still for a considerable period – made photography difficult. But with the skylight, Brockelbank assured his patrons, "pictures (can be) taken on the darkest days, and pictures of children taken in less time than has ever been previously done in Knoxville."

May 3, 1924

Knoxvillians watched and cheered on Saturday, May 3, 1924, as 2,000 youngsters paraded down Gay Street carrying their house pets.

The parade was one of the highlights of Boys' Week. That event, sponsored by the YMCA and carried out with the cooperation of various professionals and tradesmen of Knoxville, was intended to give young boys a taste of what the adult world of work was like. During Boys' Week, aspiring young bankers were invited to the offices of the city's banking executives, while would-be electricians, plumbers, doctors, coaches, policemen, railroad engineers, and city officials likewise worked side by side with grown-up practitioners of those trades.

The parade on Saturday brought all the boys together, along with their dogs, cats, rabbits, white rats, and roosters. "All of the city's domestic menagerie was lined up," one witness reported. "Folks of Knoxville who didn't see that parade missed something really worthwhile. There was a thrill every minute." Later that day there was a big hobby show where the boys showed off their handiwork.

Boys' Week came to a close the next day, Sunday. That day boys took over Knoxville's churches. Boy preachers spoke from the pulpits, boy teachers conducted Sunday school classes, and boy choir masters led the singing, while the adult pastors and their co-workers had a day of rest.

May 4, 1913

An audience of 1,200 gathered at Staub's Theater in Knoxville on Sunday, May 4, 1913, to hear a lecture by two of the South's leading anti-prostitution crusaders.

Dr. Stewart Roberts and the Rev. Dunbar Ogden, both of Atlanta, had headed up a recent campaign that resulted in the closing down of that city's notorious red-light district. Now they were on the road, spreading the word to reform-minded people in Knoxville and elsewhere about how to cure the "social evil."

The first step, Roberts told his listeners, was to recognize that prostitution was not a victimless crime. It spread disease in epidemic proportions, he said, and must be ranked with tuberculosis and alcoholism as one of the nation's leading health problems. "The wages of sin," Roberts concluded, "is death."

Ogden then outlined a plan of action like that which had succeeded in Atlanta. It involved a public information campaign, pressure on public officials, and solicitous attention to the "fallen women" in order to set them on a new path.

The lecture was an enormous success. The next day, May 5, a follow-up meeting of ministers and laypersons was held at the YMCA to begin organizing an anti-prostitution campaign in Knoxville. By 1914, the campaign had achieved victory, and Knoxville's red-light district was gone.

May 5, 1961

Depending on one's point of view, Knoxville took either a big step forward or a big step backward on May 5, 1961. On that day Knox County voters approved, by a 53.4 percent majority, package sales of liquor in Knoxville.

As late as 1957, a similar referendum had rejected liquor sales. But the increasing suburbanization of the county, and the growing conviction that Knoxville's 54-year-old prohibition law was unenforceable and hindered the progress of the city, finally achieved a majority vote for liquor sales in 1961.

Anti-liquor activists, led by the United Christian Forces, had fought to the last ditch, however. In fact, the vote outside the city went against liquor by a small margin. But the efforts of the pro-liquor forces achieved a huge margin of victory in the city.

Voters who had not registered did so before the critical liquor vote on May 5.

A News-Sentinel editorial on May 6 congratulated the citizens. "This community has at long last shed its hypocrisy and its unrealistic attitude toward the liquor business," it read.

Another battled loomed down the road, however, for Knoxville's "progressive" forces would not rest until the city had legalized liquor by the drink.

May 6, 1936

On Wednesday, May 6, 1936, the University of Tennessee was in an uproar over an egg-throwing incident.

It had all begun the previous Friday, during the traditional Carnicus parade and show. As the parade passed the Law School building, a group of freshmen law students pelted the procession with eggs. Later, at the Carnicus show in the UT auditorium, another volley of eggs was loosed, splattering the stage and the front row of spectators.

On May 6, the whole student body was called on the carpet and given a stern lecture by Dean F. M. Massey. He blamed the law students for starting the affair, but acknowledged that other students were also responsible.

Massey's remarks were restrained and temperate by comparison with the tirade he had delivered two days earlier, when he was still hot under the collar. That day he called the freshman law school class together and announced that if such incidents reoccurred he would shut down the law school. "We don't need the law school," he said. "There are too many lawyers in Tennessee now."

Asked to comment, UT President James Hoskins expressed disbelief that Massey had made such a remark, and said furthermore that no administrator "has any right to say the law school will be abolished. That is a matter for the trustees."

May 7, 1964

Knoxville welcomed a famous visitor on May 7, 1964: President Lyndon B. Johnson.

The president was on a two-day, five-state tour to promote his "War on Poverty," a key target of which was southern Appalachia. Knoxvillians turned out en masse for the visit, lining the motorcade route from the airport and crowding into the Civic Coliseum where the president was to speak.

On his way to the Coliseum, Johnson viewed an urban redevelopment project and a vocational training center that represented Knoxville's contribution to the War on Poverty.

At the Coliseum the president said that "democracy doesn't mean anything unless we are all our brothers' keepers." Furthermore, he praised TVA as a "shining example of how government and free enterprise can work hand in hand to help people," which was a major theme of his own Appalachian development program. And, no doubt looking toward his reelection, he castigated his political opponents as "men of timid faith and narrow vision."

President Lyndon Johnson at airport welcome

May 8, 1867

On May 8, 1867, a federal official submitted a report on Knoxville's blacks.

The official was an agent of the Freedmen's Bureau, which had been created at the end of the Civil War to help the newly-freed slaves in the South. The bureau carried out a wide range of duties: supervising labor contracts between blacks and whites, overseeing black schools, and providing food for the needy.

Black Knoxvillians were doing well, according to the Bureau agent's report. They were bargaining shrewdly with their white employers, and in many cases had managed to buy their own homes. Two black churches were active, both under the supervision of black preachers. Three schools for blacks were in operation, two of them under the supervision of white missionaries from the north and one under a black veteran of the Union army.

The Freedmen's Bureau and northern humanitarian agencies were providing aid to the poor in Knoxville, white as well as black. Local officials had refused to do so, having budgeted all their funds for the repair of bridges destroyed in a recent flood.

Knoxville's blacks were "generally industrious," the agent concluded. "While they have yet much to learn and much to do, as a whole in this city, they have earned a good name and deserve respect."

May 9, 1963

On May 9, 1963, the Knoxville-Knox County Civil Defense Agency began training managers for the city's fallout shelters.

The training was part of a civil defense program instituted by the government after the Cuban Missile Crisis of 1962, when the threat of nuclear war had nearly become a reality.

In Knoxville, 99 fallout shelters were established in various public and private buildings. These shelters had a capacity of 253,935 persons — more than twice the population of the city at that time. Government regulations required that shelters have a radiation protection factor of at least four — that is, 100 times more protection than a person would have outside.

The fallout shelters were stocked with medical supplies, radiation-measuring equipment, waste disposal chemicals, special waterless soap, toilet articles, and enough food and water to sustain each person for two weeks. The food was limited to a government-approved biscuit that tasted like animal crackers and had a long shelf-life.

The shelter managers, who were mostly the maintenance personnel in the buildings involved, were given instruction in nuclear weapons, attack warnings, shelter operation, emergency procedures and shelter living.

Among the shelters were those at the Andrew Johnson Hotel, with a capacity of 2,080; the Lawson McGhee Library, with 286; and The News-Sentinel building, with 1,890.

May 10, 1900

On May 10, 1900, Knoxvillians were shocked by the death of a prominent citizen in a buggy accident.

Mike Condon, a businessman and school board member, was out for a ride that day with his wife and Mr. and Mrs. M. F. Shea, who were visiting from New York. Mr. Shea had relatives who had fought in the Civil War battle of Fort Sanders, and he had asked to see that site, which in those years still stood near what is now Seventeenth Street and Laurel Avenue.

As the two-horse buggy proceeded down the steep hill from the fort toward Kingston Pike (now Cumberland Avenue), Condon — who was asthmatic — suffered a violent coughing fit. He dropped the reins, the horses went out of control, and the buggy hurtled down the hill and smashed into a telephone pole. Both Mr. Condon and Mr. Shea died of skull fractures. Both women survived.

The next day, Knoxville schools were closed as a tribute to Mike Condon, and the Chamber of Commerce held a memorial service.

Part of the reason that Knoxvillians were so shocked is that fatal vehicular accidents were very uncommon in that era of the horse and buggy. But the day of the automobile was dawning, and with it would come more and more such tragedies on the streets of Knoxville.

May 11, 1924

Knoxvillians celebrated Mother's Day on Sunday, May 11, 1924, with a number of special events.

Since 1906, when Anne Jarvis of Philadelphia had proposed setting aside the second Sunday in May to honor America's mothers, the event had grown into a nationwide observance. Among the Mother's Day festivities held in Knoxville in 1924 was a breakfast at the YMCA and a special musical program put on by the Sunday school students at Oakwood Baptist Church.

The big event was the community observance at the Lyric Theater. It featured a concert by the Amra Grotto Band and the Knoxville High School girls' glee club. Girl Scouts were on hand to present a flower (furnished free by Baum's florist shop) to each mother over 60 years old. Ages were recorded as the mothers entered, and the oldest mother present received a rocking chair provided by King Mantel Furniture Co. City manager Louis Brownlow addressed the audience of 1,200 and spoke in glowing terms of the mothers of America.

An editorial in The Knoxville Sentinel noted that "if 'Home Sweet Home' brings fond recollections today, it is because in that home a mother stood guard. . . . Our nation today . . . is great and rich because the mothers of America have made the American home the model and standard for the world."

May 12, 1846

A tongue-in-cheek letter to the editor of the Knoxville Standard on May 12, 1846, urged the formation of a "Knoxville Loafers' Club."

The letter writer, who signed himself Bob Short Jr., began by noting that the time was right for such a club, for the coming summer would no doubt bring "an unusually heavy addition to the ranks of Loaferism." The younger generation of loafers, he pointed out, would benefit from "intimate association with the older and experienced" loafers.

Bob Short warned his readers not to mistake the poor, raggedy men who lived by picking up odd jobs around town for the genuine article — the "pure, unadulterated and scientific loafer" who has developed a great talent for "killing time and living comfortably without the least possible effort." Besides being thoroughly idle, true loafers were generally well-dressed — "but at whose expense, or by what means, no man . . . knoweth."

"There are several full grown specimens about town," Short noted, "who may be seen every day of the week, lounging on the street corners . . ., puffing away at their (pipes), indulging in an occasional remark on the passersby, gazing into the ladies' faces and admiring . . . the bewitching contour of their bustles."

There is no evidence that any Loafers' Club was ever formed — no doubt its potential members decided it was too much trouble.

May 13, 1915

On May 13, 1915, The Knoxville Sentinel spoke up in support of local clothing merchants.

The merchants had complained because salesmen representing out-of-town clothing firms had recently appeared in Knoxville and were taking orders for men's shirts and women's apparel. The Sentinel, anxious to protect the commercial interests of the city — especially those that advertised in The Sentinel — denounced the outsiders and scolded those Knoxvillians who bought from them.

"It is almost inconceivable," the article declared, "how a true, loyal Knoxvillian can patronize people of this character. . . . The outside merchant, it may be well to keep in mind, pays no taxes, no salaries, no rent, no lights, no heat, and supports no one but employees in a distant city. These fellows take money from the community that could be just as well spent with the local merchant."

The merchant of Knoxville, by contrast, "helps support the schools of the city, does his part towards keeping up the streets, providing police and fire protection and innumerable other things that should be paramount in the minds of those who, through thoughtlessness or otherwise, patronize itinerant salesmen from Chicago, New York, Cincinnati, and other cities."

Furthermore, The Sentinel insisted, Knoxville merchants have "a reputation for at all times carrying merchandise of the very highest quality."

May 14, 1896

Representatives of a number of Knoxville women's groups met on May 14, 1896, and founded the Florence Crittenton Rescue Home of Knoxville.

The national foundation, of which the Knoxville Rescue Home was a part, had been established in 1883 by Charles Nelson Crittenton, a wealthy New York businessman and philanthropist, who named it in honor of his deceased daughter. The Florence Crittenton Homes were intended to shelter "unfortunate" young women — runaways, pregnant teenagers, victims of abuse, and others needing aid — and to help them establish new lives.

In June 1896, another meeting was held in Knoxville to begin the work of raising funds for the home, acquiring a building, and hiring employees. The home opened in temporary quarters on August 30, 1896. It was an immediate success and was soon sheltering an average of 13 young women a day. Some were wards of the county, which provided a small appropriation to supplement the private donations the home depended on.

In 1898, the home was visited by Charles Crittenton himself, who was traveling around the country in his private railroad car inspecting the 53 Florence Crittenton Homes. By that time the Knoxville home was located on Central Avenue, a busy location deemed undesirable given the sensitive nature of the home's mission. Soon thereafter new quarters were built in a less conspicuous part of town.

May 15, 1872

Knoxvillians gathered for a solemn ceremony on May 15, 1872, a day set aside to decorate the graves of Confederate soldiers.

A large crowd assembled that afternoon at Bethel Cemetery, where the women of the Confederate memorial society had for some time been preparing the grounds.

The speaker of the day was the Rev. E. E. Hoss. He spoke consolingly and chose his words with care, for he was keenly aware that the Civil War had ended only seven years before, that the South was still undergoing a painful reconstruction, that the antagonism between North and South had not yet subsided, and that Knoxvillians had been and still were deeply divided on the great issue of secession and war.

"This is not the place to revive profitless discussion" of the war, Hoss said. "Let politics be delegated to the politicians. . . . But I am hopeful that the time will yet come when, . . . all the bitter memories of the past having been forgotten, . . . a whole nation reunited in fraternal esteem shall give honor alike to those who fell upholding the Bonnie Blue Flag and to those whose lives were surrendered battling for the Star Spangled Banner."

Following the address, prayers were offered, the Knoxville German Band played a dirge, and the members of the memorial society placed flowers on the graves.

May 16, 1946

One of Knoxville's most renowned citizens died on May 16, 1946. Weston M. Fulton, businessman and inventor, died of a heart attack while shaving.

Born in Alabama in 1871, Fulton began his career as a U.S. Weather Bureau meteorologist. Transferred to Knoxville in 1898, he took some science courses at UT, began tinkering in the laboratory, and soon came up with an improved river gauge. It was the first of more than 100 inventions he would patent in his lifetime.

Weston M. Fulton

His most famous was the "sylphon," a seamless, corrugated bellows made of heat-sensitive metal and used as a thermostat. Eventually it was put to use in hundreds of devices, ranging from Navy depth bombs to refrigerators.

Fulton was also a brilliant businessman. He established his own company to produce the sylphon and made himself a millionaire. He sold the company (now the Fulton Sylphon Division of Robertshaw Controls) in 1930 and thereafter devoted himself to other enterprises and to philanthropy.

His mansion on Lyons View Drive, built in 1928 at a cost of $500,000, was a Knoxville showplace until it was torn down in 1967.

May 17, 1895

On May 17, 1895, the Knoxville city government was in the midst of a big squabble over the board of health.

In conformance with state law, City Council had appointed a six-man board. But one by one, the members resigned in protest.

The last member, Dr. John Boyd, turned in his resignation on May 17 with an explanation. The board, he said, was intended to advise the city government on important health matters. "But it has been ignored, no attention has been paid to it, no consideration shown it." City Council had hardly ever consulted the board members and was not supportive of the board's work. Although birth and death records had been kept as required, there had been no inspections of meat, milk, gutters or alleys as the law mandated. With the unhealthy summer months approaching, Dr. Boyd pointed out, such negligence could prove deadly.

Not until three weeks later did the council finally get around to appointing a new board of health. One council member expressed dissatisfaction with the efforts of the former board members and insisted that the new ones should be absolute fanatics on the subject of sanitation – "men who could see an epidemic of malaria in a wash basin and a million microbes in a drop of water."

May 18, 1887

May 18, 1887, was the final day of the East Tennessee Farmers' Convention in Knoxville.

The convention had opened the previous day, May 17. Meeting in the federal court room at the Custom House, the delegates — who represented farmers from all over East Tennessee — heard an opening prayer, a welcoming address by Samuel G. Heiskell of Knoxville, and a speech by their association's president, M. P. Jarnagin.

On May 18, the delegates got down to business. The state commissioner of agriculture spoke about the work of his bureau in encouraging agricultural improvement. Then the meeting was thrown open to comments and suggestions of all sorts. The question of whether the convention should endorse a prohibition amendment was debated and finally resolved in the affirmative.

The hottest arguments were over the question of why agriculture was suffering while the rest of the national economy was booming. This elicited many complaints about poor transportation facilities in the rural areas, unfair railroad rates, competition from western farmers and over-production.

Problems such as these plagued farmers all over the nation in those years and eventually sparked a radical agrarian movement, embodied in the Populist Party of the 1890s, that sought to restore farmers to their former preeminence in American life.

May 19, 1904

Knoxville lost one of its most prominent citizens on May 19, 1904, when Peter Staub died of injuries suffered in a carriage accident.

Born in Switzerland in 1827, Staub had come to Knoxville in 1856 and established himself as a tailor. Judiciously investing in real estate and an iron foundry, he became a wealthy man.

He served two terms as mayor (1874-75 and 1881-82) and remained active in public life even after his retirement from business in 1894. He took a prominent role in raising funds to help the survivors of the victims of the Coal Creek mining disaster of 1902.

Among Staub's most enduring contributions was the building of Staub's Theater on the corner of Gay and Cumberland in 1872. This was an important event in Knoxville's cultural history. Well into the 20th century, Staub's Theater hosted the finest in American opera, symphony, drama and popular entertainment.

Staub's Theater

May 20, 1886

On May 20, 1886, Knoxville threw a party for its policemen.

A group of local businessmen had come up with the idea of treating the 20-man police force to a day of fun. Thursday, May 20, was set aside for the event, and Turner Park was selected as the site.

At noon the policemen formed ranks and, with a band in the lead, marched from the Opera House to the park. By mid-afternoon hundreds of other Knoxvillians had arrived at the park to watch and join in the fun.

The festivities began with a pistol-shooting match in which all 20 officers participated. The winner, officer Dewine, received a gold badge with crossed firearms. Then the speaker of the day, W. A. Henderson, addressed the assemblage. He entertained the crowd with tales of Knoxville's first policeman, Capt. Stacks, who had carried a dogwood billy club and a cowhide whip and had for decades constituted the whole police force of the town.

Next there was a foot race and a bicycle exhibition. The festivities continued long into the evening, with dancing at the park pavilion. More prizes were awarded. Miss Lula Sutton won a silk parasol as the most graceful female dancer; Mrs. James Brown won a gold thimble as the most popular of the policemen's wives and sweethearts.

May 21, 1872

On May 21, 1872, the Knoxville Chronicle published article No. 71 in its "Facts About East Tennessee" series, which was intended to attract northerners looking for a new place to settle and make their fortune.

The topic on May 21 was "Knoxville as a Home." First on the list of Knoxville's attractions, according to the Chronicle, was the brand new public school system. To those potential immigrants who had hesitated to come to Knoxville for fear of having to pay for expensive private schooling, the Chronicle could now proclaim that "Knoxville affords to your children good free schools."

Furthermore, the article said, Knoxville is a friendly town. Although some Knoxvillians believed that "money and family connections make the man," most "are inclined to . . . take every man for the intrinsic worth he shows himself to possess." And though a few were prejudiced against Yankees, most "are kindly disposed towards northern people and anxious to have them come here to live."

Other advantages abounded, according to the Chronicle. Knoxville's churches were flourishing, the cost of living was low and the city was healthy. "All things considered, we think that there are few places anywhere in the United States presenting stronger inducements for a pleasant, healthful and cheap home than Knoxville."

May 22, 1936

Knoxville women spoke out on May 22, 1936, about some of the city's worst problems.

At a meeting of the League of Women Voters that day, several members reported the results of a public service survey sponsored by the League. Among the city's biggest needs, the survey showed, were more street signs, better garbage disposal, a slum clearance program, a medical clinic for the poor and a consumers' food cooperative.

The good news was that the city's water system was excellent and that the city was free of occupational and industrial diseases.

That same day, The Knoxville News-Sentinel carried an account of a meeting of the Knoxville Council of Social Agencies. At that meeting Louise Bignall, head of the Family Welfare Bureau, commented on a recent survey of facilities for dependent and delinquent black youths in the city. "You would be shocked and terribly ashamed if you visted some of these places," she said. "A colored child deserves just as much consideration as a white child. There should be no color line in social work."

Among Bignall's recommendations were a new facility for delinquent black girls, more nurses for the segregated black unit at General Hospital, a black social worker for the city's Children's Bureau, and a black probation officer for the Juvenile Court.

May 23, 1963

On May 23, 1963, the University of Tennessee began the greatest program of physical expansion in its history.

Since the 1820s, the campus (excluding the agricultural school) had been mostly confined to "the Hill." But the years following World War II created huge pressure for expansion.

The huge post-war "baby boom" generation began reaching college age in 1962. UT, like other schools across the nation, experienced a surge in enrollments. At the same time, massive amounts of federal money became available for colleges, in part because of public concern that the U.S. was falling behind in the technological competition with the Soviet Union.

Hemmed in by downtown on the east and by the river on the south, the university looked north and west for room to expand. But residential areas blocked the way in both directions.

On May 23, 1963, the university signed an agreement with the Knoxville Housing Authority whereby the district west of campus – although by no means a slum — was designated for urban renewal, cleared of its 341 buildings and 393 families, and turned over to the university for expansion. Over the next two years, UT constructed 17 new buildings there.

With room to grow on the west, the pressure was off the district to the north. To this day, the Fort Sanders area remains a residential neighborhood, primarily housing students.

May 24, 1793

On May 24, 1793, just a few hundred yards from the home of Gov. William Blount in Knoxville, a party of armed white men attacked three Indians without provocation, badly wounding one of them.

Blount, one of whose main tasks as governor of the Southwest Territory was to keep peace with the Indians, was appalled by the attack. The wounded Indian, John Morris, was an acquaintance of his and was well respected in the neighborhood. Blount visited the wounded man and posted a reward of $100 for his assailants.

Morris died the next day. Blount had him buried with military honors in the town cemetery and marched with Morris' family in the procession. Many white Knoxvillians turned out for the funeral, and Blount remarked, "I have rarely seen more sorrow expressed at a burial." Blount also saw to it that Morris' family and the other Indians present at the funeral were treated well. "I considered it political," he wrote, "nay, essential, that pretty liberal presents should be given."

Blount's quick action and diplomacy paid off. Local Indian leaders, convinced that Blount was sincere and that the murder was not condoned by white authorities, decided against any retribution. Thus, for the time being at least, peace was preserved with the Indians.

May 25, 1947

A News-Sentinel article on May 25, 1947, revealed that Knoxville was about to be publicly insulted.

The perpetrator was John Gunther, a prominent travel writer. In his soon-to-be-published book, "Inside USA," an advance copy of which had been provided to The News-Sentinel, Gunther had this to say: "Knoxville is the ugliest city I ever saw in America, with the possible exception of some mill towns in New England."

Gunther's book went on to scoff at the narrow-minded citizenry of Knoxville, which he called "an extremely puritanical town" that banned movies and baseball on Sundays and liquor seven days a week. "Perhaps as a result," he added snidely,"it is one of the least orderly cities in the South. Knoxville leads every other town in Tennessee in homicides, automobile thefts and larceny."

The News-Sentinel article was quick to point out Gunther's errors of fact (Sunday movies had been legal for some months and Sunday baseball for 15 years). And an editorial in the same issue denied that Knoxville was the nation's ugliest city. But at the same time, the editor confessed that Knoxville was indeed "dirty and slovenly." The editorial concluded hopefully with the reminder that outsiders' opinions, however "inaccurate and irritating" they might be, "provoke a self-analysis that sometimes leads to community improvement."

May 26, 1937

In an interview published in The Knoxville News-Sentinel on May 26, 1937, two female University of Tennessee students offered their advice to other young women on how to be popular.

The two had recently been selected, on the basis of their good looks, to be featured in full-page pictures in the forthcoming UT yearbook.

Lois Whitehead of Knoxville pointed out that popularity was more than skin-deep. "Pretty is as pretty does," was her philosophy. A popular woman is a well-rounded woman, she said, one who gives equal time to her studies and her social life. "And she must learn how to get along with people, all kinds of people."

Louise Bussart of Etowah offered the opinion that "a girl must have a good figure, and all that, but if that's all she has, people will soon get tired of her. She should be intellectual, very, but she shouldn't show off before boys." Moreover, she said, "I don't think a gentleman approves of girls smoking. And as for drinking, a girl should never consider it. Gentlemen are entirely against it. And, furthermore, a girl should not pet. That will wreck a girl's popularity quicker than anything."

And, she added as a final bit of advice, "go to church every Sunday."

May 27, 1891

Threats of a lynching circulated around Knoxville on May 27, 1891, following the arrest of a black man for the shooting of a white.

Three days earlier, Fred Carpenter had been shot and wounded while driving his buggy in West Knoxville. A description of the assailant was published, and on May 26 he was recognized and apprehended in Concord and then taken to the Knoxville jail. There, on the morning of May 27, Knoxville police questioned him, learned his name — John Patterson — and obtained a full confession.

It was quite apparent to the police that Patterson was insane and thus not responsible for his actions. Nevertheless, mutterings were heard around town about a possible lynching — a practice that was becoming increasingly common across the South in those years.

Fortunately, cooler heads prevailed. The father of the wounded man personally urged the authorities to guard the jail securely and volunteered his own services in case the jail was attacked by a lynch mob.

The Knoxville Sentinel spoke out, too. "This is a land where we are supposed to have law enough to convict any criminal," the editor declared on May 27, "and if we do not uphold and sustain these rules of social order we at once become criminals, in a deeper sense than the lone highwayman."

May 28, 1970

Religion, politics and protest took center stage on May 28, 1970, when evangelist Billy Graham and President Richard Nixon came to town.

The Billy Graham Crusade revival planned for that evening in Neyland Stadium would not normally have aroused protests but for the fact that it came at a time of great campus unrest in America as a result of the Vietnam War, and the fact that Graham had invited President Nixon to attend.

Among the 75,000 or so who jammed Neyland Stadium that evening were about 400 protesters, mostly UT students and faculty. They remained fairly quiet during Graham's introduction of the president, but when Nixon rose to speak they let loose with catcalls, boos and obscenities.

Following Billy Graham's introduction of President Richard Nixon...

Police arrested nine of the protesters that night on charges of disorderly conduct and disrupting a religious service. Several days later they made more arrests on the basis of photographs taken of the crowd. All together, 40 students, three professors, and a number of others were charged.

... protesters voiced their objections to the Vietnam War.

UT President Andy Holt expressed "shock and embarrassment . . . at the discourtesy of a small group." But the Rev. Graham responded to the incident with soothing words: "I love all those young people at the University — even the protesters. A few are being misled, using the wrong methods. . . . I am praying that some of them will find Christ."

May 29, 1846

On May 29, 1846, a state militia commander arrived in Knoxville with orders to enlist volunteers for the Mexican War.

The United States had declared war on Mexico just 16 days earlier. President James K. Polk immediately called upon the states to provide troops.

Tennessee's governor dispatched Gen. William Brazelton to Knoxville with orders to accept four volunteer companies of infantry and three of cavalry from East Tennessee. Such was the enthusiasm of East Tennesseans, however, that within a few days of Brazelton's arrival, nine companies of cavalry and three of infantry were being formed.

One of the cavalry companies was the Knoxville Dragoons. Its captain began recruiting on May 30 and within two hours had enrolled 67 men. By June 11, the Knoxville Dragoons were ready to go to war. On their way out of town they halted at the Mansion House Hotel for a farewell ceremony. Miss Margaret Ramsey, on behalf of the ladies of Knoxville, presented a flag to the troops, called them "a gallant band," and assured them that they would not be forgotten. Capt. William Caswell replied with a speech, pledging "to guard this banner as we will guard our lives." Finally, as the Dragoons saddled up to ride off to glory, a representative of the Knoxville Bible Society gave every man in the company a pocket Testament.

May 30, 1955

Knoxvillians lined up by the hundreds on May 30, 1955, to shake hands with one of America's biggest celebrities.

Fess Parker had skyrocketed to sudden fame as Davy Crockett in the Walt Disney TV series that had premiered in December 1954. On May 30, he came through Knoxville to promote a forthcoming movie based on the series. Dressed in his familiar coonskin cap and buckskin jacket, Parker toured Blount Mansion, visited with youngsters at Children's Hospital and lunched with scouts at the Andrew Johnson Hotel.

Later, he made a personal appearance at Miller's department store. There he greeted his fans and passed out autographed pictures. Parker leaned over, shook hands and gave a kind word to every fan who came through the line. Many of the younger ones wore coonskin caps.

Fess Parker

Mayor George Dempster, well known for his jokes, made an impression on Parker. "The acting profession lost a fine comedian when Mayor Dempster decided to make money instead of movies," Parker remarked.

May 31, 1861

Hundreds of East Tennesseans were gathered in Knoxville on May 31, 1861, to pledge fidelity to the Union.

The Civil War had begun the previous month, and by May most southern states had left the Union. On May 6, Tennessee's legislature drew up a "Declaration of Independence" to be submitted to the voters on June 8. Without waiting for the referendum, Gov. Isham Harris took steps to ally Tennessee with the Confederacy.

An artist's depiction of the Union allegiance meetings

Most East Tennesseans, however, rejected secession and remained loyal to the Union. In response to a call from some of the region's leading spokesmen, including Knoxvillians Frederick Heiskell, Oliver Temple and William Brownlow, 500 East Tennessee unionists met in Knoxville on May 30 and 31.

The convention opened with a prayer by Knoxville minister Thomas Humes, who beseeched God for help "in this our time of darkness and doubt. . . . Throw around the nation, we entreat Thee, the arms of Thy protection." On May 31 the delegates adopted a resolution denouncing "the ruinous and heretical doctrine of secession."

Their labor was in vain, however, for in the June 8 referendum, a majority of Tennessee voters approved secession.

East Tennessee's unionists did not give up, however, and for the next two years — until its "liberation" by the Union army in 1863 — the region remained a thorn in the side of the Confederacy.

June 1, 1860

The federal census of 1860, taken on June 1 of that year, revealed that Knoxville was well on its way to becoming a real city.

Founded in 1791, Knoxville had for many decades remained hardly more than a village. In 1800, its population was 387; in 1820, about 1,100. As late as 1850, it barely exceeded 2,000.

But after 1850, Knoxville's population began to soar. Much of this growth was due to the coming of the railroad, which tied the town into the national economy.

The 1860 census revealed that Knoxville's population had reached 3,704; of these, 752 were blacks — the great majority of them slaves. If the population of East Knoxville (at that time a separate town) is included, Knoxville's population in 1860 was 5,300.

As the town's population had grown, so had its physical dimensions. In 1791, Knoxville encompassed 32 acres bounded on the south by the river, on the east by First Creek, and on the north and west by what are now Church Avenue and Walnut Street. By 1860, the town had expanded westward to Second Creek and northward to what is now the intersection of Broadway and Central.

In the ensuing years Knoxville continued to grow, aided by further economic expansion and by the annexation of East Knoxville in 1868 and Mechanicsville in 1883. By 1900, the city — for now it could truly be called that — boasted a population of 33,000.

June 2, 1904

A racial incident in Knoxville on June 2, 1904, resulted in the death of a black man and the wounding of another black and a white policeman.

Officers Columbus Gambill and Thomas McCarty got off work about 10 that night and decided to drop by the hamburger joint owned by Alexander the Greek on Central Street. While they were eating, three or four black men drove up in a carriage, walked into the restaurant and sat down at a table. Officer Gambill then asked Alexander about his policy on serving blacks. (Segregation of public facilities was increasingly becoming the rule in Knoxville in those years.) Alexander replied that he served blacks but not while white customers were present. Gambill then told the blacks to wait to be seated until he was finished eating.

The blacks became angry and refused to comply. Gambill repeated his order, whereupon one of the blacks drew a knife and approached the officers. A scuffle ensued. One of the other blacks drew a gun and fired, hitting not the policeman at whom he aimed but instead one of his companions. By this time Gambill had his gun out and was firing, killing one of the blacks with a bullet through the brain. In a further exchange of gunfire Gambill himself was shot through the abdomen.

June 3, 1956

A quiet Sunday afternoon in Knoxville in 1956 was disrupted by an ugly racial incident.

It took place on June 3 in a "mixed" Lonsdale neighborhood near a public park that was normally used only by whites. Trouble had been brewing for some days, for blacks had begun using the park. Though most public facilities in Knoxville were segregated by law in those days, municipal parks were not.

The incident began when two black youths grabbed a baseball being used by some whites and then ran into the nearby home of a black woman. A few minutes later, three men drove by in a car and fired a shotgun blast through a window of the house.

Angry crowds of blacks and whites quickly appeared on the street. Soon there were more than 1,000, some armed with clubs and rocks. There was considerable hooting and yelling and some scuffling, and a black woman was hit with a baseball bat.

Further violence was averted by a quick police response and by the efforts of a white Baptist minister who showed up and pleaded with the crowd to disperse. Tension remained high, however, and the police had to close the park and continue to break up crowds well into the evening.

Three white men were later charged in the drive-by shooting.

June 4, 1928

On June 4, 1928, a big debate over daylight-saving time in Knoxville came to an end.

A daylight-saving law, requiring clocks to be set ahead one hour in the summer, had been enacted by Congress in 1918 but repealed in 1919. Thereafter, the adoption of daylight-saving time was a matter of local option.

In 1928, some Knoxvillians began urging that their city adopt daylight-saving time as many big cities had done. The Knoxville News-Sentinel decided to sponsor a write-in poll on the issue and publish the public's comments.

Typical of the pro-adoption arguments was, "It will give me a chance to get home from work in time to ride or walk or sit on the porch and read while it is still daylight."

But the poll ran heavily against adoption. As one man remarked, "I think it very wrong to compel people who now start work at 6 or 6:30 a.m. to get up before daylight so that some more fortunate people may play golf at 4 p.m."

On June 4, city manager Otto Roehl ended the debate with the announcement that he would not submit an adoption ordinance to City Council. "It is apparent to me that the majority of the people do not favor daylight-saving," he said.

June 5, 1980

At a meeting on June 5, 1980, Knoxville firefighters began pressuring City Council for a pay raise. Though the firefighters stopped short of an ultimatum, they voted to prepare for a "job action" and began raising money for a strike fund.

At the same time, Knoxville police were involved in a work slowdown to protest Mayor Randy Tyree's proposed budget, which included no pay raise for the police. The slowdown began on June 1, and over the next few days the number of traffic citations and non-emergency arrests in the city dwindled to almost nothing.

The police and firefighters, like all American workers at that time, were deeply anxious about their financial security. Double-digit inflation was eroding the paychecks and the morale of America's working people.

City Council met on June 10 and worked out a solution that satisfied the police and firefighters at the expense of the taxpayers. The council approved a $1.30 increase in the property tax rate that added $5 million to the budget and permitted a nine percent pay raise for all city employees.

Firefighters attended the council meeting wearing red T-shirts with the word "Strike" in white lettering. But after the meeting, the president of the Knoxville Fire Fighters Association pronounced himself satisfied and said that Mayor Tyree and council had "acted in good faith, and we will, too."

June 6, 1868

A gruesome discovery on June 6, 1868, revived memories of a long-forgotten hanging in Knoxville.

Laborers digging on Vine Avenue that day uncovered a human skeleton. Old-timers recalled a hanging there many years earlier. An elderly man who had been sheriff back in those days was called in. He confirmed that he had hanged two murderers on that site in 1828.

Other old residents then came forward with more details. One of the murderers was a 70-year-old man named Young who had killed his wife with an axe. The other condemned man, named White, had murdered his lover's husband.

In August 1828, both men were driven by wagon to the gallows, where a large crowd was gathered. The two then stood up, ropes were placed around their necks, and the wagon was driven off, leaving them dangling.

There was a bizarre denouement. A doctor and a college professor were standing by to rush White's body off to a nearby building for medical experimentation. They used a galvanic battery to apply electric shocks to the body. The crowd, which had displayed some sympathy for the youthful and handsome White, seemed disappointed when this treatment failed to restore him to life.

White's relatives then carried the corpse away. Young was buried at the foot of the gallows.

June 7, 1900

Two Knoxville lawyers got into a shouting match in court on June 7, 1900, and later carried their dispute into the street.

Samuel G. Heiskell, who happened also to be Knoxville's mayor at the time, was defense attorney in a rape case. Opposing him was state prosecutor E. F. Mynatt. The case was an emotional one, involving a 13-year-old victim, and in their closing arguments both lawyers got rather hot under the collar. Heiskell declared that "this entire prosecution is a farce and mockery on the courts of the state." Mynatt in turn denounced Heiskell for acting as an attorney while serving as mayor.

Later that day Mynatt was seated in his buggy on Clinch Avenue when Heiskell spotted him. Heiskell walked up and told Mynatt that he was upset about the remarks Mynatt had made in court. Further words were exchanged, until Mynatt's brother, who was standing nearby, told the buggy driver to get going. The buggy drove off and Heiskel returned to his office.

Some witnesses concluded that a fistfight had been narrowly averted. But Mynatt, when contacted later by The Knoxville Sentinel, denied that. "Sam Heiskell and myself . . . have been lifelong friends," he said, and would "not allow a little matter like this to come between us."

June 8, 1861

June 8, 1861, was a momentous day for Knoxville and all of Tennessee. On that day voters decided the issue of secession.

Following Abraham Lincoln's election as president in 1860, the states of the lower South had seceded from the Union. But Tennessee and the other upper South states hesitated. In April 1861, however, following the outbreak of war between north and south, Tennesseans had to make up their minds on secession.

The people of Knoxville were deeply divided. While the rural people of East Tennessee were isolated and held few slaves, and thus felt no kinship with the secessionists, many people in the town of Knoxville were slaveowners who had commercial ties with the seceding states. Knoxville had some diehard unionists, including editor William G. Brownlow, but it also had enthusiastic secessionists, such as Dr. J. G. M. Ramsey.

On June 8, the voters went to the polls. Although Knox County as a whole decisively rejected secession (3,206 votes to 1,216), in Knoxville itself the vote was close: 372 against secession, 315 in favor. But in East Knoxville (a separate town at that time) the vote was overwhelmingly in favor of secession (462 to 5).

East Tennessee as a whole voted against secession that day, but huge secessionist majorities in Middle and West Tennessee took the state out of the Union.

June 9, 1960

The effort to desegregate Knoxville began in earnest on June 9, 1960. On that day blacks began organized sit-ins at a number of downtown lunch counters.

Civil rights activists had challenged the segregation of public facilities in a number of southern cities prior to 1960, but Knoxville had thus far avoided confrontations. The older generation of the city's black leaders had taken a conservative stance. But the advent of the sit-in movement — protest demonstrations in which blacks entered white-only eating facilities and sat peacefully until removed by police — early in 1960 stirred the younger generation of Knoxville blacks into action.

Young black protesters picket Rich's Department Store.

As talk began of a sit-in campaign in Knoxville, Mayor John Duncan appointed a biracial committee to work with local merchants toward a solution. But the merchants resisted integration.

A number of local blacks — including many Knoxville College students, led by Robert Booker — finally decided to force the issue. On June 9, 1960, they began sit-ins at several downtown lunch counters, including those in Kress's, Miller's, and Walgreen's. The sit-ins were peaceful and, thanks to Mayor Duncan, the protesters were protected by Knoxville police. On July 18, after weeks of demonstrations, seven stores agreed to open their lunch counters to blacks.

This was only the first battle of Knoxville's integration struggle, however. Not until 1963 were all of the city's lunch counters, restaurants, hotels, movie houses, and hospitals integrated.

June 10, 1885

On June 10, 1885, the state legislature granted Knoxville a new charter that created a new form of government for the city.

Until then Knoxville had been governed under the 1838 charter, which set up a board consisting of the mayor and 18 aldermen, all elected annually. This board was responsible for levying taxes and enacting ordinances and for managing every detail of city administration, from the placement of fire hydrants to the hiring of policemen.

As the city took on more responsibilities over the years, such as health services, public schools, and a paid fire department, this system grew cumbersome. Furthermore, the annual elections caused a high turnover rate that hindered the development of real expertise on the board.

The new charter of 1885 modernized this archaic system. It left legislative power with the board of mayor and aldermen, but reduced the number of aldermen to nine and increased their term of office and the mayor's to two years.

Moreover, the charter created a new body, the board of public works, to handle administrative functions such as hiring and firing of employees, setting salaries and organizing departments. This board consisted of a chairman elected by the voters and two associates appointed by the mayor. All three served four-year terms.

This new system of government remained in effect until 1911.

June 11, 1895

On June 11, 1895, some of Knoxville's leading citizens were angry and embarrassed after being duped by a slick salesman.

The previous November, an agent of a Chicago publishing firm had come to Knoxville and called on prominent families. His company was publishing a collection of engravings of Knoxville scenes, he said, for $1.85. The prospectus he handed out conjured up an image of an elegant coffee table book.

The 200 Knoxvillians who agreed to buy the book included such notables as Calvin McClung and Perez Dickinson, businessmen who should have known enough to read the fine print. Apparently neither they nor any of the others did so. The contract specified that the cost was $1.85 "per part" and that each volume would consist of several parts.

Because $1.85 was about what one would expect to pay for a whole volume of fine engravings in those days, there was considerable chagrin when the salesman returned in June with the books — each consisting of 12 parts — and demanded $22.20 apiece. Some of the victims protested, but the salesman smugly — and correctly — replied that they were legally bound to pay.

Further aggravating the victims was the fact that, as The Knoxville Sentinel put it, "the books are cheap looking, . . . to say that they are a great disappointment is putting it mildly."

June 12, 1935

On June 12, 1935, a Knoxville family was battling a huge rat for control of their home on Logan Street.

Seven times in the preceding three months the children of Mr. and Mrs. John King had suffered rat bites. A seven-year-old girl was bitten on the lip. Two other children were bitten on the forehead, hands and legs. The attacks always came in the dark of night.

The family's plight came to the attention of The Knoxville News-Sentinel, which interviewed Mrs. King on June 12. From the evidence of the teeth marks she believed that one rat was responsible — a very large rat and a very smart one too. The family had set out traps baited with bologna and ham, Mrs. King said, but "he springs the traps without getting caught." She declared that "if we can't kill that rat I'm not going to stay here with my children much longer."

The crisis was solved that very night when a Knoxville woman who had read The News-Sentinel story offered the Kings the services of Dixie, her rat-killing fox terrier. Dixie, described as a natural rodent hunter who "moves like lightning," stood guard all night and the next day at the King home and put the giant rat to rout.

June 13, 1939

On June 13, 1939, Knoxville was involved in a controversy over the enforcement of the city's milk ordinances.

It began when the U.S. Public Health Service lowered Knoxville's overall health rating from 90 percent to 73.7. That decision was based on a report from the State Health Department, which had determined that the city was not properly enforcing the rules on labeling and processing milk. Knoxville Mayor Walter Mynatt announced on June 13 that this was a "serious matter" about which he was "deeply concerned."

In response, city health department chief W. H. Enneis denied that he had been lax. In the past year, he said, he had taken to City Court eight cases involving violation of milk ordinances. The problem, he insisted, was that the court was letting the offenders off. Only one case had resulted in a conviction.

City Judge John Mynatt replied that the city health department often came before him with a poorly prepared case that would not stand up in court.

In an editorial, The Knoxville News-Sentinel sided with Dr. Enneis: "This 'non-enforcement' attitude of city court is one evil that should be cleaned up immediately. Let's enforce the health laws."

The mayor announced that he would see to it that henceforth the milk ordinances would be "strictly enforced."

June 14, 1978

The Knoxville Board of Education clashed with reporters on June 14, 1978, over the Tennessee "Sunshine Law," which requires public bodies to conduct their business in open sessions.

The board's meeting that day included an appearance by an expert who was to advise the board on how to negotiate with teachers' unions. But the expert insisted that reporters should be barred from the meeting because news accounts could tip off teachers to the board's bargaining strategy.

Board member James Bell then urged the board to hold a closed meeting in violation of the law. "The law doesn't mean anything until the Supreme Court makes an interpretation," he said, perhaps unaware that the State Supreme Court had twice upheld the 1974 law.

Board member Gene Overholt sided with Bell and headed for a separate conference room where a secret session could be held. When reporters followed him he told them, "You're not welcome." But some board members had qualms about flouting the law, and none joined Overholt in the conference room.

The reporters refused to budge from the main meeting room, despite encouragement from the board members — including Robert Lash, who twice asked the reporters, "Don't you have something else to do?" Finally the board members decided not to hold a closed session, and then they all left.

June 15, 1917

Knoxville's first Liberty Loan drive came to an end on June 15, 1917.

Liberty Loans were one of the primary means by which the U.S. government financed World War I. There were five Liberty bond issues between 1917 and 1919, each accompanied by a huge publicity campaign.

The chairman of the Knoxville-Knox County Liberty Loan program throughout all five drives was T. Asbury Wright, a lawyer and banker who virtually gave up his private business to direct the campaigns. Wright organized teams of volunteers to go through Knoxville neighborhoods talking to residents and urging them to buy bonds. Furthermore, he recruited traveling salesmen, Boy Scouts and Girl Scouts to carry out similar tasks.

Wright also enlisted groups of speakers — the "Minute Women" and the "Four Minute Men" — to give brief sales pitches at movie houses, churches, street corners and anywhere else the public gathered. In addition, he organized special committees of influential men who knew how to shake the money tree in Knoxville's elite circles.

The efforts of Wright and his volunteers were spectacularly successful. The citizens of Knoxville and Knox County went "over the top" in all five Liberty Loan drives. All together they purchased over $13 million in Liberty bonds — $3 million over their government-prescribed quota.

June 16, 1920

On June 16, 1920, Knoxvillians lined up to view a grimly realistic exhibit portraying the horrors of trench warfare in World War I.

The exhibit, sponsored by the Tennessee State Library and intended to encourage donations to the proposed War Memorial Building in Nashville, was touring the state. When it reached Knoxville, The Knoxville Sentinel made space available for it in the Sentinel Building on Gay Street.

The exhibit featured war relics and photographs, but the highlight was a big model of a section of the Hindenburg Line, a German defensive work that had been breached in 1918 with the aid of American troops — including the 117th Infantry, commanded by Col. Cary F. Spence of Knoxville. Built of lumber and papier-mache, the model was complete in every detail, right down to the trenches, barbed wire, shell holes, machine gun nests and mud that had made warfare on the western front a hell on earth.

Among the Knoxvillians who viewed the exhibit were many veterans of the war. "It is worth the visit to the model," The Knoxville Sentinel said, "to hear the comments of the former doughboys as some little feature of a trench will bring to mind some exciting adventure during the days when those same boys were dressed in khaki and covered with mud."

June 17, 1892

On June 17, 1892, some 400 young Christians from all over the state met in Knoxville for the third annual convention of the Tennessee branch of the Young People's Society of Christian Endeavor.

The YPSCE was an interdenominational Protestant youth organization founded in 1885. Devoted to self-help and home missions, the YPSCE adopted the motto "For Christ and the Church" and by 1892 had 800,000 members nationwide. There were some 7,000 members in Tennessee, including several hundred in Knoxville, where there were 16 local branches based in various churches.

The Tennessee delegates convened at the Second Presbyterian Church in Knoxville on Friday, June 17, to begin their three-day meeting. That day and the next they heard business reports and inspirational lectures. On Saturday, they ended their session early and boarded a train for an excursion to Fountain City. The convention concluded Sunday morning with an address by the Rev. F. H. Smith entitled "The Greatest Work in the World."

After the delegates departed, The Knoxville Sentinel reported that the convention had been "very interesting as well as beneficial to all who have had the good fortune to participate. . . . The society is one of great good and growing usefulness, and the people of Knoxville feel that they were honored by having an opportunity to enjoy the services and entertain the visitors."

June 18, 1915

A meeting of the city commission on June 18, 1915, was attended by dozens of Knoxville blacks interested in the education of their children.

The commission was voting that night on a proposed five-cent tax that would raise $40,000 for the construction of a new black high school. Some 75 black Knoxvillians were present as the commission took up the matter. A number of them stepped forward to address the commissioners, thanking them for their cooperation thus far and urging final passage of the tax. Among the speakers were some of Knoxville's most prominent black citizens, including educators Charles W. Cansler and John W. Manning and newspaper editor W. L. Porter. Mrs. G. W. McDade spoke on behalf of the city's black women.

Mayor Samuel G. Heiskell and the four commissioners received the visitors graciously and responded to their entreaties by passing the tax and approving the construction of the new school. The audience greeted the vote with a round of applause. The only point of contention was the site of the school. Three different locations were proposed by the citizens present, but the mayor put off discussion of the issue for the time being.

The new school, known as Colored High School, was built that year and remained in use until 1928, when Austin High School was opened on Vine Avenue.

June 19, 1889

On June 19, 1889, the mortal remains of one of Tennessee's great heroes came home to Knoxville.

John Sevier — Revolutionary War hero, first governor of Tennessee and a resident of Knoxville for the last 18 years of his life — had died in 1815 in Alabama while on a surveying expedition.

There his body remained, in an unmarked grave, for more than seven decades. Eventually, however, a movement was begun to retrieve his remains and re-inter them in Knoxville. In 1889, the Tennessee legislature appropriated funds for the removal, the Knox County court provided a plot on the courthouse square, and a committee of citizens arranged for the removal and began raising money for a monument.

A special railroad car left Knoxville for Alabama on June 14, 1889. Five days later, it returned with Sevier's remains. A crowd of 30,000 citizens was on hand for the event. Pallbearers escorted the coffin to the courthouse, where Gov. Robert L. Taylor gave a eulogy, a poem was read, and the coffin was buried with all due ceremony and solemnity.

The monument — a tall, marble shaft honoring Sevier as "One of the Founders of the Republic" — was erected at the gravesite in 1893. In 1922, the remains of Sevier's second wife, Catherine, were re-interred next to Sevier's. In 1946, a monument to his first wife, Sarah, was erected on the site.

June 20, 1897

On June 20, 1897, Knoxville's black community paid homage to the memory of a dedicated teacher, Emily Austin.

Austin was one of a large number of idealistic white northerners who went south after the Civil War to help the emancipated slaves. She came to Knoxville from Philadelphia in 1870 and, despite hostility from local whites who regarded Yankee reformers as troublemakers, for the next 30 years she worked tirelessly to educate the black children of Knoxville.

Emily Austin

In 1879, having helped raise $6500 in donations from the north, she turned the money over to the city of Knoxville for the construction of a black school, which became the Austin School on Central Avenue. In 1885, having secured another $6,000 from local and northern donors, she established the Slater Training School on Payne Avenue to teach young blacks industrial and domestic skills as well as academic subjects. She remained active in black education in Knoxville until her retirement in 1891.

She died in Philadelphia in May 1897. On June 20, memorial services were held at Knoxville's Logan Temple with a large audience of blacks in attendance. Later, an inscribed tablet was placed in the Austin School that described her as "a devoted friend of the freedmen, fearless of criticism, shrinking from no duty, unswerving in fidelity." Her memory is still honored in Knoxville in the name of Austin-East High School.

June 21, 1932

On June 21, 1932, Knoxvillians were pondering the liquor question.

The front page of The Knoxville News-Sentinel that day was full of news about prohibition. The proposed repeal of the federal prohibition laws in effect since 1919 had become an issue in the 1932 presidential race.

That issue meant little to Knoxvillians, however, for their city had had its own prohibition law since 1907 and would remain "dry" for decades after national prohibition was repealed. Most Knoxvillians in 1932 were adamantly anti-liquor, a fact underscored by the appearance of "Ten Nights in a Bar Room" — a classic melodrama about the evils of drink — at the Bijou Theater on June 21.

At the same time, the Knoxville police were trying to deal with an epidemic of drunkenness in the city. Records showed that 190 people had been jailed on drunk charges between June 1 and June 21. Billy Gallaher, who drove the city drunk wagon, told a News-Sentinel reporter, "I've hauled so many drunks in, I'm just getting sick every time I see one." Asked if jailing people helped keep them sober, Gallaher replied, "Heck, no. We've been hauling the same persons to jail for 20 years. It might be that when they are in jail they are kept from being run over by automobiles, or killed by other means, but it certainly does not reform them."

June 22, 1855

A long-sought dream became reality on June 22, 1855, when Knoxville's first train steamed into town.

As far back as the 1830s, progressive Knoxvillians, led by J. G. M. Ramsey, had encouraged the building of a railroad to their isolated city. By linking Knoxville to the outside world, they believed, the railroad could make the city a great commercial center.

But it was not until the 1850s, when the East Tennessee and Georgia Railroad began constructing a line from Dalton, Georgia, northward, that the iron rails began to approach Knoxville. The project faltered when the line reached Loudon in 1852, however. But then the state legislature stepped in and provided funds to ensure the extension of the tracks to Knoxville.

When the first train came into Knoxville on June 22, 1855, one local newspaper called it "a new era for Knoxville." The city organized a special "Jubilee," but postponed it until July 4 to coincide with the national holiday. On that day the railroad offered a special round-trip excursion to Dalton for $4.

The arrival of the ET&G Railroad meant that Knoxville was now linked to Charleston and other important points to the south. With the completion of the East Tennessee and Virginia Railroad from Knoxville to Bristol in 1858, Knoxville was also linked to the northeast.

June 23, 1948

On June 23, 1948, the Knoxville Naval Reserve office announced that it would accept no more draft-age recruits.

The Naval Reserve, along with the local National Guard, had been flooded with enlistees for several days past. Congress had just enacted a conscription act with the intention of drafting 200,000 young men. But the act exempted anyone who joined a Guard or Reserve unit before President Harry Truman signed the bill into law.

As the bill sat on the president's desk, thousands of young American men headed for their local Guard and Reserve headquarters. By June 23, the National Guard office in Knoxville had signed up 60 men and the Naval Reserve about 150.

Among these enlistees were some 23 members of the UT football team who boarded a bus with one of their coaches, drove to the Guard headquarters and enlisted as a group. They included all the draft-age players on the 55-man varsity team who were not service veterans (the majority of the team members were veterans who were exempt from the draft). One of the 23 was Robert R. Neyland Jr., son of the head coach.

The conscription law — the first peacetime draft since 1940 and only the second in American history — was part of the nation's growing commitment to defend the "free world" against communism in the early days of the Cold War.

June 24, 1873

On June 24, 1873, the nation was in the grip of a deadly cholera epidemic, and Knoxvillians were worried.

No signs of the disease had yet been noticed in Knoxville, but just to be on the safe side, eight ministers in the city asked Mayor William Rule on June 24 to declare an official day of "fasting, humiliation and prayer" so that the citizens could give thanks.

The mayor complied, designating June 26, and on that day most of the city's churches held special services. But it was too late, for the cholera epidemic had already claimed its first Knoxville victim on June 25.

As the summer progressed there were at least 23 more deaths. Among the victims was one of Knoxville's most distinguished citizens, the 61-year-old lawyer and statesman, Thomas A. R. Nelson.

It was fortunate that there were not more deaths, considering the deplorable sanitary conditions in the city and the primitive state of medical knowledge. This was in fact the fourth outbreak of cholera in Knoxville since 1849. There was no real sewage system in those years, and the city's water supply was in constant danger of contamination. Animals were butchered openly in the market place, and livestock roamed the streets. There was no permanent city health department — outbreaks of disease were handled on an ad hoc basis.

June 25, 1900

On June 25, 1900, Knoxville authorities were busy cracking down on the city's saloons.

Saloons were still legal in Knoxville at that time (they were outlawed seven years later). But selling liquor on Sunday and keeping slot machines were not legal, and many of the city's 100 or so saloons were flagrantly violating those laws.

In early June, a Knoxville grand jury began calling witnesses and issuing indictments. Over the next four weeks, the grand jury found true bills against 25 or so saloon keepers who kept slot machines and a number of others charged with Sunday selling.

One of the star witnesses was the Rev. R. J. Bateman of the People's Tabernacle on Cumberland Avenue. On one Sunday, he reported, "I observed at least 100 men going in and out the rear entrance of DeArmond's saloon," and on that same day he saw "a constant stream of men going in and out of the Shamrock saloon. . . . It seems they have a system of signaling to get into DeArmond's saloon. When one goes to the door and knocks, it opens a few inches and the doorkeeper passes upon the seeker for admission. If he is 'all right' he is admitted, but last Sunday I saw a few turned away."

June 26, 1950

"North Koreans Drive Beyond Seoul," announced The News-Sentinel's headlines on June 26, 1950. On that day, Knoxvillians received the first complete reports of the previous day's invasion that triggered the Korean War.

Armored forces of communist North Korea had crossed the border and quickly broken the resistance of the South Korean army. The South Korean government was hastily evacuating the capital city of Seoul.

It was uncertain what action the U.S. would take. President Harry Truman denounced North Korea's "unprovoked aggression," and Gen. Douglas MacArthur in Tokyo ordered supplies and equipment, including fighter planes, to be sent to the aid of South Korea. But many Americans opposed sending U.S. troops. Republican members of the Senate told the president that this country had no obligation to go to war in Korea.

Knoxvillians were disturbed to learn that some of their own were in the war zone. Army Capt. Wolfred J. White, assigned to the Korean Military Advisory Group, was stationed in Seoul; his family was with him. A former Knoxvillian, the Rev. E. T. Boyer, was a missionary in South Korea, living in Soonchung.

A News-Sentinel editorial, reflecting the concerns of many Americans in this crisis, urged that the United Nations act quickly "to prevent this now localized conflict from touching off a third world war."

June 27, 1903

A dramatic jailbreak in Knoxville's history occurred on June 27, 1903.

Harvey Logan of Montana, alias Kid Curry, was a notorious Wild West bandit and a former member of Butch Cassidy's "Wild Bunch." Following his capture he was tried in Knoxville's federal court, convicted of forgery, and given a 20-year sentence. He was being held in the Knox County Jail pending his removal to a federal penitentiary.

Harvey Logan

On June 27, Logan engaged his unarmed guard in conversation and, when the guard turned his back while standing in front of the cell, Logan put a wire around the man's neck, threatened to strangle him, and tied him to the bars.

Using a long pole with a hook, Logan reached through the bars and secured two revolvers that were stored nearby. When the jailer arrived, Logan forced him at gunpoint to open the cell door and lead him to the sheriff's horse. Then Logan was off, headed presumably for the mountains in Blount County.

Posses were organized, and Sheriff J. W. Fox offered a $500 reward for Logan's capture, "dead or alive." It was to no avail. Harvey Logan was gone.

June 28, 1965

June 28, 1965, was the kick-off day for Knoxville's Head Start program.

Project Head Start was part of the federal "War on Poverty" begun during the administration of President Lyndon Johnson. The purpose of Head Start was to provide a culturally nourishing environment for pre-school-age children from poor families, and thus to prepare those children for elementary school. It was based on the belief that poverty led to a kind of cultural deprivation that put poor children at a disadvantage in school.

Activities in the Head Start classes included story-telling, drawing, games, and simple alphabet and numbers exercises. In addition, there were field trips to zoos, parks, farms, and similar places that children from poor families might otherwise never see.

The first day of classes in Knoxville was a little disappointing. Though 900 children had been expected, only 729 showed up. Officials attributed that to a "wait and see" attitude on the part of some parents and expressed optimism that interest in the program would grow. Patricia Hardin, head of the Knoxville Head Start program, stated that "As far as the overall picture is concerned, we're very pleased. Everything went very well. A few youngsters found it difficult to say good-by to mother on the first day, but of course that can be expected."

June 29, 1920

On June 29, 1920, a Knoxville businessman announced his intention to make war on the city's flies.

Flies were a significant health problem in those days, when garbage removal was unsystematic and window screening was not in universal use. Public health officials blamed much sickness and death in Knoxville on the fly problem. In some tenement houses, it was not unusual to find infants literally covered with flies.

B. M. Gaston, manager of the Knoxville office of the Metropolitan Life Insurance Co., proposed that the city undertake an anti-fly campaign as part of its annual ''Clean-up Week.'' A key part of the campaign would be to encourage landlords to screen the windows of their rented properties.

In addition, Gaston announced that he was planning to put 30 of his employees to work distributing leaflets that Metropolitan Life had prepared. The leaflets provided information on the life cycle of the fly and on fly-related health problems and offered suggestions on controlling flies by eliminating breeding areas. Among the suggestions were removing rubbish from yards and cellars, cleaning carpets and drapes, scrubbing floors and unvarnished woodwork with soap and hot water, ventilating damp cellars, repairing leaky roofs and plumbing, and reporting stagnant pools and refuse piles to the health department.

June 30, 1940

On June 30, 1940, The Knoxville News-Sentinel sponsored a write-in forum on the international situation.

The world was at war. The totalitarian nations of Germany, Italy, and Japan were on the march. The U.S. had so far stayed out of the struggle, but many Americans had concluded that the nation should join the fight against totalitarian aggression.

Among them were a number of Knoxvillians who sent in comments published in a special section of The News-Sentinel. One reader denounced the inaction of the U.S. government and blamed the climate of the times, which he called the Age of Talk. "The democratic nations talked themselves stupid and became easy victims of . . . the totalitarian nations." It is time, he said, for the Age of Action.

Another commentator pointed to the English, who were struggling almost alone against Hitler's Germany: "Are we going to wait until they are whipped and then start protecting the good old U.S.A.?," he asked.

Despite the bellicosity of The News-Sentinel's commentators, isolationist sentiment remained strong in the nation as a whole. Not until the Japanese attacked the American base at Pearl Harbor, Hawaii, a year and a half later, did the United States commit itself fully to the war.

July 1, 1974

City garbage workers went on strike July 1, 1974, and Mayor Kyle Testerman reacted swiftly.

The garbage workers, members of Local 1898, American Federation of State, County and Municipal Employees, were protesting a reduction in work hours and demanding a retroactive pay raise. Mayor Testerman took a tough stance from the start of the controversy, refusing to recognize the union or even to meet with union representatives.

When 300 garbage workers walked out on July 1 and began picketing at the city garage and landfill, Testerman immediately fired all 300 and got a temporary restraining order against picketing. He then told the fired workers that they could have their jobs back if they ended the strike and reapplied for their positions. To those who refused, Testerman said, "I wish you luck in your future employment."

Kyle Testerman pitches in during the garbage strike.

About half the workers returned to their jobs by the next morning. Nevertheless, the mayor declared the city to be in a state of emergency and ordered firemen, policemen and other city employees to help handle the garbage collection. The trucks were soon rolling again, accompanied by police cars. Among those toiling in the summer heat was the mayor himself.

Testerman's forceful response broke the strike and ended the hope of labor organizers for a strong and militant garbage workers' union.

July 2, 1852

On July 2, 1852, word reached Knoxville of the death of one of America's preeminent statesmen.

Henry Clay of Kentucky, the "Great Compromiser," had died three days earlier. While his passing was not unexpected — he had long been in failing health — it plunged Knoxville and the nation into mourning.

When Knoxvillians heard the news, all businesses in the town closed and bells tolled. That evening the citizens gathered to give public expression to their grief. Mayor George White called on William Reese to preside. Reese gave a brief but beautiful and heartfelt speech, then appointed a committee to draw up a resolution.

Clay's death, the resolution read, "has sent a thrill of sorrow through every American heart, and has cast a gloom and sadness over a nation. . . . We deeply deplore his loss as a national bereavement."

Then and since, Clay's death has been viewed as a symbol of the passing of a whole generation of American leaders, a generation born in the Revolutionary era and possessed of a profoundly nationalistic outlook. It was succeeded by a younger generation of leaders who had come of age in an era of growing conflict between North and South and who seemed less willing, or less able, to halt the nation's headlong rush toward civil war.

July 3, 1847

On July 3, 1847, Knoxville welcomed home its Mexican War heroes.

Preparations had begun a month earlier, when it was learned that the Knoxville troops who had marched off to war in the spring of 1846 were coming back, having had a prominent role in the victory over Mexico. A committee was appointed to solicit donations for a public welcome, and a resolution was passed commending the soldiers who "in the fiery storm of battle . . . bore aloft the unsullied flag of the state."

Everything was ready by July 3. That day a procession formed on Gay Street, headed up by Knoxville's War of 1812 veterans. They were followed by the faculty and students of the university and a large crowd of citizens. The column marched out to the troops' campground for the formal welcome; then the whole assemblage moved to a grove, where they heard a grand oration by Alexander Anderson. Then toasts were drunk to the United States, the Constitution, the president, the army and the navy.

Other toasts followed: to the triumphant generals; to the volunteers ("their heroic deeds . . . have added luster to the untarnished glory of Tennessee"); and to the memory of those who died ("let us ever hold their virtues and heroism in grateful remembrance"). Finally, all the troops were treated to a big dinner.

July 4, 1876

On July 4, 1876, Knoxvillians joined all Americans in celebrating the nation's 100th birthday.

It was a gala event in Knoxville, with festivities from dawn to dark. It began with the booming of cannons — a 13-gun salute fired at daybreak by the university cadets. Then church bells pealed, and soon the streets of the city began to fill up with citizens.

At 10:00 a.m., a flag ceremony was held at the courthouse. The big procession formed an hour later. It included city officials, military companies, floats representing the city's trades and industries (including the Knoxville Cigar Manufactory, whose float sported a seven-foot cigar) and a marching band wearing three-cornered hats. They all marched down Gay Street and Jackson Avenue, where the buildings were festooned with flags and bunting. A crowd of 15,000 was on hand to cheer them.

Afternoon events included a public ceremony at the Female Institute, where a band played patriotic songs, a chorus sang "The Red, White and Blue," the audience sang "My Country 'Tis of Thee," and the Declaration of Independence was read aloud.

Festivities concluded that evening with the release of balloons, another cannon salute and fireworks. "The display was beautiful," one witness wrote, "and a fitting termination of the day so enthusiastically celebrated throughout the length and breadth of this country."

July 5, 1905

A new law requiring the segregation of white and black passengers on Knoxville's streetcars went into effect on July 5, 1905.

Across the South in those years, state laws and local ordinances were creating a rigid system of segregation in public facilities, which theretofore had been only informally segregated or, in many cases, actually integrated.

The Tennessee legislature's streetcar law of 1905 required that signs be posted in each car designating the front seats for whites and the rear seats for blacks. A few exceptions were made: black invalids and black nurses accompanying white children were allowed to sit in the white section.

On July 5, the Knoxville Traction Company, which ran the streetcar system, began enforcing the new law, setting aside the two rear seats of each trolley car for blacks.

Knoxville's blacks immediately protested with a boycott. Their leaders were arrested on assault charges on July 8, however, after trying to enforce the boycott on members of their own race. The boycott soon fizzled out.

A number of white Knoxvillians complained about the new law, too: some because they had always preferred sitting in the back; others because they were now separated from black friends; and still others because they thought blacks should be relegated to separate cars.

July 6, 1984

On July 6, 1984, workmen tore up a downtown Knoxville parking lot to make way for Krutch Park.

The park was to be the realization of the dream of Charles E. Krutch, a native Knoxvillian who had died in 1981 at the age of 94. Krutch, a long-time TVA photographer and brother of the famed drama critic and naturalist Joseph Wood Krutch, had accumulated a fortune in his lifetime through careful saving and investment.

Determined to leave a lasting legacy to the city, he bequeathed $1 million in stocks and bonds to establish a downtown park that would be "a quiet retreat with trees, shrubs, flowers and other plantings for the pleasure and health of the general public."

By the time city officials began to take steps to implement Krutch's plan, the value of the bequest had grown to more than $1.5 million, which would not only cover the property acquisition and design and construction of the park but also provide a trust fund to maintain the park.

Workman Tyrone Thomas helps in the first stages of construction on Krutch Park.

Krutch Park was opened in June 1985, complete with a stream, paved walks, benches and tables and ornamental shrubbery. Every day, hundreds of Knoxvillians find it a welcome and "quiet retreat" from the downtown hustle and bustle.

July 7, 1823

A thousand citizens gathered at the courthouse in Knoxville on July 7, 1823, to endorse a candidate for president of the United States.

They drew up a formal resolution: "We . . . desire to select some citizen distinguished by his intrinsic worth and his merited renown," they declared, a man of "strict integrity, sound judgment, unwavering principles." Having spelled out their criteria, the citizens then named Andrew Jackson as their man.

Jackson, the hero of the battle of New Orleans in 1815 and a prominent Tennessee politician in the years since, had become one of the leading figures of the American west (which at that time meant everything west of the Appalachians).

"His intrinsic merit will . . . render our country happy at home," the resolution continued, "while his fame abroad will cause us to be respected by the other nations of the earth." This latter point was very important to many Americans, for in that era the United States was a small, young nation struggling for international respectability.

Having resolved in conclusion "that by all fair and honorable means" they would support Jackson's candidacy, the citizens ended their meeting and went home.

Their labors were in vain, for Jackson lost the election of 1824. Four years later, however, he triumphed and went on to become one of the nation's greatest leaders.

July 8, 1949

A city official's report to City Council on July 8, 1949, revealed that conditions in Knoxville's beer joints were, on the whole, very unsatisfactory.

Transportation inspector William N. Albert had just completed a personal inspection of some 200 of the city's 317 beer joints. About 10 percent, he said, were above reproach, another 10 percent were "deplorable," and the rest varied between "deplorable and good."

Albert witnessed gambling in one form or another — chiefly on pinball machines and punchboards — at 70 percent of the establishments he had visited. Other violations included unsanitary food service, filthy toilets, obscene pictures on the walls, fighting, and drunks and teenagers being served. In one place, he heard a policeman boast of having the prize-winning pinball score for the week.

Albert's report provoked councilman Cas Walker to declare that "if beer dealers continue their policy of not cooperating with the council in its efforts to clean up the beer situation," then he would recommend that all city beer permits be canceled and a moratorium on beer sales be enacted.

Instead, City Council responded by appointing Albert chief beer inspector and naming three assistants to work under him. Their duties, as specified by City Council, were limited to citing beer licensees for violations. "Police will continue to handle disturbances and rowdiness at beer places."

July 9, 1824

An article in the Knoxville Register on July 9, 1824, gave Knoxvillians some surprisingly modern-sounding advice on bringing up children.

Titling the article "Duty of Parents," the anonymous advice columnist prescribed five rules for mothers and fathers. First, begin the instruction of children early. "Very young children are capable of learning many things. . . . The infant mind opens faster than we are aware."

Second, be patient with children, using Christ's teaching of his disciples as a model. "Be patient with their ignorance, their backwardness . . . their mistakes, their forgetfulness."

Third, use persuasion, not compulsion, to encourage the young to learn. And don't coop them up studying for too long or give them overly difficult tasks. "To most children, learning may be made an alluring object," if parents promote it with the proper attitude.

Fourth, teach by example. "Children do little besides imitating others. Reading parents will have reading children. Industrious parents will have industrious children."

Last, encourage children to put their knowledge to use. "The human mind is not a mere vessel into which knowledge is to be poured. It is better compared to a bee, fed during the first periods of its existence by the labors of others; intended ere long to lift its wings in the active employment of collecting sweets from every field within its reach."

July 10, 1817

A local landmark was inaugurated on July 10, 1817, with the announcement that the Knoxville Hotel had opened its doors to the public.

Construction of the building, which stood on the southwest corner of present-day Gay Street and Cumberland Avenue, had been initiated a year or two earlier by the owner of the lot, a prominent early Knoxville merchant named Thomas Humes. Humes died in 1816, but his widow finished the project and rented the building to Archibald Rhea.

Rhea opened the hotel in 1817 with a public announcement to potential guests, boasting of his establishment's "elegant rooms" and pledging that "traveling gentlemen and ladies shall have every attention paid them and shall be furnished . . . with some of the most respectable newspapers for their perusal."

Rhea had reason to boast, for by the standards of that time and place the Knoxville Hotel was truly elegant. The three-story brick building contained 13 large guestrooms, each with its own fireplace, as well as a bar, a ballroom and a dining room.

The hotel immediately became one of the town's social centers, and over the following decades it hosted many travelers, among them Andrew Jackson. Later it was renamed the Lamar House. And, with additional construction completed in 1909, it assumed a new role in the 20th century as the Bijou Theater.

July 11, 1823

A letter to the public in the Knoxville Register on July 11, 1823, called on Tennesseans to stop spending money on imported items.

The letter-writer, who signed himself "Western Mechanic," was worried about the continuous drain of currency out of the state to pay for hats, bridles, saddles, shoes and other items that were shipped in from the east but could just as easily be made in Tennessee. Local merchants, he said, should refuse to stock any goods not manufactured here. When they sell such items they "drain off money and impoverish the community."

But the customers themselves were at fault, too, "Western Mechanic" insisted. They were "infatuated by fashion and in love with extravagance" and thus preferred the fancy goods from the east to the plain but serviceable items of local manufacture. Tennessee goods may lack a "glossy outside appearance," he said, but they are strong and durable and will "stick to you through rough and through smooth while your eastern friend will too often desert you in the hour of danger."

The underlying tone of the letter was one of resentment toward the east, a common sentiment among westerners in that era. "The eastern states have long had the ascendancy over the western," the letter concluded, "though we have tried hard to get on an equal footing with them."

July 12, 1913

Knoxvillians learned on July 12, 1913, that the great National Conservation Exposition scheduled to open at Chilhowee Park on Sept. 1 of that year would indeed be ready on that date.

The exposition was the culmination of the dreams of some of Knoxville's most progressive citizens. These local boosters hoped to draw national attention to their city in order to further its growth and development.

Until July 1913, none of the promoters felt assured that the project would succeed. Problems with funding, federal approval, public and private participation, and so on, kept cropping up. But on July 12, exposition president T. Asbury Wright announced that the event would open as scheduled on Sept. 1 and would be free of debt.

The exposition was a huge success, drawing over a million visitors during its two-month run. It featured exhibits in nine big buildings at Chilhowee Park. The most important exhibits focused on the conservation of the nation's natural resources, an issue that was becoming increasingly important in those years.

The Liberal Arts Building at the exposition

July 13, 1891

On July 13, 1891, members of the National Afro-American League arrived in Knoxville in preparation for their annual meeting.

Founded in Chicago in 1890, the National Afro-American League was a black civil rights organization devoted to remedying the plight of southern blacks. Its founder, T. Thomas Fortune, was a New York newspaper editor and a very prominent black leader. Fortune was deeply disturbed by the violence and discrimination to which southern blacks were increasingly being subjected in that era.

Fortune and the other NAAL members opened their meeting on the morning of July 14, 1891, at a black Methodist church in Knoxville. They were welcomed to the city by Samuel R. Maples, a black lawyer. Other prominent Knoxville blacks in attendance included Charles W. Cansler, William F. Yardley and the Rev. Job Lawrence.

At the meeting, a resolution was passed in favor of a federal election law that would prevent southern states from unfairly disenfranchising blacks. Another resolution condemned the segregation of blacks in railroad cars as "a gratuitous indignity — an insult to our manhood. . . . It is an injustice that should not quietly be acquiesced in."

In commenting on the meeting, The Knoxville Sentinel denounced the NAAL members for promoting "ultra-radical ideas."

July 14, 1956

No News-Sentinel writer, past or present, ever developed a following of readers like Bert Vincent, whose "Strolling" column was a mainstay in the newspaper for nearly 40 years.

Six days a week, Vincent dished out homespun humor, told "haint" stories, shared fan mail, swapped tall tales, helped people locate lost relatives and found homes for stray animals. This column excerpt from July 14, 1956, was typical of Vincent's gentle, laid-back style:

"Mrs. Hazel Hoffman, 2828 Carson Ave., let her heart and sympathy get her into a lot of trouble.

"Weeks back, she found a baby bird, likely a starling, along Clinton Highway. She took the baby home and played mama to him, feeding him and caring for him until he was grown. Then she pitched him out the door.

"But little birdie, Bee-Bee, as she called him, liked being babied. So now he comes back three or four times a day, and he pesters Mrs. Hoffman until she feeds him some hardboiled egg and bird seed. He is even so spoiled he wants her to put the food in his mouth.

"'And don't you know,'" says Mrs. Hoffman, "'he pecks on the kitchen door as early as 4 o'clock in the morning. I worry about the winter months. Will he by then realize he is a bird, or will he be back and wanting to roost in the house out of the cold?'"

July 15, 1965

On July 15, 1965, Mayor Leonard Rogers spoke at a meeting of the Knoxville Police Department and told the 123 officers assembled there that he expected them "to enforce the law without fear or favoritism."

Rogers was responding to complaints that some policemen had been reprimanded after arresting certain "friends" of the mayor. "My friends have never asked me to fix as much as a $1 traffic ticket," Rogers insisted. "They know I wouldn't. Those who claim I have done differently are telling a falsehood."

Leonard Rogers

Rogers went on to suggest that politics was behind this controversy. "I know many of you didn't vote for me, and even worked for my opposition." And he implied that his decision to roll back certain promotions and institute a merit system in the department had also created some ill-will. ''There are those of you who are kicking in the traces,'' he said sternly. "If this continues, you will be dealt with."

But Rogers also proffered an olive branch. He would work for a salary raise for police, he promised, and for a new Safety Building. Furthermore, "I'll back you to the hilt when you are right. . . . All I ask of you is to make Knoxville a better place to live and do business in."

July 16, 1846

On July 16, 1846, the Knoxville Board of Aldermen appointed a committee to procure a building to house the town's fire engine.

The town had acquired the fire engine in 1822. Although it represented a major advance in Knoxville's fire-fighting ability, it was a primitive contraption by today's standards. It was horse- or hand-drawn, of course, and had no hose — just an eight-foot nozzle through which water could be pumped from a reservoir inside the engine.

When a fire broke out, all citizens were expected to report to the scene with their buckets (an ordinance required each family to keep two leather two-gallon buckets). The men formed a line on one side of the street from First Creek to the fire engine; women and children formed a line on the other side. Full water buckets were passed up from the creek by the men, emptied into the engine's reservoir, then passed down by the women and children for refilling.

The inefficiency of this system encouraged the town authorities to order the construction of a cistern near the courthouse in 1828. This did not, of course, eliminate the need for the bucket brigade; it just reduced the distance water had to be carried.

The old fire engine remained in use until 1859, when the board of aldermen purchased two new engines.

July 17, 1901

One of Knoxville's great merchants died in the city on July 17, 1901, at the age of 88.

Perez Dickinson came from Massachusetts to Knoxville in 1829 to attend the university. After graduation, his life followed a path like that of a Horatio Alger hero. He got a job as a clerk in Cowan's grocery store at $8 per week. Through hard work he rose in the business and became a partner. The firm of Cowan & Dickinson eventually became one of the leading wholesale houses in the state.

By the time of the Civil War, Dickinson was rich. Although his northern origin did not deter him from adopting southern customs (for one thing, he was a slave owner), it no doubt influenced his decision to remain faithful to the union after Tennessee seceded in 1861.

After the war, Dickinson bought a farm south of town, called Island Home. He developed it into a model farm, a must-see for every important visitor to the city.

Dickinson was also renowned for his generosity. He gave away so many Christmas presents to children that his business associates called him Santa Claus. At his death in 1901 the City Council formally resolved that, "the city has lost one of its most useful, most prominent and most respected citizens."

July 18, 1934

Commercial airline service to Knoxville began on July 18, 1934, when a two-engine Condor biplane carrying mail from Washington landed at Downtown Island Airport.

Luddington Airlines, which owned the plane, was later informed by the government that the Condor was too big for that airport. Consequently, the Condor was replaced by a single-engine Stinson which could carry six passengers along with the mail.

A view of McGhee Tyson Airport taken from the control tower in the 1940s

American Airlines took over Luddington and began service to Downtown Island early in 1936, using a 16-passenger DC-2. After McGhee Tyson Airport opened in 1937, American moved its operations there and began using the larger DC-3. Delta Airlines began service to McGhee Tyson in 1940, also using DC-3s.

Delta, American and a third carrier (Pennsylvania-Central) monopolized Knoxville's air service until after World War II. Piedmont Aviation came to the city in 1952 and Southern Airways in 1960. United Airlines bought out Pennsylvania-Central's successor (Capital Airlines) in 1961 and thereafter became an important part of Knoxville's air travel service.

Jet service came to Knoxville in 1966. This was considerably later than in many other cities, one reason being that the early jets were large, four-engine aircraft that could be profitably employed only over long routes between large cities. The introduction of lighter, two- and three-engine jets such as the DC-9 and Boeing 727 allowed smaller cities, including Knoxville, to be brought into the jet age.

July 19, 1930

The first Knoxville contender in the nationwide tree-sitting craze went aloft on Saturday, July 19, 1930.

Inspired by the example of a Wisconsin boy who had stayed up in a tree for 96 hours, 10-year-old Pearl Walker of 517 Baxter Avenue climbed up a catawba tree at 8 a.m. and announced her intention of staying until she broke the record.

Assisted by a ground crew of other neighborhood children, and wearing a bell around her neck that would awaken her if she began to fall while sleeping, Pearl cheerfully endured boredom and discomfort in her quest for national recognition. She was enthusiastically supported by her mother, who prescribed a diet of coffee, French toast, and a tomato for breakfast; cold milk at 9 a.m.; boiled vegetables for lunch; and ice cream and cake for dinner, all carried up to her by her loyal ground crew.

Pearl's adventure ended abruptly a week later after she developed an infection in her hand. When a city nurse determined that she was running a temperature, her mother made her come down out of the tree. Her first words upon alighting were, "Gosh, I feel so low down here."

In the meantime, however, a number of other youths around Knoxville had climbed into their own trees, and the competition continued.

July 20, 1891

On July 20, 1891, Knoxville was in an uproar over the great Tennessee Coal Miners' War.

Some days earlier, miners in Anderson County had rebelled in protest against the use of leased state convicts in the coal mines there. The miners, convinced that the convicts were taking away their livelihood, forcibly removed them from their guarded stockade, put them on a train, and sent them to Knoxville along with their guards. Gov. John P. Buchanan then ordered the state militia to escort the convicts back to the mines. On July 20, however, armed miners again removed the convicts and sent them back to Knoxville.

"Not since the dark days of '65," reported The Knoxville Sentinel, "have there been such thrilling scenes on the streets of Knoxville." Hundreds of militiamen summoned by the governor were in town marching, drilling and waiting for orders. Meanwhile, the convicts were crowded into temporary quarters in a building on Gay Street, where they threatened a rebellion of their own if they were not fed properly.

The governor eventually defused the crisis by negotiating with the miners and promising to work with the state legislature to abolish the convict lease system. Later in the year, however, after the legislature had failed to act, the miners again revolted. Only in 1893 did the legislature finally abolish the system.

July 21, 1943

A fire in a large boarding house on Wall Avenue on July 21, 1943, sent seven people to the hospital and highlighted the serious problem of overcrowding that Knoxville was experiencing during World War II.

The boom in war-related industries brought thousands of workers and their families into Knoxville. Finding room for them posed a big problem. All sorts of buildings were pressed into service, some of them offering nothing more than rows of cots. Many of these buildings were endangered not only by overcrowding and inadequate fire escapes but also by makeshift stoves and amateurish electric wiring.

The fire in the Wall Avenue boarding house — where 57 of the 78 roomers were war-plant employees — started in a coal-burning stove, probably due to an explosion of accumulated coal dust. Four boarders and three firemen were injured.

Ironically, The News-Sentinel had already prepared an editorial to run that very day on the housing problem. "The saturation point has just about been reached in Knoxville," the editorial pointed out. "But we are fortunate in that the congestion is nothing like as bad as in the densely packed industrial cities up north."

The incident stimulated the city fire inspector to work out a cooperative arrangement with Knoxville's federal rent-control director by which the fire code could be more effectively enforced.

July 22, 1940

A News-Sentinel story on July 22, 1940, told how quick-thinking Knoxville police detective Joe Kimsey ended up with egg on his face — and water in his billfold — after "saving" the life of a 6-year-old boy.

Kimsey, a noted outdoorsman of his day, was enjoying an afternoon at Andersonville Dock on Norris Lake. Suddenly a woman began screaming, "My baby! My baby! He's drowned!"

Kimsey dashed to the edge of the dock and saw the horrified woman pointing to a child's hat in the water. Fully clothed, he leaped in and began searching for the tyke.

Three times, the policeman dove to the bottom of the cove and felt his way through rocks, stumps and mud. But his attempts proved futile.

The woman's husband, who had heard the screams from some distance away, came running onto the dock. In his arms, he carried the boy.

It seems the lad had thrown his hat into the lake moments earlier. As punishment, his father had taken him away.

Kimsey — a colorful and popular officer, but often the center of political controversy — headed Knoxville's police department for 18 years. He retired in 1960. Sixteen years later, at the age of 75, he died of cancer in Florida.

July 23, 1897

In an election held on July 23, 1897, voters approved a measure that more than doubled the size of Knoxville.

The move consolidated Knoxville with West Knoxville and North Knoxville, which were at that time separate towns. North Knoxville, which stretched from the intersection of Broadway and Central north to Woodland Avenue, had been incorporated by the state legislature in 1889. West Knoxville, which stretched from Second Creek west to Third Creek and included what is now the Fort Sanders area and the university campus, had been incorporated in 1888.

Early in 1897 a bill was introduced in the legislature requiring Knoxville to absorb North and West Knoxville. But Knoxville's mayor and aldermen were unenthusiastic about the bill. They sent a resolution to the legislature declaring that North and West Knoxville were hardly meeting their own expenses and that consolidation would impose a financial burden that Knoxville could not support.

Nevertheless, the bill passed, subject to the approval of voters in the three towns. That approval came in the July 23 election. North Knoxvillians voted 154 to 87 in favor of consolidation, and West Knoxvillians voted 142 to 61 in favor, while the voters of Knoxville — rejecting the pleas of their mayor and aldermen — endorsed consolidation by the biggest margin of all: 699 to 35.

July 24, 1923

A bizarre case in Knoxville's probate court on July 24, 1923, involved a woman who claimed to have a "heaven-made marriage" to a local minister.

For three years the woman had been convinced that she was married to her minister by a special act of God. Needless to say, this caused the minister — who already had a wife and children — considerable embarrassment. But no amount of reasoning could convince the woman otherwise. She began sending notes and long letters to the minister, eventually adopted his name and persisted in using that name even though she was fired by two employers for doing so. Through it all, she maintained that God had united her and the minister and that no man or law could sunder that bond.

At the hearing on July 24, the woman showed up dressed entirely in white and attributed all of her actions to "heavenly inspiration and divine guidance." Several witnesses confirmed the unusual nature of her behavior, and a physician gave it as his opinion that she was mentally incapacitated, "especially concerning religion."

The probate court jury agreed, declared the woman mentally ill and recommended that she be assigned a guardian and get treatment in a sanitarium.

July 25, 1885

In a ceremony on July 25, 1885, the cornerstone of the new Lawson McGhee Library building was laid.

The origins of the Lawson McGhee Library go back to 1873, when a group of citizens founded the Knoxville Library and Reading Room Association. This private club began with a membership of about 50 persons who paid a subscription fee and dues. Some 150 books were donated to get the library under way. In 1879, this association was incorporated as the Public Library of Knoxville, and shares were sold.

Lawson McGhee Library, 1885-1904

Until 1885, the library had no building of its own. Temporary quarters were found in various buildings around town. But that year, Charles McClung McGhee, a wealthy Knoxville railroad magnate, decided to build a permanent home for the library at the corner of Gay and Vine as a memorial to his late daughter.

This gift put the long-struggling institution — now reorganized as the Lawson McGhee Library — on a sound footing, for income was secured by renting out the bottom two floors of the three-story structure.

Thereafter the library thrived. In 1892, the trustees hired one of the nation's first professionally trained librarians, Mary Louise Davis of Massachusetts. By 1899, the book collection numbered over 11,000 volumes. It was not until 1911, however, when the city began appropriating funds for it, that Lawson McGhee became a truly public library.

July 26, 1955

A highly publicized trial in Knox County Criminal Court ended on July 26, 1955, with two convictions, one acquittal, and a lecture from the judge.

The case grew out of a labor strike the previous May against Southern Bell telephone company. During the strike, dynamite blasts had destroyed two telephone company terminal boxes in Knoxville. Two men, both in their 20s, were arrested and charged with destruction of property; both gave confessions. A third man was charged with supplying the dynamite.

The trial lasted over a week. The defense was crippled from the start by the ruling of Judge J. Fred Bibb that the confessions were voluntary and admissible. The jury found the two men charged with destruction of property guilty, but acquitted the third man.

After the verdict, Judge Bibb commented that all along he had thought the three defendants were "good folks." The two men convicted were, he said, "two overgrown boys who got out and got likkered up and listened to a lot of violent talk. They are actually not bad boys." The lesson of the trial, he continued, was that organized labor was hurt by such acts of violence. "The organizations of labor in this community have been seriously injured by the fool acts of two or three, or four or five, fellows."

July 27, 1913

On July 27, 1913, Dr. William R. Cochrane of the city board of health warned the people of Knoxville to start boiling their drinking water.

Cochrane had just learned that approximately one million gallons of untreated Tennessee River water had been allowed into the city water mains a few days earlier. He was unaware of the water release until his office began receiving complaints about muddy tap water in some sections of the city.

Investigation revealed that on July 23, the city water department, headed by city commissioner Charles P. McTeer, had deliberately let unfiltered river water flow into the city water supply for about 45 minutes. McTeer defended his action by pointing out that high summer demand for water and inadequate filtration facilities had left the city reservoir nearly empty. To allow the reservoir to go dry would, McTeer reasoned, have created a fire safety problem even more serious than the health problem that unfiltered water posed. Thus, he had chosen the lesser of two evils.

Despite the public's fears, the untreated water quickly passed and no typhoid epidemic resulted. In fact, the water scare may have been beneficial in the long run, for it spurred the city government to push ahead with plans to expand the water filtration plant.

July 28, 1874

On July 28, 1874, one of the leading authorities on Tennessee's resources published a glowing description of Knoxville.

J. B. Killebrew, commissioner of the state Bureau of Agriculture, declared that "for healthfulness the location of Knoxville could scarcely be improved. . . . The climate is truly temperate; neither the long and dreary winters of the northern states, nor the equally long and burning summers of the southern states. . . . All things combine to insure the healthfulness of Knoxville, while the transcendent beauty and picturesqueness of the scenery give it attractions beyond almost any city in the Union as a place of residence."

The city had other attractions, too, according to Killebrew. Rents were low, wages high. Public schools were "tolerably good," and "year by year they grow better and stronger."

Furthermore, Knoxville's economic future was bright, for its industry and commerce were booming. "The city will long continue to grow with healthful rapidity until it becomes one of the great internal cities of the South."

Killebrew's gushing description of Knoxville had an ulterior motive. He hoped to attract immigrants and investors to Tennessee to help develop the state. In fact, he wrote comparable descriptions of every Tennessee city and county, and rarely had a bad word to say about any of them.

July 29, 1925

On July 29, 1925, Knoxvillians paid tribute to one of the nation's great statesmen and orators, William Jennings Bryan.

Bryan had died in Dayton, Tenn., on July 26 — just five days after the conclusion of the famous "Monkey Trial" where he had spoken out against the theory of evolution. The Dayton trial was the capstone of a long career in which Bryan had distinguished himself as a friend of the common man, an advocate of international peace, and a spokesman for religious fundamentalism.

The train carrying Bryan's body left Dayton on July 29 and passed through Knoxville on its way to Washington. A crowd of 10,000 Knoxvillians gathered at the Southern Railway depot that afternoon. During the 20 minutes that the train sat in the station, 500 people passed through the special Pullman car where Bryan's flag-draped bronze casket lay. Outside the car, grieving onlookers deposited wreaths. Acting Mayor Charles Baker called on all citizens to cease work while the train was in the city as a token of respect for one of America's outstanding leaders.

Edward Meeman, editor of The Knoxville News, published an editorial that day lauding Bryan as "a man who all his life tried to bring to public life what he conceived to be the righteousness enjoined by his religion."

July 30, 1951

Knoxvillians by the hundreds opened their hearts, as well as their homes, to two small children on Monday, July 30, 1951.

The day before, The News-Sentinel had carried a long, emotional story about "Jimmy" and "Bobby," 3- and 6-year-old brothers, respectively, who had been declared wards of the state. The Children's Bureau wanted to place them in an adoptive home, but no couple was willing to take both boys.

All that changed after publication of their plight.

Beatrice Garrett, head of the bureau, received more than 200 telephone calls the next morning. Dozens more came to The News-Sentinel's switchboard. Some of the callers were from out of town, a few even from neighboring states.

"The Children's Bureau is making a list of the couples who want Jimmy and Bobby," a front-page story read. "The bureau will follow its usual procedure of carefully studying the offered homes and the children, to be sure they will suit each other.

"The bureau has several other brothers and sisters and older children who need good homes. Those calling in about Jimmy and Bobby will have an opportunity to adopt these other children."

July 31, 1943

In Knoxville on July 31, 1943, a federal agency began hearing cases of gasoline-rationing violations in East Tennessee, and among those found guilty was a Knoxville filling station owner.

Gasoline was strictly rationed during World War II — not to save gasoline, which was plentiful, but to preserve tires, for rubber was in short supply. Citizens were issued coupons for a certain amount of gasoline, and dealers were ordered to dispense no gasoline unless a coupon was presented.

Some cheating was inevitable, of course, and so the federal Office of Price Administration policed the rationing system. At the hearing on July 31, E. S. Strader was ordered to explain the 800-gallon shortage of gasoline that inspectors had discovered at his Magnolia Avenue filling station. Strader claimed that he had suffered repeated thefts of gasoline, and he brought in three city detectives to confirm his story. But the OPA commissioner was unconvinced and ordered Strader's station closed for 30 days.

A number of other East Tennessee gasoline dealers were similarly punished during the two-day hearing. An editorial in The Knoxville News-Sentinel commented that the public should "feel gratified at the action of OPA in cracking down on those who have been chiseling. . . . He who chisels on the gas rationing is sabotaging our war effort."

Aug. 1, 1947

Aug. 1, 1947, marked the end of Knoxville's streetcar era.

The advent of streetcar systems in the late 19th century was an important development in American history, permitting cities to expand enormously and encouraging the growth of suburbs.

Knoxville's first streetcar, a horse-drawn car running on Gay Street between Main and Jackson avenues, began operating in 1876. In the following decades the streetcar system expanded in all directions and fostered the development of such suburbs as West Knoxville (now Fort Sanders), South Knoxville and Fountain City. By the turn of the century, Knoxville had one of the most extensive systems in the South.

The first electric streetcars were introduced to the city in 1890 on a line running out Magnolia Avenue to Lake Ottossee (now Chilhowee Park). Soon thereafter all lines were converted to electric power.

At its height in the 1920s, Knoxville's streetcar system had 53 miles of tracks and carried nearly 20 million passengers a year. Soon thereafter, however, automobiles and buses rendered streetcars obsolete. From 1930 on, more and more streetcar lines were replaced by bus routes. By 1937, Knoxville's streetcar track mileage was down to 23.

The demise of the streetcar in Knoxville, Aug. 1, 1947

In 1947, the city decided to abandon streetcar transportation altogether. The "last run" was set for Aug. 1. On that day, a procession of 12 cars moved slowly down Gay Street as thousands of citizens watched and waved goodbye.

Aug. 2, 1963

A number of construction projects throughout Knoxville and East Tennessee were shut down by a strike of the Laborers Local Union No. 818 on Aug. 2, 1963.

Harrison Ray, president of the 17-member Building and Construction Trades Council of Knoxville, said 1,400 laborers were idle and had set up picket lines at various job sites.

At issue was wages. Although contractors were paying $2.20 per hour, agreed upon in a recent settlement with the International Laborers Union, the local was dissatisfied with the amount and had voted to strike the night before.

The job action did not stop all construction in the area, however. Many union skilled workers did not participate, although picket lines were being honored at some job sites. TVA projects were not affected since the agency had a separate contract with its laborers.

The $350,000 remodeling job at the Mercantile Building in Knoxville was idled, as was work on a school in Oak Ridge. At the University of Tennessee, laborers walked off the West Hall girls' dormitory project, although skilled workers stayed on the job.

"This is a serious interruption," said Tom Nicholson, vice president of Nicholson Construction Co., "because we understand UT has already made rental contracts with girls for the fall term in this building."

Aug. 3, 1871

An important step in the development of Knoxville was begun on Aug. 3, 1871, when a county-wide referendum approved the construction of a bridge across the Tennessee River.

Until the time of the Civil War, ferries provided the only connection between Knoxville and the south bank of the river. Union troops occupying Knoxville built a bridge during the war, but it was used only a few years before it was washed away in the great flood of 1867. After that, ferries were put in service again.

The 1871 referendum authorized a bridge to be built at Knox County's expense. The vote total was 1,919 to 886. (The vote outside the city was actually against the bridge, but the Knoxville vote was so overwhelmingly in favor — 1,156 to 35 — that the bridge was approved.) The bridge, which connected Gay Street to the south bank, was completed in 1874. The very next year, however, it was destroyed by high winds. Again, the ferries were put back in service.

Another bridge was begun in 1879 using the piers of the previous bridge. It was finished in 1880 and used until 1898, when a new bridge (the current Gay Street bridge) was completed. Over 1,500 feet long and 42 feet wide, built of steel and concrete at a cost of $211,000, this bridge has served Knoxville for almost 100 years.

Aug. 4, 1893

A prominent Knoxville man got involved in an embarrassing escapade on Aug. 4, 1893.

Frank Seaman was the commander of the East Tennessee district of the Grand Army of the Republic, a brotherhood of Union Civil War veterans. It was a position of considerable distinction, for the GAR was a powerful and much respected organization in those years.

It seems, however, that Seaman had a drinking problem. "His faults were known at the time" he was elected commander, The Knoxville Sentinel reported, "but almost everyone believed that Seaman would be able to pull through one term without getting drunk and disgracing himself and the (GAR)." They were wrong. "On Aug. 4," the story continued, "Commander Seaman got drunk and was found on Gay Street a little the worse for wear. . . . He was not disorderly, but was simply too far gone to navigate." He was taken off in the police paddy wagon, paid a $6.75 fine and was released.

The story might have been kept from the public, but a Chattanooga newspaper, having learned about it from some indignant GAR members in that city, broke the news. Only then did The Knoxville Sentinel comment on the incident, calling it "an unfortunate spree" and pointing out that it was Seaman's first such lapse since taking office in March.

Aug. 5, 1933

On Aug. 5, 1933, Knoxville was gearing up for participation in one of the most important programs of President Franklin Roosevelt's New Deal: the "Blue Eagle" campaign of the National Recovery Administration.

The NRA represented a bold attempt to bring America out of the Great Depression by means of a huge cooperative effort among employers and workers. Each industry would draft codes of fair practices which all producers were encouraged to subscribe to voluntarily. These codes could set industry-wide prices, wage levels, working conditions, etc., all without fear of federal antitrust action. It was hoped that by this means prices and wages could be stabilized and production and employment could be increased.

On Aug. 5, it was announced that 1,250 Knoxville business concerns had pledged to abide by the NRA's blanket codes and were thereby entitled to display the NRA Blue Eagle sign, with its motto, "We Do Our Part." Meanwhile, representatives of a number of Knoxville's businesses were making plans to meet and discuss the adoption of specific codes. These included the city's grocers, shoe repairmen, laundry operators and theater owners.

An editorial in The Knoxville News-Sentinel urged housewives to avoid patronizing any store not displaying the Blue Eagle. Otherwise, "the work of the National Recovery Administration will be meaningless."

Aug. 6, 1945

On Aug. 6, 1945, Knoxvillians were doubly astounded to learn that an atomic bomb had been dropped on Japan and that the bomb's uranium had been enriched in the nearby super-secret town of Oak Ridge.

During World War II, as part of the Manhattan Project which developed the first atomic bomb, the federal government had built a whole city from scratch in an isolated section of Anderson County. By 1945, there were 75,000 residents in Oak Ridge, making it the fifth largest city in the state — nearly two-thirds the size of Knoxville.

Knoxvillians knew little or nothing of what was going on in Oak Ridge during the war, but with the revelation of Aug. 6, many were quick to claim for Knoxville a share of the credit and to prophesy a great era ahead. A News-Sentinel editorial on Aug. 7 predicted that "Knoxville may well become known as the capital city of atomic energy." The editorial provoked a wave of replies from Oak Ridgers, many of whom had found Knoxville a none-too-hospitable town during the war.

Trailers, wooden boardwalks and dirt roads made up the hurriedly populated residential section of Oak Ridge in the 1940s.

Aug. 7, 1916

Knoxvillians who hoped to encourage automobile tourism got some good news on Aug. 7, 1916.

J. L. McGhee, an official of the Automobile Club of America, was in Knoxville as part of an extensive trip to map the highways of the South. In an interview with The Knoxville Sentinel on Aug. 7, he spoke highly of Knoxville's attractions.

"I have been agreeably surprised," McGhee said. "Knoxville is the hub center of one of the best road-provisioned sections in the South. . . . People in the North and East and West wish to see the southern country. . . . (But) they have not been fully advised as to the splendid motoring opportunities here. The purpose of my trip now is to give them full information. . . . If the American motor tourists are informed as to what you have in natural beauty here, they will come in great numbers."

What Knoxville really needed, McGhee continued, was "another large and very modern hotel. Auto tourists usually are people of means and they are willing to pay real money for the best that is to be had in hotel accommodations."

McGhee's remarks showed foresight, for auto tourism would become a major Knoxville industry in the future — not, however, until the construction of the state highway system in the 1920s and, more importantly, the interstate system in the 1960s.

Aug. 8, 1893

On Aug. 8, 1893, a Knoxville Sentinel reporter with a flair for dramatic prose published a description of his recent visit to the county jail.

"There is a sort of melancholy interest about a jail," the article began. "The grim surroundings of bare stone walls and iron gratings possess one with a peculiar sensation as he enters them." In one cell, stretched out on a cot, was the notorious bad-check man, Dan Benick, who "looked cool and comfortable, wearing clean underwear and had his hair elaborately dressed." Among the jail's other occupants was Wash Boyer, serving 20 years for killing his father. "Boyer is far less unruly now than he was formerly, before his encounter with jailer (George) McIntyre, who first licked him and then put him in the dungeon. Boyer moped sullenly in the dungeon for seven weeks, and then got tired of it and apologized to the jailer, and was let out under the promise that he would behave himself." Jailer McIntyre reported conditions much improved in the jail, for the prisoners' "former practice of robbing new arrivals of money has been stopped." Nevertheless, he still "has to keep his eyes wide open. The prisoners are always concocting some scheme for escape."

Aug. 9, 1906

One of America's foremost labor leaders visited Knoxville on Aug. 9, 1906.

John Mitchell, president of the United Mine Workers, was in town to address local UMW members who were meeting at the county courthouse. Mitchell had risen to national prominence four years earlier during the great Anthracite Coal Strike, when his determined leadership had gained a signal victory for organized labor.

Mitchell, a sort of boy wonder, was only 36 years old in 1906 (he had become UMW president at the age of 28). A Knoxville Sentinel reporter who interviewed him described him as "an impressive man, quiet and dignified, but with a pleasant word and a hearty handshake."

In his address to the mine workers, Mitchell displayed both modesty and moderation. "When I was less experienced than I am now," he said, "I thought that I could readily reach a proper solution of the (labor) question. But now I am imbued with the idea that after me and my children and their children have passed away, this question will still be discussed." What he sought, he said, was a fair and "humane" resolution of labor conflicts. His policy was not to automatically condemn management and defend labor but to consider "quietly and impassionately all questions that are involved."

Aug. 10, 1816

On Aug. 10, 1816, the editors of the new Knoxville Register set forth their policy and their philosophy.

Frederick S. Heiskell and his brother-in-law, Hugh Brown, had begun publication of the weekly Register on Aug. 3. In the second issue, dated Aug. 10, they devoted front-page space to a statement of their aims, a statement that reflected the values of the generation that had fought and won the American Revolution.

"The general diffusion of information is indispensable," they said, to "a free government. . . . Hence the great importance of newspapers in a republican government." But, they continued, depending on how a newspaper was conducted, its influence might be either "salutary or pernicious." Heiskell and Brown intended to present an impartial review "of all the facts and arguments" on every topic, and thus help "destroy that dependence of the many on the few which is utterly inconsistent with . . . liberty and equality." This was in contrast to other editors who "conceive themselves the miserable tools of a party, whose interests they . . . support, if necessary, by the propagation of falsehood or the concealment of truth."

The Register, which was available to subscribers for $3 a year, "payable in advance," was an immediate success. Though Brown left in 1829 and Heiskell retired in 1837, the newspaper was carried on by others until 1863.

Aug. 11, 1937

On Aug. 11, 1937, all of Knoxville was talking about the controversy over the flogging of prisoners at the Knox County workhouse.

The issue had arisen when it was learned that four workhouse prisoners had been whipped for refusing to work at the quarry to which they were assigned. When questioned about the incident, the county commissioner who had ordered the whippings replied that "you have to rule (prisoners) with an iron-clad hand." He was supported by a second commissioner, who said, "I'm in favor of whipping them at the workhouse. . . . I favor the return of the public whipping post of 100 years ago. That's what I would like to see."

These pronouncements provoked a storm of public indignation. The Young Republican Club of Knox County passed a resolution calling the floggings "brutal and inhuman, futile and unnecessary." A similar resolution by the Knoxville Industrial Union Council called the county commissioners' remarks "contrary to right and decent public practice . . . and conducive to the lowering of the moral and spiritual standards of a free and democratic people." The controversy ended abruptly on Aug. 11, when the Knox County assistant attorney general declared that neither the county commissioners nor anybody else had authority to order the flogging of prisoners.

Aug. 12, 1984

With a dazzling display of lights and fireworks, Michael Jackson ended his three-night stand in Knoxville on Aug. 12, 1984.

At that time Jackson was unquestionably the hottest entertainer in the nation. Excitement had been mounting for months, ever since it became known that Knoxville was on the list of cities to be visited by the "Victory Tour."

Hundreds of workers labored several days to erect the five-story stage in Neyland Stadium on which Jackson was to perform. A total of 2,640 lights illuminated the stage, which resembled a NASA launch pad. Dry ice — 1,000 pounds per show — was stockpiled nearby to provide smoke effects.

Fans wait in the rain for Victory Tour tickets.

The rigid security measures in force made some people wonder if Jackson was expecting a terrorist attack (he had in fact received death threats). Security was also tight at the Airport Hilton, where Jackson and his entourage had rented an entire floor — 54 rooms.

Over three days, 133,000 fans thrilled to Jackson's performance. They were not the only ones who were pleased. Knoxville city authorities were also smiling: the city's take from the amusement tax was about $150,000.

Aug. 13, 1875

Public executions were a common spectacle in 19th-century America, and Knoxvillians were treated to one on Aug. 13, 1875.

A gallows had been erected on Clinton Pike for the hanging of John Webb, recently convicted of murder. The execution was scheduled for the afternoon, but spectators began assembling as early as 8 in the morning. Some came on foot, some in wagons, and some by train. Eventually the crowd numbered 10,000 or more, all of whom had come, as one newspaper reporter put it, "to satisfy that morbid appetite to see a man hanging in mid-air at the end of a rope, dying." (The reporter ironically noted that only 5,000 had turned out for the recent funeral of Andrew Johnson.)

The crowd's expectations were gratified when the prisoner was escorted to the site sometime after noon, accompanied by his wife and 50 guards armed with shotguns. Before ascending the gallows he protested his innocence, then shook hands with the defense and prosecution lawyers and the trial witnesses, who were among those present.

His last words were, "Well, I thank you all for coming out to see me hung. I forgive all, and hope God will forgive me. Goodbye, God bless you." And then, to his wife, "I'll try and meet you in heaven."

Aug. 14, 1821

James White, the founder of Knoxville, died on Aug. 14, 1821.

Born in North Carolina about 1747, White was a militia officer during the Revolution. In 1785, he crossed the mountains into the Tennessee country and settled at the junction of the Holston and French Broad rivers. The next year, however, he moved downriver, settling on a 1,000-acre tract that he had acquired on the north bank. This was the future site of Knoxville, and there he built a settlement, fortified against Indian attacks, known as White's Fort.

White was active in politics at each succeeding stage of East Tennessee history. He served in the legislature of the state of Franklin, which attempted to assert the Tennessee country's independence from North Carolina. After the failure of the Franklin movement, White served in North Carolina's legislature and constitutional ratification convention. After North Carolina ceded the Tennessee country and a territorial government was established, White served in its general assembly.

White was a friend and business associate of Territorial Gov. William Blount, who in 1791 chose White's Fort as the site of the territorial capital, which he named Knoxville. In 1796 White helped draft the Tennessee constitution and later served in the state legislature. He never held a national office, but his son, Hugh Lawson White, became a famous national political figure.

Aug. 15, 1953

Members of a Knoxville family cried for joy on Aug. 15, 1953, upon learning that Pvt. Carl Keller, U.S. Army, had been released from a communist prisoner of war camp and would soon be coming home.

Keller, a Knoxvillian, was among the first American prisoners released under the armistice agreement that had ended the Korean War three weeks earlier. Ordered to Korea at the outbreak of the war in 1950, he had survived two wounds only to be reported missing in action in May 1951. His family endured months of suspense before it was confirmed that he was a prisoner.

At a repatriation center in South Korea following his release, Keller told a reporter about the abominable mistreatment of prisoners by their communist captors. Forced "confessions," political indoctrination, staged "war crime" trials, dysentery and starvation all made prison life a hell, he said. But "the hardest battle was boredom and discouragement." Keller's account was among the first of many stories of brutality in the Chinese and North Korean prison camps that would outrage the American public in the postwar period.

Meanwhile, Keller's family in Knoxville made plans for his return. His sister declared her intention to "bake the biggest banana pudding I can make" for Keller, who, she said, "could eat more banana pudding than anybody I know."

Aug. 16, 1935

On Friday, Aug. 16, 1935, The News-Sentinel reported the death of humorist Will Rogers and pilot Wiley Post in a plane crash in Alaska the day prior.

Cowboy-philosopher Rogers "was the biggest box-office attraction we ever had in Knoxville," said the manager of the Tennessee Theater. "Everyone loved him. All ages and all classes, they flocked to see his pictures."

Rogers had made a few personal appearances in Knoxville as well, the first being at the Appalachian Exposition in 1910, doing his rope act in "Zack Mulhall's Wild West Show." He returned in 1926 for "a wise-cracking performance" in which he poked fun at Knoxville's "traffic coops" on Gay Street — referring to the officers who regulated traffic flow from elevated booths at each intersection.

The News-Sentinel carried daily dispatches from Rogers and published his final report — about hundreds of gold miners rushing into Alaska and creating a terrible housing shortage — along with the news of his death.

Almost simultaneously with the arrival of his report came a letter from the newspaper syndicate that handled Rogers's pieces. Ironically, it explained that in the future "Will's pieces might not come as regularly as before, since he was passing through places that had no telegraph service."

Aug. 17, 1855

A torchlight procession in Knoxville on Aug. 17, 1855, honored Tennessee's newly reelected governor, Andrew Johnson.

Johnson had arrived that day by stage from his home in Greeneville, on his way to Nashville to begin his second term as governor. That night a group of loyal Democrats who had helped elect him marched to the Coleman House Hotel where he was staying. They carried banners and torches and brought along a band.

Johnson, always ready with a speech, appeared before his followers and spoke for more than an hour. He denounced the Know-Nothing party, whose candidate he had narrowly defeated in the recent election. In fact, according to the Knoxville Standard (a very partisan Democratic newspaper) Johnson "dealt Know Nothingism some crushing blows. He showed up the inconsistencies of the Know Nothings in a way that will not soon be forgotten by those who heard him." A few disgruntled Know Nothings in the crowd tried to shout down the governor, but were unsuccessful. At the conclusion of his remarks, Johnson "retired amid prolonged and loud cheers."

"We have never seen a more orderly and peaceable gathering of the people," the Standard concluded. "Everything passed off quietly and the crowd dispersed at an early hour." The next morning Johnson boarded a train and was off to Nashville.

Aug. 18, 1920

"Knoxville Women Are Elated," blared the headlines of The Knoxville Sentinel on Aug. 18, 1920; "Red Letter Day for America." It was indeed a significant moment in American history, for on that day Tennessee became the 36th state to ratify the Nineteenth Amendment, giving women the right to vote. Woman suffrage thus became the law of the land.

The Sentinel that day carried an editorial praising the "glorious work" of the state legislature in approving the amendment. The editorial also sang the praises of the female suffrage activists who "have made this heroic fight for political freedom."

Sentinel reporters asked Knoxville women for their reaction to the news. "Good work!" was the comment of Mary Utopia Rothrock; "I am delighted." Mrs. B. S. Williams called it "the most glorious thing that has ever come to the women of the United States." Mrs. L. Crozier French, one of Knoxville's leading "suffragettes," declared that "the crowning of 40 years of aspiration, organization and work gives me this profound feeling of satisfaction. . . . Votes for women will . . . make for true democracy." Not all the comments were so enthusiastic. "I think women's sphere is in the home," said Mrs. Walter Barton, "and for that reason I have never approved of woman suffrage."

Aug. 19, 1914

On Aug. 19, 1914, Knoxville was feeling the effects of the great war that had broken out in Europe just a few weeks earlier. Although the U.S. would not enter World War I until nearly three years after its outbreak, many Knoxvillians and other Americans were touched by the conflict from the moment it began.

On Aug. 19, 1914, Mrs. Walter Lutz of Knoxville went to her husband's furniture plant on South Morgan Street and assumed direction of the business. Her husband, a native of Switzerland, had just been summoned back there to take his position in the Swiss militia. "It nearly broke my heart to see him go," Mrs. Lutz said. "I shall stay here . . . and take care of his business while he is gone."

Meanwhile, several Knoxvillians were stranded in the war zone. They included some who were traveling in Europe and others who were in school there. Family members in Knoxville were frantically contacting the State Department for information about their loved ones.

The first Knoxvillian to return from the war zone was F. C. Reeder, a Fulton Co. engineer who had gone to England on business. Advised by the U.S. embassy to get home as quickly as possible, he returned as a steerage passenger on a tramp steamer.

Aug. 20, 1953

The second "Kinsey Report" on sexual behavior in America was released on Aug. 20, 1953, and The Knoxville News-Sentinel had some words of caution about it.

The Kinsey Reports of 1948 and 1953, based on thousands of interviews conducted by Dr. Alfred C. Kinsey, gave Americans their first scientific knowledge about actual sexual practices in their society. Among the shocking findings were that nearly half of all married women were not virgins when they married; that 26 percent of wives and 50 percent of husbands had been unfaithful to their spouses; and that 20 percent of women and 37 percent of men had engaged in homosexual acts.

The revelation that such practices were widespread made them seem less "unnatural" than conventional morality had always depicted them. Along with the contraceptive pill, the Kinsey Reports are regarded as one of the foundations of the "sexual revolution" that rocked late-20th century American society.

In commenting on the second report, a Knoxville News-Sentinel editorial warned that "scientific" facts are sometimes found to be completely wrong. "Therefore the layman may well look at Dr. Kinsey's findings critically, and not be too quick to accept it all." Furthermore, "We do not believe any clinical studies, no matter how useful, will displace the wisdom of the ages or experience of religion."

Aug. 21, 1971

"Operation Aquarius" got underway on Aug. 21, 1971, and before the day was over dozens of persons in Knoxville had been arrested on drug charges.

The arrests were the culmination of seven weeks of undercover police work, during which agents had made drug buys of everything from marijuana to heroin. Heading up the operation was the new city safety director, Randy Tyree.

Randy Tyree with the remains of a marijuana raid

Warrants had been issued for 102 persons, and by midnight about 60 had been arrested, mostly in East Knoxville and in the Cumberland Avenue "Strip" area. Very few of those arrested were UT students, however.

"We want to let people know that they are not going to get away with peddling drugs in our city," Tyree announced as the operation was in progress, adding that "there is a major drug problem in Knoxville." The operation was code-named Aquarius, he said, because it would "bring peace and tranquility to the city of Knoxville." Mayor Leonard Rogers praised the drug raids and said that they would put "people on notice that we're not going to allow drugs in Knoxville." The abatement of the "drug problem" proved only temporary, however. A more enduring result of Operation Aquarius was that it boosted Randy Tyree's prestige and helped him four years later when he ran successfully for mayor.

Aug. 22, 1889

"The most horrible tragedy ever to befall our town," as one Knoxvillian described it, occurred on Aug. 22, 1889.

It happened, oddly enough, not in Knoxville but in Grainger County, through which the new Knoxville, Cumberland Gap & Louisville Railroad passed. Construction of the railroad had begun in 1887, after the city of Knoxville agreed to help underwrite its cost.

The railroad made a special inaugural run on Aug. 22, 1889. On board the train were a number of Knoxville dignitaries.

As it passed over Flat Creek one of the cars went off the track and plunged into the creek. Five Knoxvillians were killed or mortally injured, and at least two dozen others were hurt. The dead were George Andrews, an eminent lawyer; S. T. Powers, a prominent merchant; Alex Reeder, a former sheriff and state representative; Isham Young, chairman of the board of public works; and F. Hockenjos, a city alderman.

Word of the tragedy quickly reached Knoxville, and an anxious crowd gathered at the depot to await the return of the dead and injured. "The assembled multitude greeted the incoming train in silence and with bowed heads," one witness wrote. "Many eyes glistened with tears. . . . The rain . . . settled into a steady downpour, as if nature herself was weeping for the great calamity that had befallen the city."

Aug. 23, 1899

A fatal accident on Aug. 23, 1899, raised concerns about the safety of the Knoxville streetcar system.

The victim, W. O. Carback of Grainger County, had been waiting on the west side of Gay Street for a streetcar. When a northbound car approached, he crossed the street and tried to board the car from the street side rather than the curb side. He slipped, however, and fell into the path of a southbound car running on a parallel track. He died instantly. Some witnesses said that the southbound car was speeding (a city ordinance limited the speed of streetcars to four miles per hour).

Carback was a merchant who was in Knoxville stocking up on store supplies. Ironically, part of his business involved selling cross ties to the Knoxville Traction Company, which operated the streetcars.

The accident — the second such in Knoxville in the space of two months — inspired an editorial in The Knoxville Sentinel. "The lesson of last night's fatality," it read, "seems to be that, first, the public should . . . learn to be careful in crossing the tracks at any time. And, second, that the Traction Company should require its motormen to reduce their speed on Gay Street. . . . At the speed at which the cars are run at present there is daily danger of fatalities."

Aug. 24, 1973

On Friday, Aug. 24, 1973, University of Tennessee officials revealed the details concerning what was probably the biggest art theft in Knoxville history.

The previous Tuesday night, burglars had broken into the main library at Fifteenth and Cumberland and gained access to the valuable Audigier Art Collection, housed in the tower of the library.

The burglars apparently knew exactly what they wanted. They took 82 small or easily transportable objects but ignored larger items; and they used packing material to avoid breaking the stolen pieces. UT delayed reporting the theft until the whole collection had been inventoried.

The Audigier Collection was given to UT in 1932 by L. B. Audigier in honor of his wife, Eleanor. Both were Knoxville natives who lived most of their lives in Italy and collected art there.

The missing items were valued at $20,000 to $30,000. They included an 18th century Turkish rug, a 15th century Italian crucifix, a Napoleonic era French coffee pot, a Swiss statuette, a Russian candlestick, an Arabian dagger, an Egyptian bracelet and a pair of Welsh book holders made from carved walrus tusks. The burglars also got away with a set of the library's master keys.

No arrests were ever made in the case, and none of the stolen items was ever recovered.

Aug. 25, 1794

The first regular session of the territorial legislature met in Knoxville on Aug. 25, 1794, and among its members was one of Tennessee's great heroes, John Sevier.

A descendant of French Huguenot colonists and a native of Virginia, Sevier (born in 1745) settled in East Tennessee before the American Revolution. In the years that followed, he won fame as an Indian fighter and a Revolutionary War hero, especially after he led American forces to victory over the British at the battle of King's Mountain in 1780.

John Sevier

When the Tennessee settlers asserted their independence against North Carolina in the 1780s, they elected Sevier governor of their short-lived state of Franklin. After North Carolina formally ceded the Tennessee country in 1789, Sevier was appointed a general of the territorial militia and later a member of the territorial legislature.

Sevier did not actually establish his residence in Knoxville until 1797, after Tennessee had become a state (with Knoxville its capital) and he had been elected its first governor. Sevier served six terms as governor and then became a U.S. congressman from 1811 until his death in 1815.

Aug. 26, 1899

On Aug. 26, 1899, a Knoxville minister spoke out against the desecration of the Sabbath.

The Rev. M. D. Jeffries was incensed at the news that entertainment shows would be put on at Chilhowee Park on Sundays. "Knoxville has a hundred years of history as a quiet, law-abiding, Sabbath-keeping city," Jeffries said. Knoxville theater owners had always kept their theaters closed on Sundays. "Anyone who knows anything of Sunday theaters knows they are generally the roughest kind, attended by the roughest element. . . . If we begin now with the open Sunday theaters, we shall soon have the open saloon. . . . We are threatened with changes in our moral habits that will be far-reaching and serious."

Jeffries was seconded by the Rev. W. A. Saville, who said that shows like that to be performed at Chilhowee Park are "not fit for decent virtuous people to look at. . . . Let all who love the Sabbath frown down on any such attempt to destroy the sacredness of the day."

Despite the preachers' protests, the show went on as scheduled the next Sunday, before a large crowd. One man who attended remarked that he had spotted "several people in the audience who, had they not been there, would have been in much worse places."

Aug. 27, 1844

An ad for Mansfield's drugstore that appeared in the Knoxville Post on Aug. 27, 1844, offered Knoxvillians some of the latest in patent medicines.

The 19th century was the golden age of patent medicines, most of which were worthless and some of which were actually harmful. Not until the early 20th century did state and federal authorities begin regulating the production and sale of such drugs.

The ad in the Post touted the efficacy of Fahenstock's Vermifuge, "a never-failing cure for worms," for only 25 cents per vial. Also available at Mansfield's was a complete line of Allebasi's Medicines, "among the most popular and valuable medicines in this country." These included Allebasi's Salve, which was guaranteed to heal fever sores, ulcers, abscesses, tumors, cuts, burns, scalds, swellings, inflammations and muscle pains; Allebasi's Pills, good for fevers, ague, jaundice, acid stomach, constipation, "impure blood," and "general debility"; Allebasi's Toothache Drops, which "will cure every ordinary case of toothache in from 3 to 10 minutes"; and Allebasi's Plasters, "for pain or weakness in the back, side, chest, bowels, loins, muscles, feet, chronic rheumatism, nervous affections, coughs, colds, asthma, fever and ague, weakness in woman, such as falling of the womb, etc., etc." Included with each was a pamphlet containing information on the drug and testimonials to its effectiveness.

Aug. 28, 1941

Knoxville kicked off its great sesquicentennial celebration on Aug. 28, 1941, with a parade.

The commemoration of the 150th anniversary of Knoxville's founding was a gala five-day event culminating on Sept. 1. Each day was packed with ceremonies and shows. The first day's "Parade of Progress" down Gay Street was followed by a special luncheon at the S&W Cafeteria, a flag presentation at Blount Mansion and a 600-piece band concert at Shields-Watkins Field.

After the concert came the first performance of the big outdoor historical spectacle, "Echoes of Progress," which dramatized Knoxville's history from prehistoric times through World War I.

This souvenir booklet was distributed during the sesquicentennial.

Other events of the birthday celebration included historical lectures, a boat regatta on Norris Lake and a coronation ball featuring the crowning of "Miss East Tennessee." Downtown stores presented historical displays in their show windows. Knoxville's oldest residents were honored each evening before the "Echoes of Progress" performance. Among them was Amanda McTeer, oldest living descendant of Knoxville founder James White.

The purpose of the whole event, as noted in the official brochure, was to celebrate "150 years of progress and achievement. This celebration is not a series of shows based merely on pride, but rather a demonstration of the earnestness of our own efforts to build a greater and more wholesome city."

Aug. 29, 1968

George Wallace visited Knoxville on Aug. 29, 1968, during his presidential campaign tour.

Wallace, a former Alabama governor and an outspoken critic of racial integration, was running as a third-party candidate. His right-wing rhetoric appealed to many Americans, especially in the South, during the 1960s — an era of intense social and political conflict in America.

"The people of the United States are tired of both the Republican and Democratic parties and their attitudes," Wallace said after greeting the crowd of 400 who met him at the Knoxville airport on Aug. 29. In particular he criticized forced integration of schools and residential neighborhoods.

That night at the Civic Auditorium, as an enthusiastic crowd of 7,000 cheered and a band played "Dixie," Wallace gave a rousing speech. He predicted a "throat clearing" in the November election because Republican party leaders have "rammed everything there is to ram down the South's throat." And he denounced the liberal establishment, especially the ''ivory tower professors . . . people with pointed heads who can't even park a bicycle straight." He also blasted communists, gun control, the Supreme Court, and Vietnam War protesters. "If an anarchist lays down in front of my car when I'm president," he declared, "it'll be the last car he ever lays in front of." Moreover, Wallace said, he was "tired of being called a redneck."

George Wallace at the Knoxville Civic Auditorium

Aug. 30, 1919

The worst racial violence in Knoxville's history occurred on Aug. 30, 1919.

Although race relations in Knoxville appeared amicable in the early years of the century, trouble was brewing. The black population of the city grew enormously in those years, spilling over into previously all-white neighborhoods. The economic dislocations following World War I further aggravated social tensions.

The race riot that broke out on Aug. 30 began with the arrest of a black man, Maurice Mayes, charged with murdering a white woman. A white lynch mob, unaware that Mayes had been sent to Chattanooga, stormed the Knox County jail. After releasing a few white prisoners and consuming the confiscated whiskey stored in the jail, the mob moved out into the streets, broke into stores and stole guns and then headed toward the black section of town.

National Guardsmen were quickly brought to the scene, but not soon enough to prevent a bloody shootout between blacks and whites. Before the riot was over, one guardsman and one black were dead and 13 people injured.

Order was restored the next day, thanks to the presence of the military and the appeals for peace by white and black leaders. Meanwhile, however, hundreds of blacks had fled the city in terror. A number of white rioters were later arrested, but a jury exonerated them.

Aug. 31, 1854

A letter to the editor of the Knoxville Register, dated Aug. 31, 1854, took up the controversial question of reviving the African slave trade.

The importation of slaves from Africa to the U.S. had been outlawed since 1808. Northerners and southerners alike had come to agree that the overseas trade in human beings was a horror that could no longer be justified.

In the 1850s, however, a few southerners began to call for an end to the ban on importations. The price of domestic slaves was rising, they argued, putting them out of the reach of most whites. Moreover, because the North's population was outstripping the South's, the North would soon dominate Congress unless the South's population could be increased (slaves counted as three-fifths of a person for purposes of Congressional representation).

On Aug. 31, 1854, after reading of a proposal to revive the African trade, Joseph H. Martin fired off a letter to the Register. He regarded such a proposal, he said, as "too base and iniquitous for men of principle and honor to listen to for a moment. It is a scheme to be instantly repudiated, . . . just as a chaste and virtuous woman would scorn a proposal insulting to her purity. . . . Is there a man in the state of Tennessee who does not brand with indignation this unholy plan?"

Sept. 1, 1863

On Sept. 1, 1863, Knoxville was "liberated" by Union troops.

The outbreak of the Civil War in 1861 had bitterly divided the people of Knoxville. Although Tennessee was officially a part of the Confederacy, many Knoxvillians remained steadfastly loyal to the Union.

Confederate troops occupied the town until 1863. They ruthlessly suppressed Union sentiment and forced the town's most outspoken Unionist, newspaper editor William G. Brownlow, to flee to the north.

The Confederates evacuated Knoxville in August 1863, however, and on Sept. 1, Union troops under Gen. Ambrose Burnside marched in and seized the town. ''Long shall (that day) be remembered among us,'' wrote one pro-Confederate woman. ''It was the day when we beheld for the first time our most dreaded foe, the Yankees.''

Many other Knoxvillians cheered the Union troops, however. ''The people seemed frantic with joy,'' wrote one northern soldier who was there. Long-hidden American flags were brought out and flown from windows. The soldiers were showered with gifts of food.

Union troops held Knoxville for the rest of the war, despite an attempt by Confederate forces to recapture it in November 1863. Brownlow returned and resumed publication of his newspaper. Many Confederate sympathizers in the town eventually resigned themselves to defeat and took an oath of allegiance to the Union.

Gen. Burnside's march into Knoxville, as depicted in Harpers' Weekly

Sept. 2, 1876

On Sept. 2, 1876, the town was abuzz with the news that a Knoxville man had entered the race for governor.

William F. Yardley

What made William F. Yardley's candidacy especially remarkable was the fact that he was black. Indeed, he was the first black ever to run for governor of Tennessee.

Yardley was only 32 years old in 1876. He had been born not a slave but free (his mother was white). He learned to read and write before the Civil War. After the war he studied law under a white attorney and in 1872 became Knoxville's first black lawyer.

Displeased by the domination of state government by conservative white Democrats, and by the failure of the Republicans to protect black rights, Yardley declared his candidacy as a Republican. He called his candidacy "a new departure" undertaken "for the good of my party and my race."

Yardley had no chance to win (few whites supported him, and even many blacks were skeptical), but he fought the good fight. Not unexpectedly, the Democrats swept the elections. Yardley received only 2,165 votes out of more than 200,000 cast.

Sept. 3, 1894

Knoxville's first official Labor Day celebration, on Sept. 3, 1894, was a grand success.

Knoxvillians had organized labor parades and festivities before, but this was the first since Congress had declared Labor Day a national holiday.

It began that morning with a huge parade in which all of Knoxville's craftsmen and organized laborers were represented. Thousands of people lined Gay Street to watch the mile-long procession of workers, who marched two abreast from downtown to Fountain City.

The policemen led the parade, followed by the firemen with their horse-drawn engines. Behind them came the men of the tinners' union and the cigar-makers' union. On a handsome float rode the stonecutters, chiseling and polishing Tennessee marble.

On they came: railroad engineers and conductors, painters, bricklayers, typesetters, tailors, plumbers, harness makers, cabinet makers, and more.

The parade ended at Fountain City, where a big picnic was enjoyed by thousands. Contests were held, including a tug-of-war (married men vs. single men), a 100-yard dash for union men, a 50-yard dash for married women and an apple-eating competition for boys. Prizes were also awarded to the best woman rifle shot, the best woman whistler and the ugliest man. In the baseball game that afternoon, the railroad workers beat the iron workers 21-6.

Sept. 4, 1871

Knoxville's first public schools opened on Sept. 4, 1871.

Before that time, the only education available to the children of Knoxville was in private subscription schools and academies. Knoxville and many other southern communities were far behind the rest of the nation in providing free public schools.

But in the post-Civil War years, many Knoxvillians and other southerners came to see the benefits of public education. In December 1870, the Knoxville City Council took up the question, and in January a voter referendum approved (by a vote of 433 to 162) the establishment of tax-supported schools. A contribution from the Peabody Fund, a philanthropic organization devoted to improving southern education, also helped get Knoxville's school system underway.

Nine schools opened on Sept. 4, 1871, with 17 teachers and 1,000 students. Among the rules enforced was that "no teacher shall be allowed to teach sectarian views in religion or partisan or sectional views in politics." There were no black students at first because Knoxville's black children were already being taught in schools run by northern humanitarians. By 1872, however, public schools for blacks were in operation. In 1874, the head of the city board of education declared it was his policy to "educate white and black, rich and poor, Catholic and Protestant, exactly alike."

Sept. 5, 1939

On Sept. 5, 1939, Knoxville was already being touched by the war that had begun in Europe just days earlier.

The outbreak of World War II created uncertainty about the future of food prices in the U.S., leading food producers to withhold commodities from the market. On Sept. 5, Knoxville wholesalers and processors reported that they were unable to procure wheat or dried beans. East Tennessee farmers stopped bringing their hogs to market.

The specter of food shortages and rising prices prompted panicky Knoxville consumers to begin hoarding, thus further aggravating the problem. "It's a sort of mental hysteria," said a Knoxville White Stores official. Within a matter of days, the price of flour in local grocery stores climbed from $7.20 to $8.40 per barrel, shortening from 35 to 45 cents a carton, pork loins from 25 to 35 cents a pound.

The panic inspired The Knoxville News-Sentinel to print a front-page editorial addressed "To Knoxville Housewives." "There is no food shortage," it declared. "Don't get hysterical and buy a big supply of food. That is one sure way to shoot the price skyward. Buy only what you would normally buy. And when you come on an item that has shot upward all out of proportion, simply refuse to buy it."

Sept. 6, 1972

On Sept. 6, 1972, bowing to the inevitable changing of fashion, the Knoxville police department dropped its attempt to punish a police officer who refused to shave his mustache.

Patrolman Mike Gillespie had been charged with conduct unbecoming a police officer after he insisted on wearing a mustache in violation of the department's dress code.

A Civil Service hearing was scheduled for Gillespie, but before it could be held the authorities had a change of heart. Police Chief Joe Fowler — having been apprised of the recently liberalized dress codes of big-city police departments and the U. S. military, and having discussed the issue with Mayor Kyle Testerman — announced that charges against Gillespie were being withdrawn. Furthermore, Fowler said, the police department would give its dress code a "revamping."

A Knoxville News-Sentinel editorial applauded Fowler's decision, noting that "hair is everywhere (these days). . . Excess hair has little to do with a person's performance of his duties or his loyalty to God and Country. We can see nothing wrong with a little decorative fuzz here and there if it's kept neat and clean. . . . What we don't appreciate is a tangled, unkempt mass which is symbolic of an irresponsible person who is unwilling to join the mainstream of the 1970's."

Sept. 7, 1917

Knoxvillians turned out by the thousands on Sept. 7, 1917, to say goodbye to the men of the Third Tennessee Infantry.

The Third Tennessee was a regiment of East Tennesseans, 900 strong, who were heading off for combat service in France.

Knoxville, like cities all across the nation, was delirious with patriotic enthusiasm in those early days of America's participation in World War I. As the troops marched to the railway station a band played, flags waved and cheering crowds lined the streets.

Col. Cary Spence of Knoxville, the regimental commander, told the crowd that "the men of the Third Regiment will uphold past traditions of the Volunteer state by making a name for themselves which will be marked in the annals of history."

The Knoxville Sentinel that day extolled America's noble mission, which was "to stamp out the evils of the old world and to write in the history of the universe a new chapter of progress."

Col. Spence's confidence was not misplaced, for the Third Tennessee did indeed distinguish itself on the battlefields of France in the months to come. But the public idealism reflected in The Sentinel's remarks would fade in the postwar era, as Americans began to wonder if the war had been worth fighting after all.

Sept. 8, 1830

A distinguished visitor was in Knoxville on Wednesday, Sept. 8, 1830: President Andrew Jackson.

Word had earlier been received that the president would arrive in Knoxville on Tuesday en route to Washington. Such an event was sure to spark a celebration in just about any town in the nation in those days, and Knoxville was no exception.

Andrew Jackson

Citizens assembled at the courthouse Tuesday morning, formed a welcoming committee and resolved to honor the president with a banquet.

Later that day Jackson and his entourage arrived. Amid the booming of cannons, a big crowd rode out to meet him. They handed him a letter expressing "a hearty welcome" and lauding "the purity and usefulness of your administration." Jackson replied with a note of his own, declining the offer of a banquet but agreeing to attend a reception and shake some hands.

The next morning, he breakfasted at the home of U.S. Sen. Hugh Lawson White, where another big crowd of Knoxvillians turned out to greet him. Later that day he headed on to Washington.

Sept. 9, 1886

On Sept. 9, 1886, Knoxvillians were engaged in a generous effort to help the victims of a terrible natural disaster.

Charleston, S.C., had recently been hit by an earthquake, one of the most catastrophic in U.S. history. The disaster evoked great sympathy all across the nation.

In Knoxville, as in many other places, citizens undertook to raise money for the suffering people of Charleston. Mayor James C. Luttrell Jr. appointed a committee to oversee fund-raising in Knoxville. On Sept. 9, the committee reported that in just two days over $1,000 had been procured. The Southern Express Co. agree to forward all donations free of charge.

Fund-raising events were held in town, too. On Sept. 14, the Crouch Band (a 23-member community orchestra that had been organized in Knoxville a year earlier) put on a benefit concert at Staub's Theater, which owner Peter Staub had made available at no cost. An hour-long program of classical music, highlighted by a selection from Verdi, delighted the audience, who contributed another $270 to the relief effort.

That was not all. It was announced that a "grand moonlight fete" would be held at Lyon's View Park on Sept. 21 for the benefit of the Charlestonians. "Come one, come all," said the promoters, "and help the distressed."

Sept. 10, 1794

On Sept. 10, 1794, the territorial legislature chartered Blount College, Knoxville's first institution of learning and the forerunner of the University of Tennessee.

The charter named Samuel Carrick, a Presbyterian minister, as president and 18 other men as trustees. Among them were some of the most famous figures in Knoxville's early history, including William Blount, John Sevier, James White, Charles McClung and George Roulstone.

The legislature's intent, as spelled out in the charter, was to create an institution "where youth may be habituated to an amiable, moral and virtuous conduct, and accurately instructed in the various branches of useful science, and in the principles of ancient and modern languages."

The little college struggled for years. No building was erected until 1795. Only an emergency contribution of $1,000 from the trustees prevented the dissolution of the school in 1803. By 1804, there were only five students, and none graduated until 1806.

Only in 1807 was some stability achieved. In that year the state legislature created East Tennessee College, approved its absorption of Blount College and provided a land grant for financial support. But still there were lean years ahead, and in fact the school pretty much ceased to function between 1809 and 1820. Not until 1826 did the college move to its present location on the Hill.

Sept. 11, 1894

Two Knoxville lawyers got into a squabble on Sept. 11, 1894, and one of them tried to settle it with a gun.

The dispute arose during a trial in which Samuel G. Heiskell was prosecutor and Horace Van Deventer was defense attorney. At one point Van Deventer insulted Heiskell — or so Heiskell believed.

After court adjourned, Heiskell confronted Van Deventer in the judge's office. Words were exchanged, and suddenly Van Deventer struck Heiskell with his fist. Heiskell drew a revolver, but Van Deventer grabbed him by the wrist and turned the gun skyward. Two shots hit the ceiling. Van Deventer then wrestled Heiskell to the ground and held him until the police arrived. Heiskell was arrested and charged, posted $2,000 bond and went home.

Commenting on the incident, The Knoxville Sentinel said, "It is a barbarous and exceedingly dangerous practice for men to go armed. Especially is it to be condemned in lawyers, who are supposed to be defenders of the law."

Apparently no permanent damage was done to anyone's reputation. A year later, Heiskell was elected mayor of Knoxville, the first of many terms he would serve in that office. Van Deventer likewise went on to become one of Knoxville's most prominent citizens, distinguishing himself in law, politics and civic affairs.

Sept. 12, 1910

Knoxville's great Appalachian Exposition opened on Sept. 12, 1910.

The Appalachian Exposition was the brainchild of a group of progressive Knoxville businessmen, including William J. Oliver, Lawrence D. Tyson and W. M. Goodman. Inspired by the successful expositions held in Philadelphia, Chicago, Buffalo and St. Louis between 1876 and 1904, the Knoxvillians hoped to promote the modernization of their region by bringing the great natural resources of southern Appalachia to the attention of the nation.

The promoters raised money, signed up exhibitors and constructed a number of buildings at Chilhowee Park, which they had leased for the event. Everything was ready by Sept. 12.

During the exposition's one-month run, hundreds of thousands of visitors enjoyed the biggest spectacle Knoxville had ever hosted. There were not only commercial and educational exhibits but also a midway and shows of all sorts, including the first airplane flights ever seen in East Tennessee. The only amusements not to be found were liquor, games of chance and girlie shows, all strictly prohibited.

A number of prominent visitors added luster to the exposition, among them former President Theodore Roosevelt.

So successful was the exposition that its promoters brought it back again in 1911. And in 1913 they put together an even bigger extravaganza, the National Conservation Exposition.

Sept. 13, 1952

A squirrel monkey's two-week escapade in Knoxville ended sadly on Sept. 13, 1952.

The monkey had escaped from the Knoxville Zoo one day while a News-Sentinel photographer was trying to get a picture of him through an open cage door. For two weeks he ran free through the neighborhoods around the zoo, defying the best efforts of police and zookeepers to trap him. He feasted from time to time off crab apples stolen from trees.

On Sept. 13, the monkey was spotted by a 10-year-old boy on Woodbine Avenue. The boy climbed onto a garage roof to try to catch him, but the monkey eluded him by climbing onto a power line. Regrettably, the monkey then decided to perch on a transformer. In the explosion that followed, power was knocked out all over the neighborhood and the monkey was incinerated. He was buried with appropriate services at the city garage.

The News-Sentinel announced that it would pay for a new squirrel monkey out of the Birthday Park Fund that it administered. The Birthday Park Fund was the means by which the zoo had been established in 1948. It was supported by the donations of boys and girls who, on their birthdays, contributed a penny for each year of their age.

Sept. 14, 1981

On Sept. 14, 1981, the Knoxville Board of Education found itself entangled in the thorny issue of religious recruiting in the schools.

The question had arisen the previous February when Jewish students at Bearden Middle School complained of harassment by representatives of Youth of Knoxville Evangelism (YOKE), who came to the school cafeteria to encourage students to come to after-school YOKE meetings.

YOKE ended its solicitations after the complaints, but the school board was under pressure to revise its standing policy, which permitted such recruiting by religious groups.

Involving as it did deeply-felt beliefs about religion, the family, and the Constitution, this issue stirred up considerable debate. For months the board wrestled with the problem. It came up again at the Sept. 14 meeting.

A proposal to ban religious recruiting provoked opposition from some board members, one of whom cited statistics on broken homes and declared that "We've got to have some people seeking these children out and giving them some religious background." Other board members feared Constitutional complications, however, and they were seconded by a representative of the American Civil Liberties Union, who said that the current policy was "patently unconstitutional."

Uncomfortably perched on the horns of a dilemma, the board ended its meeting without taking any action.

Sept. 15, 1923

On Sept. 15, 1923, Knoxville held its first elections under the new council-manager form of government.

The first important act of the 11 new city councilmen elected that day was to appoint a city manager. The basic purpose of the new form of government was to put the management of the city into the hands of a professional administrator, an efficient, businesslike manager, untainted by politics. The councilmen chose Louis Brownlow, a former Knoxvillian who had distinguished himself as a city manager in Virginia.

As Knoxville city manager, Brownlow accomplished some major reforms, including the enactment of a plumbing code, improvements in fiscal management, installation of traffic signals and the creation of a city planning board.

But the very qualities that made Brownlow an outstanding city manager led to his political downfall. He was aloof from the rough and tumble of politics and projected an elitist image, for he distrusted politicians and the public. Opposition to him began to grow, particularly among the working-class voters represented by councilman Lee Monday, whom Brownlow characterized as a "hillbilly." Monday denounced Brownlow as "King Louis I."

Brownlow's opponents eventually wore him down. Harassed by City Council and by pressure groups, and broken mentally and physically by the strain, he resigned in 1926.

Sept. 16, 1898

On Sept. 16, 1898, the city of Knoxville reorganized its board of health.

The city had experimented with various forms of health regulation over the years, usually in response to an epidemic of some sort. The reorganization of 1898 may have been a reaction to an outbreak of smallpox in the city earlier that year, during which some 80 cases appeared, though with only one fatality.

Under the new regulations, a six-person board of health was created. One member had to be a lawyer, one a businessman, and four physicians, one of whom was the official city physician. The board was given the authority to enforce all city health regulations. In times of epidemics, its jurisdiction could be extended 10 miles beyond the city limits.

Furthermore, the office of city health inspector was abolished, and city policemen were ordered to report all unsanitary conditions in their respective beats.

The new system had its first real test the very next winter. Between December 1898 and February 1899, there was an outbreak of what the city physician termed "cerebro-spinal meningitis," which struck mostly the young. Apparently the city's health efforts paid off, for the disease was confined to a few dozen cases — fortunately so, for it killed about 75 percent of its victims.

Sept. 17, 1866

On Sept. 17, 1866, a group of Knoxville businessmen organized the Kingston Turnpike Company, whose object was to improve the road now known as Kingston Pike.

The road originated in frontier days, having been laid out in the 1790s by Charles McClung at the request of the Knox County Court. Its original purpose was to connect Knoxville with the settlements at Campbell's Station and beyond. By 1800, the road extended all the way to Kingston, and later it formed part of the great national highway from Washington to New Orleans.

But the road was a rough dirt one, and travel on it was slow. In 1866, however, the Kingston Turnpike Company began macadamizing the road. The company's charter permitted it to erect toll booths every five miles and to collect tolls, which were set at 60 cents for a six-horse wagon, 15 cents for a one-horse cart, five cents for a man on horseback and one-half cent for each sheep or hog "in drove." Ministers and anyone going to or from church traveled toll-free.

The whole 15 miles to Campbell's Station was macadamized by 1893, cutting travel time between there and Knoxville from five to two and a half hours. Soon thereafter Knox County bought out the company and became sole owner of Kingston Pike.

Sept. 18, 1948

Knoxville's Democrats turned out in force at the Lyric Theater on Sept. 18, 1948, to see and hear their U. S. Senatorial candidate, Estes Kefauver.

Kefauver, fresh from his triumph in the Democratic primary — in which he had defeated the candidate endorsed by the powerful "Boss" Crump of Memphis — was in Knoxville to kick off his campaign against his Republican opponent.

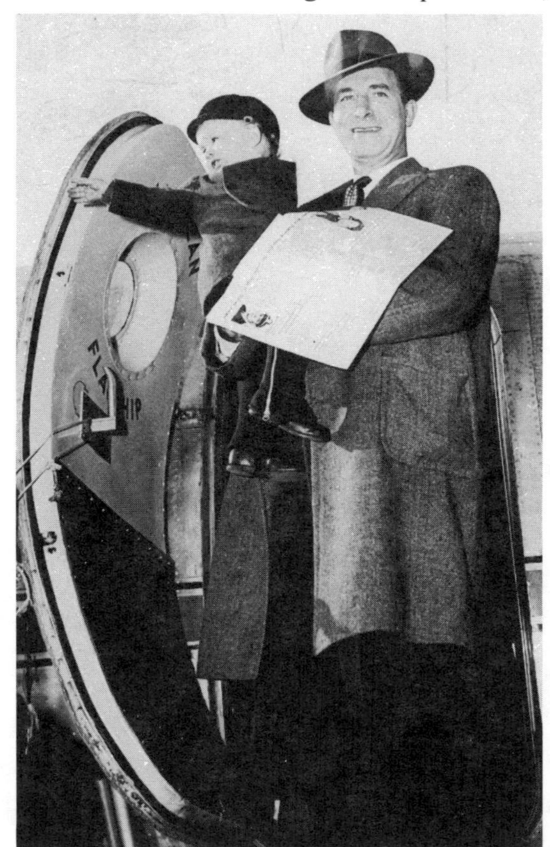

Estes Kefauver and son David arrive in Knoxville.

This campaign, Kefauver's first run for the Senate, resulted in victory. Twice reelected, he served with distinction until his death in 1963. He was a serious contender for the Democratic presidential nomination in 1952 and 1956.

In his Knoxville appearance in September 1948, Kefauver touched on some of the themes that would become his hallmarks in the years to come. One was the Tennessee Valley Authority, which he strongly defended. "The old guard Republicans," he reminded his audience, "have sought to cripple and damage and destroy the TVA."

Kefauver also addressed the racial issue, criticizing President Harry Truman's civil rights programs — ironically, because in later years Kefauver would become known as one of the few Southern politicians to support civil rights for blacks.

And, like many Democratic (and some Republican) office-seekers in those years of anti-communist hysteria, Kefauver was forced to respond to baseless charges that he was a communist tool.

Sept. 19, 1901

On Sept. 19, 1901, services were held in Knoxville to honor America's martyred president.

William McKinley had died five days earlier, assassinated by a foreign-born anarchist. Knoxvillians, like all Americans, were not only grief-stricken but angered. On the day of the president's death, Knoxville Mayor Samuel G. Heiskell declared that "a blow has been stricken not only against William McKinley, but against the government and people of the whole United States."

At a public meeting that night, Heiskell denounced "the spirit of hatred among certain foreigners for the flag of this great and free country." Another speaker called for restrictions on immigration, for America had become "the dumping ground for the other nations of the world."

Many memorial services were held in Knoxville on Sept. 19, the day of the president's funeral. By then the public anger and xenophobia had subsided a bit. The services were devoted to honoring McKinley rather than denouncing his assassin. At Church Street Methodist Church, the slain president was extolled as "a great and good man." The congregation at Third Presbyterian was reminded that McKinley's "prophetic vision . . . made our nation one of the great world powers." A speaker at the University of Tennessee declared that "no man was ever more of an American than McKinley."

Sept. 20, 1954

An incident of vandalism in Knoxville on Sept. 20, 1954, was blamed on "communists" but turned out to be merely the work of two young servicemen on a spree.

A tent, set up to accommodate evangelistic services at the First Nazarene Church on North Central Avenue, was chopped down late that night. After the deed was discovered, the evangelist, the Rev. Vernon Gortner, told a reporter, "I believe with all my heart the work was done by communists."

The guest speaker that evening, said Gortner, was an anti-communist crusader who claimed that a number of his recent lectures had been followed by acts of vandalism. His lecture that evening was on "Why Russia Always Wins at the Peace Conferences."

But even as Gortner spoke, the police had the real culprits behind bars. They turned out to be two 18-year-old airmen stationed at McGhee Tyson airbase. They had been apprehended just after midnight on Cumberland Avenue. Both had bloody hands and wrists. They confessed not only to cutting down the tent, but also to smashing windows along a path of destruction from North Central to West Cumberland.

"They had been drinking a little," the arresting officer reported, "but not very much. They were very nice and calm when I arrested them."

Sept. 21, 1877

President Rutherford B. Hayes and members of his cabinet visited Knoxville on Friday, Sept. 21, 1877.

Hayes was the second president to visit Knoxville while in office (the first was Andrew Jackson). As president, he had officially brought the painful Reconstruction era to a close by withdrawing the last federal troops from the South. Now he was on a goodwill tour of the southern states.

Thousands of Knoxvillians turned out to greet Hayes and his entourage upon their arrival. The crowd thronged Gay Street and surrounded the speakers' platform erected in front of the Lamar House. Bunting and evergreen boughs decorated every building. McCrary and Benson's art gallery displayed a big canvas portrait of the president. A peddler went through the crowd hawking smaller presidential portraits for a nickel.

A formal welcoming ceremony was held on the speaker's platform (but not until a drunken woman had been removed therefrom and taken to jail). After the ceremony the president left for Atlanta. He returned to Knoxville two days later, however, attended services at First Methodist Church and took a carriage tour of some of the city's points of interest. That night, Hayes and company departed Knoxville on the train, expressing great reluctance at leaving a town where they had been so enthusiastically welcomed.

Sept. 22, 1833

A fire on Sept. 22, 1833, inspired one newspaper to make some hilarious observations on how Knoxvillians behaved in an emergency.

There was no fire department in the town in those days. All citizens were expected to turn out to fight any conflagration. When fire broke out in a woodshed on Gay Street, the Knoxville Republican reported, a number of citizens took quick action and put it out.

There was a far more numerous group, however, "running about and commanding those who were at work, and talking as if they expected to overcome (the fire) by windy words."

And then there was another group, the "superfine gentlemen," "who never fail to make their appearance at a fire." At the sound of a fire bell these men would rise from their beds, carefully don ruffled shirts and gloves, "abuse the servants for not putting the shine upon their boots," and finally, after checking themselves in the mirror, wander down to the scene of the fire.

"Arrived at the spot, they all take their stand just near enough to be comfortably warm, and there they remain fixed in admiration, until the grandeur of the scene is destroyed by the vulgar crowd who continue throwing water upon the flames."

Sept. 23, 1927

Beginning with the issue of Sept. 23, 1927, The News-Sentinel offered to its readers 24 hours of wire service from The Associated Press.

Heretofore, the newspaper announcement said, "this complete service has been enjoyed by only a few large metropolitan newspapers of the north and east." Its extension resulted from "the constantly growing and healthy prosperity of the communities south of the Mason and Dixon line, and the consistent progress of the southland toward its proper place in national affairs."

The extended service — previously The News-Sentinel received dispatches between 7 a.m. and 2 a.m. — enabled The News-Sentinel to present a greater variety and volume of news than ever before.

The News-Sentinel writer who prepared the announcement about the extended service waxed poetic about its benefits: "Tried and tested correspondents in the frozen wastes of Siberia, in the jungles of India, on the border lines of the new states of Europe where the world's map is being made over, . . . are at all hours of the day and night carefully watching the life of the world for its progress, its tragedies and its lighter moments, for all the interesting happenings which are brought in over the cables, laying deep in the bed of the ocean, or through the air by wireless, to supply Americans with material for the daily newspapers. . . ."

Sept. 24, 1870

Sept. 24, 1870, was the day of the big dedication ceremony at the Knoxville fairground.

The fairground, two miles east of downtown, was the site of the annual East Tennessee Agricultural Fair. (The Chilhowee Park fairground of today is not the site of this old fairground, nor is the present-day Tennessee Valley Fair related to the old Agricultural Fair.)

In 1870, the fairground was refurbished. A three-story exhibition hall was built, along with new stalls for livestock and a mile-long racetrack.

Knoxvillians planned a grand ceremony to inaugurate the renovated fairground. On Sept. 24, a large procession assembled on Gay Street and marched out to the fairground. The procession included a brass marching band, carriages carrying city officials and other dignitaries and three hook and ladder companies. (The band members climbed into a big four-horse wagon to make the crossing at First Creek ford, so as not to get their feet wet.)

Hundreds of citizens were waiting at the new exhibition hall. The ceremony included prayer, music and speeches. Among the Knoxville notables who addressed the assemblage were businessman Perez Dickinson, the Rev. Thomas W. Humes and Judge T. A. R. Nelson.

Then everybody adjourned to the racetrack, where the day's festivities concluded with a lively horse race.

Sept. 25, 1793

The little frontier settlement of Knoxville was almost wiped from the map by an Indian attack on Sept. 25, 1793.

The town was only two years old at that time and had but a few dozen inhabitants. Although the 1791 Treaty of Holston had officially worked out a boundary settlement with the Indians, there were continuing conflicts between Indians and white settlers.

On Sept. 25, a large party of Cherokees and Creeks (estimated at from 900 to 1,500) attacked a white settlement at Cavet's Station, eight miles downriver from Knoxville, killing 13 people. When word reached Knoxville, preparations were hurriedly made to protect the town from the anticipated attack.

At that moment there were only 40 men in the town. The two oldest were left behind to man the blockhouse while the other 38, led by James White, gamely marched out to meet the enemy. They took position on a ridge about a mile west of town, where they planned to fire one musket volley at the Indians and then retreat to the blockhouse.

Their courage was never put to the ultimate test, however. Although the Indians apparently did intend to move against Knoxville and wipe it out, three of their chiefs had a falling out on the way. The attack was called off and Knoxville was saved.

Sept. 26, 1930

A Knoxville hold-up man was released from jail on Sept. 26, 1930, amid a great outpouring of sympathy for his plight.

Like many Americans in those years of the Great Depression, A. L. Persell was poor and desperate. He had lost his job, his rent was overdue, his wife was pregnant. His family was living off charity.

Then, on Sept. 25, Persell got word that the charity agency was out of funds. When his four children began crying from hunger, he resolved to do something. Using a broken revolver, he held up a grocery store. He was recognized, however, and was immediately arrested.

Persell's story provoked much pity. City officials intervened to get him released from jail, and a lawyer volunteered to defend him for free. Donations of money and groceries were sent to his home.

The manager of the grocery store expressed compassion for Persell but decided to prosecute the case. An editorial in The News-Sentinel sided with the store manager. "All must feel sympathy for A. L. Persell," it said. "No one wants him to be punished as harshly as the ordinary hold-up man. . . (Nevertheless), Persell's act must be rebuked. . . . No jobless man must think that he has a right to bring fear and possible death to other men."

Sept. 27, 1871

A murder in Knoxville on Sept. 27, 1871, illustrated the bitter personal and political conflicts that characterized the Reconstruction era.

The victim, James H. Clanton of Alabama, was a former Confederate general and a leader of the conservative Democrats who were fighting Radical Reconstruction. He was in Knoxville on legal business. He had a reputation as a thin-skinned hothead.

On Sept. 27, Clanton was walking down Gay Street, where he met David M. Nelson, a lawyer from Cleveland, Tenn., also in town on legal business. Nelson was a former officer in the Union army and the son of Thomas A. R. Nelson, a prominent Knoxville Unionist.

Nelson, who was apparently drunk, offered to take Clanton on a tour of the town, "if you are not afraid." Clanton, bristling at this gratuitous insult, replied, "I am not afraid of anything or any man." Further words were exchanged, and finally Clanton (who habitually carried a gun) challenged Nelson to a duel. Nelson then ran into a nearby store, grabbed a shotgun and fired at Clanton. Clanton drew his gun and fired back, missing Nelson, who then finished off Clanton with a second shot.

Nelson was tried in 1873 but was acquitted after convincing the jury that his first shot was accidental and that he fired the second shot in self-defense.

Sept. 28, 1966

The Knoxville News-Sentinel published a strongly worded and unusually personal and subjective news article on Sept. 28, 1966.

"I witnessed a sickening incident this morning," wrote News-Sentinel reporter James C. Ward, "that is a glaring example of why law enforcement officers do not have the full respect the people should give them."

According to Ward, he was in the Knox County courthouse about 7 a.m., where he saw "a stocky city policeman beat up an unresisting Negro, apparently drunk." As Ward watched, the officer slammed the man against a post. When Ward protested, the officer ignored him and kept shoving the man around.

"After watching this officer, incapable of handling an unresisting drunk, I wondered how he would have fared in a real emergency. No matter what the man had done before the courthouse incident, he was not resisting or fighting the officer there."

Ward declined to bring charges against the policeman, but urged that he "be given some instructions on how to handle — not manhandle — a situation like this."

That very afternoon the black man was brought into court. Six police officers testified that he had acted "wild, drunk, and hysterical," had resisted arrest and had struggled with the arresting officer. The judge fined the man $50 for public drunkenness and $50 for resisting arrest.

Sept. 29, 1923

Thousands of Knoxvillians thronged Chilhowee Park on the night of Sept. 29, 1923, and watched in awe as the Ku Klux Klan held a huge ceremony.

The Klan enjoyed great popularity among white Protestants in those years. Its reactionary political and social agenda appealed to many, but so did its social-club camaraderie, gaudy uniforms and secret rituals.

The ceremony was the biggest Klan event ever held in Knoxville, and it attracted thousands of Klansmen from all over Tennessee and adjoining states. It coincided with the closing night of the East Tennessee Division (now Tennessee Valley) Fair, and thus a big crowd of spectators was on hand. The Klan even set up an information booth at the Fair, and Klansmen handed out lapel buttons and red, white, and blue pennants that read "100 per cent American."

The highlight of the evening was the initiation of new Klan members by the light of a 20-foot burning cross beside Chilhowee Lake. The white-robed Klansmen formed a semi-circle around the novitiates, among whom were a number of women. Presiding over the event was the King Kleagle of Tennessee, Dr. R. Bullard. Along with the initiation rites there were speeches by the Klan dignitaries, including one on "Ideals of Klankraft."

Sept. 30, 1794

On Sept. 30, 1794, the first regular session of the territorial legislature, meeting in Knoxville, adjourned after a 37-day session.

Knoxville was a mere frontier village at the time, and it offered few amenities to the lawmakers assembled there. The 13 members of the lower house had to meet at Carmichael's tavern or in a room of the military barracks. The five members of the upper house met in another room of the barracks or at the house of John Stone. On the one occasion when the two houses met jointly, they went to the Knox County courthouse (a single-story building, 30 feet long and 25 feet wide) because it was the only place in town big enough to seat all 18 men.

Despite the roughness of the accommodations, the legislators worked diligently and enacted some important legislation that helped prepare the Tennessee territory for statehood. They established a system of courts, instituted taxes (on land, slaves, polls and stud horses), created the office of public printer, chartered Greeneville College and Blount College and officially incorporated the town of Knoxville (which had been founded three years earlier).

Knoxville served not only as the territorial capital but also as the first state capital, following Tennessee's admission to the Union in 1796.

Oct. 1, 1928

On the afternoon of Oct. 1, 1928, an excited crowd of Knoxville moviegoers was ushered into the brand-new Tennessee Theater on Gay Street.

Built at a cost of $2 million, the 2,200-seat Tennessee Theater was one of the glitziest exemplars of the golden age of movie palaces in the 1920s. The Knoxvillians who showed up for the grand opening were dazzled by the splendor they beheld. They stared awestruck at the marble stairs, brass railing, plush carpeting, mirrored walls, chandeliers, leather seats and the magnificent Wurlitzer organ that rose majestically out of the stage to entertain them before the show.

The feature that day was "The Fleet's In," starring the popular Clara Bow. But even Clara Bow couldn't hold the attention of the audience, which kept looking around in amazement even after the movie started.

A News-Sentinel editorial praised the Tennessee, calling it a "palace of democracy": "Amusement palaces such as the Tennessee mark the ascent to the throne of Mr. Average Man. . . . Nearly anybody can find 60 cents, which is the admission fee; and no matter how many times 60 cents you may have, you can procure no different entertainment than the man who has only 60 cents. . . . Thus does democracy triumph."

The Tennessee Theater as it looked in 1928

Oct. 2, 1916

Oct. 2, 1916, was opening day of the first East Tennessee Division Fair, the forerunner of today's Tennessee Valley Fair.

In 1916, a group of prominent Knoxvillians, encouraged by the success of the big Knoxville expositions of 1910, 1911 and 1913, conceived the idea of an annual fair. Led by Hugh Faust, they leased Chilhowee Park (the site of the expositions), secured a corporation charter, raised funds and lined up exhibitors and shows. Everything was ready by Oct. 2.

That first fair set the pattern for all those to come by striking a balance between fun and serious business. The fair not only served as a showplace for the products of East Tennessee's farms and businesses, but also offered midway games and rides, bands, acrobats and other attractions.

The Knoxville Sentinel told its readers that "no lover and well-wisher of this city . . . should neglect to visit the fair" and expressed the hope that it would become a "permanent institution."

Forty thousand people attended the 1916 fair, and the fair did indeed become a permanent institution. With the exception of a four-year hiatus due to World War II, the fair (which in 1933 was renamed the Tennessee Valley Agricultural and Industrial Fair) has entertained tens of thousands of East Tennesseans at Chilhowee Park every autumn since 1916.

Oct. 3, 1791

Oct. 3, 1791, is the date commonly accepted as Knoxville's birthday.

Because it is hard to define when a town began its existence, however, there are other dates that might be considered.

The site on which Knoxville stands was actually first settled in 1786, when James White built a fort there. The fort became an important frontier rendezvous point, and it was there that Territorial Gov. William Blount signed the Treaty of Holston with the Cherokees in the summer of 1791.

About that same time, Blount chose White's settlement as the site of the territorial capital and named it Knoxville in honor of Secretary of War Henry Knox. Knoxville was not officially incorporated, however, until the territorial legislature took that step in 1794.

What, then, actually happened on Oct. 3, 1791? That was the day a lottery was held to assign the lots into which the town site had been divided. Once it was decided that the site was to be the territorial capital, James White, who owned the land, had his son-in-law, Charles McClung, survey the site and lay it off into 64 half-acre lots. Among the lottery subscribers who purchased the lots were some of the most important figures in Knoxville's early years, including Blount, the Rev. Samuel Carrick, and George Roulstone.

Oct. 4, 1940

On Oct. 4, 1940, a Knoxville judge threw the book at a high school student accused of post-game rowdyism.

The incident had occurred the night before, following a Knoxville High School football game. A policeman driving down Gay Street was bombarded with ripe tomatoes thrown by a young man. He stopped, arrested the youth and called the paddy wagon. While awaiting the wagon, the policeman was pelted by more tomatoes thrown by other high schoolers gathered on the sidewalk.

The arrested youth spent the night in jail. The next day he went before City Judge Bob Williams, who fined him $50 and then sent him back to jail when he couldn't pay the fine.

The judge also delivered a stern lecture from the bench. "I know this boy isn't a bad boy," he said. "But we're going to have to stop this throwing missiles after football games. . . . We're going to have football, but we're going to have it civilized and orderly."

A News-Sentinel editorial approved the young man's harsh punishment: "It will take a few stiff fines such as Judge Wiliams handed out to make football celebrations here what they should be — enthusiastic but within the bounds of safe conduct. . . . Partisanship is one thing but . . . rowdyism and unsportsmanlike conduct is another."

Oct. 5, 1927

The whole city of Knoxville was in mourning on Oct. 5, 1927, following the death of Gov. Austin Peay.

Peay was one of Tennessee's great governors. His accomplishments included a major reorganization of the state government, a road-building program that gave the state a modern highway system, important reforms in public education and the establishment of the Great Smoky Mountains National Park.

Austin Peay

Peay died suddenly in 1927, his fifth year in office. On Oct. 5, the day of his funeral in Clarksville, Knoxvillians expressed their grief.

All business was suspended in Knoxville. Banks were closed, as were government offices. UT classes were cancelled, and students and faculty held a memorial service. Public schools closed at noon. At 2 p.m., the moment when Peay's funeral began, all the church bells in Knoxville tolled.

A News-Sentinel editorial noted, "the achievements of Gov. Peay were real and substantial. . . . (But) Gov. Peay himself was significant, apart from his acts. . . . He proved that accomplishments in the public service are the best recommendation a man can have to the American electorate."

Oct. 6, 1896

The Woman's Home Missionary Society of Knoxville held its annual meeting on Oct. 6, 1896.

The society had been organized six years earlier, with 20 members. By 1896, it had 45. It was one of many women's benevolent organizations in that era. Such organizations provided one of the few opportunities for women to use their talents outside the home.

The society's stated purpose embodied the highest ideals of Christian charity: "to care for the needy, to rescue the perishing, to give comfort to those who are in sorrow, seeking to save the lost for whom Christ died."

In pursuit of these goals the society employed a "deaconess." At the Oct. 6 meeting, the deaconess gave a report of her activities for the previous year. She had made 1,589 calls at the homes of the poor and the sick and at the jail, the workhouse and the hospital. She had accomplished 12 conversions and found jobs for 10 people. Moreover, she had provided books and tuition for a young man studying for the ministry.

Children were a special concern of the society. The deaconess had bought school books for six children, had brought 25 children into Sunday school, had provided free lunches for 125 kindergarteners and had enrolled 100 youngsters in the society's free industrial arts classes.

Oct. 7, 1926

On Oct. 7, 1926, Knoxville College announced it had enrolled the largest freshman class in its history: 75 students.

The school had come a long way since its founding in 1875. Like many other black schools in the South, Knoxville College was established by northern whites who came south to help the freed slaves after the Civil War. In the case of Knoxville College, these white founders were agents of the United Presbyterian Church.

From the beginning, Knoxville College enrolled women as well as men. And, until 1901, when it was officially chartered by the state and legally restricted to blacks, it also enrolled some whites (children of the faculty). In the 1890s, the college began educating black students formally enrolled at the University of Tennessee, which was required to accept blacks but which refused to allow them on its campus.

Until the 20th century, the Knoxville College student body actually consisted mostly of primary and secondary students. The school offered a three-year primary program, followed by a four-year "manual arts" program. Beyond that there was a four-year "normal" program that prepared the student to teach or to go on to college. At the college level the school offered six programs: agricultural, mechanical, scientific, classical, theological and medical.

Oct. 8, 1918

On Oct. 8, 1918, Knoxville and the nation were in the grip of a deadly influenza epidemic.

That day the city health director, Dr. W. R. Cochrane, reported 801 flu cases in Knoxville and three deaths so far. One-fourth of the cases were in the military camps at the University and Chilhowee Park (the U.S. was involved in World War I at the time).

Many other cities had already suspended schools and public gatherings, and Cochrane warned that if the disease spread Knoxville would have to do the same. But for now he simply urged citizens to "stay home if possible, avoid large assemblies, and take advantage of all fresh air possible while working or sleeping."

Patent medicine dealers publicized their own remedies. An ad for Calotabs in The Knoxville Sentinel assured the public that "the first step in the treatment of a cold, cough, influenza or grippe should invariably be a brisk calomel purgative."

The next day, convinced that the epidemic was spreading, Cochrane suspended schools, churches and other public assemblies — including the East Tennessee Division (later Tennessee Valley) Fair, which had been under way for three days. However, he relaxed the order enough to allow patriotic meetings, including Liberty Loan and Red Cross rallies.

Oct. 9, 1890

For three days ending on Oct. 9, 1890, Knoxville hosted a big reunion of veterans of the Civil War battle of Fort Sanders.

The citizens of Knoxville had arranged a grand reception for the veterans, who began arriving by the trainload on Oct. 6. Among those who came was Gen. James Longstreet, commander of Confederate forces in the 1863 battle.

All the city's hotels were packed. Flags and bunting decorated every building downtown. West of town, where Fort Sanders still stood, a huge tent was erected. Speeches, toasts, and fireworks highlighted the three-day extravaganza.

The event was marked by a spirit of friendship between those who had worn the blue and those who had worn the gray. Bands played both "Dixie" and "Marching through Georgia." "The best of humor prevailed," one witness reported, "notwithstanding (the fact that) some of the vets had been to the (whiskey) canteen once too often."

The Knoxville reunion, like others in that era, helped reunite a nation still divided by memories of the war. As one Knoxvillian wrote, "There is not a northern man who was here who will not go back to his home . . . with a friendlier feeling towards the south. There is not a southern man here who has not a more fraternal feeling for his northern brother."

Oct. 10, 1792

The first issue of the Knoxville Gazette actually printed in Knoxville appeared on Oct. 10, 1792.

The Gazette, Tennessee's first newspaper, was published by George Roulstone, a prominent figure in Knoxville's early history. A printer by trade, Roulstone was born in Boston and later lived in North Carolina. He came to the Tennessee country in 1791 at the bidding of Territorial Gov. William Blount, who saw the need for a printing press in the territory.

Though Blount had designated Knoxville as the territorial capital, Roulstone settled first in Rogersville, where he began publishing the Knoxville Gazette in November 1791. Within a year, however, he moved to Knoxville, where he owned two lots (acquired in the lottery of Oct. 3, 1791, that marks the town's founding).

Roulstone quickly assumed a leadership role in Knoxville. When the territorial legislature met there in 1794, he was named legislative clerk and public printer. After Knoxville was officially incorporated that year, he became one of the town's commissioners and, a little later, its first postmaster. When Tennessee became a state in 1796, he was designated the official state printer. He was also among the original trustees of Blount College, the forerunner of the University of Tennessee.

Roulstone's career was cut short, however, by his death in 1804 at the age of 36.

Oct. 11, 1897

Thousands of people crowded into a big circus tent in Knoxville on Oct. 11, 1897, to see Buffalo Bill's Wild West Show.

The town came to a standstill that day. Anyone who visited the courthouse, for example, found that no business could be done because all the judges and officials were at the show.

The crowd was delighted by the feats of riding and shooting and the mock battles that highlighted the show. The only unpleasant incident occurred when a drunken county constable watching Buffalo Bill's display of marksmanship pulled out his own gun and fired, almost into the crowd.

Among those attending was a group of Eastern Cherokee Indians. Later they visited the Sioux Indian performers in their tent and passed the peace pipe.

Buffalo Bill's show was intended to be not only fun but educational, a recreation of life on the plains before civilization swept away the buffalo, the Indians and the cowboys. The Knoxville audience, most of whom had never seen such a show, seemed generally well pleased. But one observer, more experienced than the rest, was disappointed. "It has degenerated from a genuine wild west show into a motley sort of circus," he said. "Buffalo Bill . . . is but a relic of his former self."

Oct. 12, 1985

The eighth annual Saturday Night on the Town was held on Oct. 12, 1985, but whether it was successful was a matter of dispute.

A record-breaking crowd of 175,000 turned out that night for what its organizers called "the largest street party in the South." Downtown Knoxville streets were closed to traffic and opened to revelers. Beer, exotic and not-so-exotic food, live music and dancing were all available.

Some had too much fun that night. Police made 35 arrests, many for public drunkenness. Even worse, there was a robbery and at least six fights, one of which resulted in a fatal stabbing.

Nevertheless, a police spokesman declared that "for a crowd this size, you can virtually say there were no problems." He did, however, suggest that beer be prohibited in the future.

Event organizers likewise denied that there were serious problems and called the evening a big success. One said, "There is more violence at a high school football game. It was a huge party, it was Knoxville's party."

But others disagreed, including a food vendor whose moneybag containing $6,000 was stolen. He blamed it on inadequate police protection. "They (officials) tried to say it was successful," he remarked. "It was not successful, it was a disgrace. We lost everything."

Oct. 13, 1931

On Oct. 13, 1931, Knoxville charity workers began a two-day "Emergency March" to meet the Community Chest goal.

At that time America was in the depths of the Great Depression. Never had the need for charity been greater, but never had the public had so little to give. Knoxville's Community Chest had fallen $57,000 short of its goal of $170,000

In a last-ditch attempt to meet the goal, Chest organizers sent out two squads of volunteers — the Blue Crusaders and the Red Invaders — to knock on doors in every neighborhood in town.

Massive publicity accompanied the drive. A parade was held on Gay Street, featuring the Knoxville High School Band. Mayor John T. O'Connor issued a special plea to the public: "This task cannot be shirked, if we do not want our people to be weakened by illness, distress, and neglect. . . . Give until it hurts." A News-Sentinel editorial insisted that "everyone can give something. . . . Those who have given once should not hesitate to give again."

The people of Knoxville responded as best they could. Donations poured in — not just cash, but useful goods, including 50 gallons of buttermilk. Still, it was not enough. The Emergency March raised only about $13,000. Knoxville's needy families would face a bleak winter.

Oct. 14, 1844

Caldonia F. Johnson, the most successful black entrepreneur in 19th-century Knoxville, was born in Knox County on Oct. 14, 1844.

Cal Johnson in front of Cal Johnson Park, built in 1922

Born a slave, "Cal" Johnson managed to accumulate a little money by the time slavery was abolished (it was not unusual for masters to allow their slaves to earn spending money on the side). He invested in a small grocery store in Knoxville, but he extended credit to too many unreliable customers, and the business failed. No doubt this was an important lesson to Johnson who, though illiterate, soon developed a real talent for making money.

After accumulating another small nest egg by doing odd jobs around town, Johnson bought a wagon and team of horses. This enabled him to bid (successfully) on a contract to exhume and re-inter the bodies of Civil War soldiers.

In 1880, Johnson went into the saloon business. His patrons included many of the city's most prominent men. With his profits he invested in real estate, including a race-track which became a popular resort for Knoxvillians. (It was well that he expanded his investments beyond the liquor business, for in 1907 saloons were outlawed in Knoxville.)

In his later years Johnson was worth over $150,000, making him one of Knoxville's wealthiest citizens. He died in 1925.

Oct. 15, 1952

Republican presidential candidate Dwight D. Eisenhower visited Knoxville on Oct. 15, 1952.

About 6,000 supporters turned up at the airport that evening, where Eisenhower was scheduled to fly in, give a speech and fly out. The plane arrived right on time, and Eisenhower was escorted with much fanfare to the speaker's platform.

To the embarrassment of all, however, just seconds after Eisenhower launched into his speech, the microphone went dead. For several minutes the candidate stood there, awkward and helpless. Finally an NBC News engineer came to the rescue, sticking a screwdriver into the blown fuse receptacle and holding it there while Eisenhower resumed his speech.

Dwight D. Eisenhower responds to the crowd at the airport.

In his opening remarks the candidate felt obliged to take the defensive, angrily refuting charges that he was anti-TVA and anti-Social Security.

Eventually, however, he took the offensive against the Democrats, particularly on the issues of the Korean War and the supposed infiltration of the government by communists. "We have a right to be worried," he said, "that the same leadership which led us into the Korean War may bungle us into still greater conflict. We have a right to be suspicious of the judgment of leaders who failed to see the Red stain seeping into the most vital offices of our government."

Oct. 16, 1934

A rodeo came to Knoxville on Oct. 16, 1934, but the event was marred by mishaps from beginning to end.

First of all, city firefighters (who were sponsoring the show) hoped to use the Caswell Park baseball field. But the park operator refused. Only after the firefighters began building their own arena did the park operator change his mind.

Next, a public outcry was raised when the rodeo's promoter announced it would feature a bullfight. Despite his insistence that "positively no baiting or other form of cruelty is engaged in" and no "instruments of torture" would be used, protests continued. When the attorney general and humane society officials announced their intention to watch the show closely and enforce the letter of the law, the promoter cancelled the bullfight.

Then, on Oct. 16, the day the rodeo opened, a lawyer showed up with a legal order to attach $447.54 of the show's proceeds, representing an unpaid debt owed to former employees of the rodeo.

Finally the show got under way. But in the first two days, the performers suffered seven injuries, four requiring hospitalization. "South American revolutions have been staged with fewer daily casualties," commented a News-Sentinel reporter in an article headlined "Rodeo Riders, Not Animals, Need Humane Society Help."

Oct. 17, 1823

On Oct. 17, 1823, the editor of the Knoxville Register worked himself into a lather on the subject of debt.

A bill had just been introduced in the state legislature permitting debtors to delay repayment of their debts. In response, the Register's editor — presumably a creditor himself — delivered an editorial tirade.

"Has the creditor no rights?" he demanded. "There always are and always will be men in society of an imprudent, indolent disposition, willing to contract debts without the means of payment, . . . and whose maxim is to get money, honestly if they can, villainously if they must. Are these adepts in profligacy, these lovers of civil rapine, who desire to retain and riot upon what is not their own, to be the sole objects of legislative favor? Will our Assembly protect these mendicant gentlemen in the possession of other men's property? Will our legislators by law promote dishonesty and the infraction of contracts? Will they cure imprudence and lazy pride by giving it countenance and encouragement?"

"What will be the effects of this law?" the editor asked rhetorically. "It will give dishonesty the sanctity of law. . . . The system of fraudulent speculation will be permanently established. Farewell . . . to honor, integrity and the performance of contracts."

Oct. 18, 1969

Knoxville was part of a statewide Civil Defense exercise conducted on Oct. 18, 1969.

The exercise, based on the premise that an atomic bomb had hit the nearby ALCOA plant, revealed (according to the local coordinator) that the Civil Defense program was "96 percent effective" in maintaining lines of communication.

What the exercise did not reveal was the deplorable state of Knoxville's Civil Defense shelters. The News-Sentinel had conducted its own test of the shelters during a recent civil defense drill, and it reported the results on Oct. 18.

Eight reporters had walked around town as the sirens wailed, asking people about the location of fallout shelters, which were supposed to be maintained in several buildings.

Only two of four people questioned in the post office knew the location of the shelter there. No sooner did the reporter find the shelter than he was ordered out by postal employees who said the room was off limits.

The story was much the same elsewhere. Only one of 10 persons queried at the Hamilton National Bank knew that there was a shelter there. When the reporter finally located it, she found the door locked.

Phone calls to the police, Highway Patrol and the Civil Defense office itself likewise revealed much confusion about the location of shelters.

Oct. 19, 1946

Thousands of UT alumni were in Knoxville on Saturday, Oct. 19, 1946, to celebrate homecoming.

It was the biggest homecoming in UT history up to that time. Everyone was in the mood for a grand celebration, for they were no longer distracted — as they had been during the previous four homecomings — by World War II.

As always, the football game was the highlight of the homecoming weekend. Volunteer fans were anxious, for the Alabama Crimson Tide was coming to Knoxville with an experienced team and a record of 14 straight victories, including a Rose Bowl triumph. The Tide was favored by a touchdown over the Vols, whose starters were all new that year — all of them war veterans.

Nevertheless, Gen. Bob Neyland's Vols pulled off a stunning upset that Saturday afternoon, turning back the Tide by a score of 12-0 before 50,000 screaming fans.

Robert Neyland

The jubilant alumni crowded into Memorial Gym that night for the big Reunion Dance, which featured music by the Reggie Childs Orchestra. The weekend activities concluded Sunday on a more solemn note, however, with a memorial service for the 315 UT men who had lost their lives in the war.

Oct. 20, 1922

On Oct. 20, 1922, radio station WNAV of Knoxville began broadcasting under new ownership.

WNAV was not only Knoxville's first radio station, but the first in Tennessee and among the first in the nation. It began broadcasting in 1921. Its ownership changed hands at least twice before it was acquired by Scripps-Howard Radio in 1935.

Lowell Blanchard announces for WNOX.

In the meantime the call letters had been changed to WNOX, and under that name the station became a familiar presence to generations of Knoxvillians.

The heyday of WNOX came in the 1930s, '40s and early '50s, the golden age of radio. The station's Mid-Day Merry-Go-Round show, hosted by Lowell Blanchard, was especially popular. The show featured live country music performed in front of an audience consisting of anyone who felt like dropping by the studio auditorium.

Among the performers who appeared on the Mid-Day Merry-Go-Round (or on WNOX's other shows, Tennessee Barn Dance and Stars of Tomorrow) were some who later achieved national fame, including Archie Campbell, Chet Atkins, Homer and Jethro, the Carter Family and Roy Acuff.

Not long after Blanchard's death in 1968, some of the stars he had helped make famous appeared in a memorial show in the Civic Coliseum. Archie Campbell conceived the idea for the show, which was billed as One Last Merry-Go-Round.

Oct. 21, 1896

On Oct. 21, 1896, the first annual Free Street Fair and Trade Carnival got under way in Knoxville.

The street fair was the brainchild of a Knoxville newspaper publisher, J. B. Pound. Its purpose was to encourage rural and small-town East Tennesseans to come to Knoxville and patronize the city's stores.

Pound's idea appealed to the many Knoxvillians who hoped to make their city a centerpiece of the "New South," a great commercial and manufacturing center rivaling Nashville and Atlanta. The Chamber of Commerce and the Manufacturers' Association immediately leaped on the bandwagon. A citizens' meeting was called, funds were raised, and on Oct. 21, just six weeks after the movement began, the street fair opened.

The highlight of the three-day event was the arrival of the "Prophet of the Great Smokies," a Rip Van Winkle look-alike who rode on a great float to the courthouse, where he received the keys to the city and then delivered his prophecy, which expressed "the hope for a greater Knoxville." This was followed by a grand parade of floats down Gay Street — dozens of them, each representing one of the city's trades.

The overwhelming success of that first street fair surprised even its most optimistic promoters. All agreed that it should become an annual event.

Oct. 22, 1859

The Knoxville Tri-Weekly Whig, in its issue of Oct. 22, 1859, gave Knoxvillians a full account of the momentous events at Harpers Ferry, Va. There, on the 16th, a group of armed abolitionists led by John Brown had seized a federal armory and attempted to stir up a slave insurrection.

The Whig reprinted dispatches from the scene indicating that the plot had failed, that some of the conspirators had been killed by federal troops rushed to the scene, that Brown and others had been captured, and that no revolt among the slaves had occurred.

In a later issue of the Whig, editor William G. Brownlow called the conspirators a "deluded pack" who misunderstood the nature of slavery. "We are not alarmed in the South. Not a single slave joined . . . in this miserable Harpers Ferry enterprise, (because) they are not dissatisfied with their condition."

Despite Brownlow's boasts, a great many white men and women in Knoxville and across the South were deeply alarmed by John Brown's raid and were less than confident about the loyalty and contentment of the slaves. Many who had theretofore turned a deaf ear to the secessionists now began to believe that the South's only safety lay in withdrawing from the Union.

Oct. 23, 1962

On Oct. 23, 1962, Knoxvillians and all Americans were anxiously watching the latest developments in the Cuban Missile Crisis.

The night before, President John F. Kennedy had appeared on television to reveal that the Soviets were placing missiles in Cuba capable of hitting the U.S. with nuclear warheads. The U.S. could not permit this, he said, and would institute a naval blockade of Cuba.

No one could predict the Soviet response. The crisis might trigger a war. But the people of Knoxville seemed to be solidly behind the president, as indicated by man-on-the-street interviews conducted by The News-Sentinel on Oct. 23. "Boy, it looks bad," one man remarked, "but he's doing the right thing. We can't just sit and do nothing."

A News-Sentinel editorial that day also strongly endorsed the president's policy. If the Soviets "are testing our courage and trying to see how far they can go without war," it said, "they have had their answer."

Meanwhile, members of local military reserve units readied themselves for action. "We've already started preparing, just in case," said one Marine officer. "Our equipment is set up, our supplies packed."

To the relief of all, however, the crisis ended a few days later when the Soviets backed down and agreed to remove the missiles.

Oct. 24, 1861

On Oct. 24, 1861, Knoxville newspaper editor William G. Brownlow wrote his last editorial before fleeing Knoxville under the threat of arrest.

An ardent unionist, Brownlow had continued to fly the American flag and to denounce secession even after Tennessee seceded from the Union and Confederate troops occupied Knoxville.

He eventually wore out the patience of the Confederate authorities, however. On Oct. 24, believing that he was about to be arrested for treason, Brownlow fired his final editorial blast. He called the South's war for independence "the most wicked, cruel, unnatural and uncalled-for war ever recorded in history" and he condemned the Confederate government's "acts of tyranny, usurpation and oppression" against unionists.

A few days later he went into hiding in the Smoky Mountains. But he was eventually caught and imprisoned by the Confederates, who in March 1862 banished him to the North.

In the north, Brownlow continued to write and speak out vehemently against the Confederacy. When Knoxville was captured by the Union army in September 1863, he returned to the city and resumed publication of his newspaper, the Knoxville Whig, adding "and Rebel Ventilator" to its name.

Having secured his reputation as one of Tennessee's most prominent unionists, Brownlow was elected governor when the state government was reconstructed in 1865.

Oct. 25, 1929

On Oct. 25, 1929, Knoxvillians learned with dismay the full details of the stock market crash that heralded the Great Depression. The huge sell-off, which had begun on the 24th and was continuing without respite, had stunned Wall Street observers.

"It was heartrending to see the reckless selling," a correspondent for The Knoxville News-Sentinel reported. "The word 'panic' was used freely." Billions of dollars of wealth had simply evaporated.

Knoxvillians and all Americans were alarmed by the crash — the worst in Wall Street's history — but none could know that it foreshadowed worse problems to come. In fact, confidence in the economy remained high in the days that followed the collapse of the market.

In Washington, President Herbert Hoover assured the nation that "The fundamental business of the country . . . is on a sound and prosperous basis."

The News-Sentinel's editorial page echoed the official optimism. "There is every reason to accept (the president's) assurance as something more than false courage to prevent panic," editor Edward J. Meeman wrote, "to accept it as a welcome statement of fact." But he went on to criticize the unhealthy credit situation that encouraged stock market "sprees," and he warned his readers not "to laugh off the danger involved in repeated collapses of inflated markets."

Oct. 26, 1794

On Oct. 26, 1794, a traveler from the East visited the little frontier village of Knoxville (then only three years old) and wrote a description of it.

"The town has had a rapid growth," said Abishai Thomas. "Here are frame houses and brick chimneys. . . There is in it ten stores and seven taverns, besides tippling houses, one courthouse, no prison, which they boast of as not being an article of necessity."

Two and a half years later another traveler left a description of Knoxville. Louis Philippe, the future king of France, recorded this entry in his diary for April 29, 1797: "Nasty, inhospitable country, sparsely settled. We reached Knoxville early. It would be quite picturesque if not for the wearying regularity of streets and houses (typical of) American towns. . . . Five years ago there was not a single house here. Now there are over a hundred. We are lodging in one of the oldest, but laziness has so pervaded the way of life that they have not yet plugged up the holes in the outer walls cut for scaffolding when they built the house. . . . Our horses are indifferently cared for, but the common board (where we are obliged by local custom to take our meals) is not bad."

Oct. 27, 1919

On Oct. 27, 1919, Tennessee Gov. A. H. Roberts called for federal troops to help put down labor violence in Knoxville.

The 250 unionized employees of the Knoxville Railway & Light Company, which operated the city's streetcar system, had struck for higher wages on Oct. 17, bringing streetcar service to a halt.

Eight days later Knoxville Mayor E. W. Neal appealed to both sides to "get together and adjust their differences," noting that the walkout was "causing great inconvenience to the general public and a great financial loss to our merchants." The company refused to deal with the union, however, and brought in strikebreakers to operate the cars. Violence erupted on Oct. 26, when union sympathizers attacked the streetcars and dragged the strikebreakers into the street.

The governor immediately called in the national guard and on Oct. 27 asked for federal troops. Then, the next day, he visited Knoxville and spoke out against "labor agitators," whom he regarded as un-American. "The issue is clear," he said. "Either you stand with the flag or you stand against it."

Roberts's speech helped turn the tide of public sentiment against the strikers. Though intermittent acts of violence and sabotage continued for some days, the strike was soon broken. Full streetcar service resumed on Nov. 5.

Oct. 28, 1861

A near-riot occurred in Knoxville on Oct. 28, 1861, when pro-Union citizens attacked Confederate soldiers.

Although Tennessee seceded from the Union and joined the Confederacy in 1861, many Knoxvillians remained loyal to the Union and bitterly resented the Confederate troops in their town.

When rumors reached Knoxville in October that Union troops were approaching, the pro-Union citizens grew cocky and restive. On Oct. 28, some eight or ten of them made an unprovoked attack on a group of Confederate soldiers near the Lamar House Hotel on Gay Street. The brawl quickly mushroomed into a serious confrontation.

Confederate infantry and cavalry units were immediately dispatched to the scene. Their arrival broke up the fight, but the unionist troublemakers got away.

Despite this show of Confederate force, the unionists of Knoxville remained openly defiant. One was heard to boast that the Confederates might be in control for now "but in less than 10 days the Union forces would be here and run them off."

Though that threat did not materialize (in fact, the Union army did not occupy Knoxville until 1863), the authorities feared more trouble. On Dec. 11, the Confederate commander, declaring that "the exigencies of the time" made necessary "the sternest measures of military policy," put Knoxville under martial law.

Oct. 29, 1902

A brief visit by a famous female prohibitionist stirred up a ruckus in Knoxville on Oct. 29, 1902.

Carry Nation, who had gained national notoriety by attacking saloons with a hatchet, stopped that day at Knoxville's Southern Railway station en route to Asheville.

She took advantage of the stop to go out onto the street and address the passers-by. As word spread that she was the famous Carry Nation, the crowd grew. For about five minutes she harangued her listeners on her favorite topic — the evils of the saloon and the "liquor power."

At one point a man in the crowd interrupted her with the question, "Did not Jesus Christ make wine?" When he continued heckling her, some traveling salesmen who were present asked him to desist. When he refused, one of the salesmen beat him up.

Nation rewarded the salesman with a lapel pin shaped like a hatchet and inscribed "Death to Rum." Then she boarded her train and departed, but not before tongue-lashing some young men who were smoking cigarettes. "Aren't you ashamed of yourselves?" she demanded.

The heckler, having recovered from his pummeling, also headed for Asheville, leading some to speculate that he was an agent of the "liquor power," paid to follow Nation around and harass her.

Oct. 30, 1978

Two colorful speakers faced off on Oct. 30, 1978, in what was billed as the "Great Debate" on metro government.

A movement to unify Knoxville and Knox County government had begun earlier that year. A county-wide referendum was scheduled for Nov. 7 to let the voters decide the issue.

In a public debate at UT on Oct. 30, Knoxville politico Cas Walker, a leader of the anti-unification forces, took on UT administrator Walter Lambert, spokesman for the pro-unification interests.

Walker hurled charges that were already familiar to readers of his newspaper, The Watchdog. Metro government, he said, would mean higher taxes and forced busing of schoolchildren.

Lambert contradicted Walker on both counts. Then he pointed out that the proposed unification charter required that any new services for which county citizens were taxed had to be provided within a year. Without unification, he said, the city would simply continue to annex parts of the county with no assurance that services would be extended.

The debate ended on a light note. Lambert took off his coat and tie and unbuttoned his shirt, revealing a T-shirt that read "I have the urge to merge!"

His urge would remained unfulfilled, however. In the Nov. 7 referendum, the metro charter went down to defeat.

Oct. 31, 1820

An editorial in the Knoxville Register on Oct. 31, 1820, scolded the people of Knoxville for their inattention to the danger of fires.

Taking note of a small fire (quickly extinguished) that had broken out two days earlier in a densely built-up part of town, the editor asked, "Ought this not rouse the citizens of Knoxville to some exertion for their safety?" In perhaps no other town of such size, he continued, have the people "been more careless and unconcerned" about fires. The volunteer fire company organized a few years previously had dissolved. The town's only fire engine was in disrepair. Nor was there even a real ladder in the town, except a few being used in smokehouses, and they were only six feet tall.

"As citizens so much exposed to destruction by fire," he said (alluding to the preponderance of wooden over brick structures in Knoxville), "we are inexcusable in not using some little precaution at least." For a relatively small amount of money the town could procure hooks and ladders and buckets, fix the engine and organize a fire company. Surely no good citizen "would refuse to contribute to such an object. Let a meeting be immediately requested to organize a company. This is the season to be prepared."

Nov. 1, 1907

On Nov. 1, 1907, Knoxville officially became a "dry" city.

The battle between the "wets" and "drys" (pro- and anti-liquor forces) had raged for years in Knoxville, but by 1907, the "drys" had the upper hand. In a referendum on March 11 of that year, Knoxvillians endorsed (by a vote of 4,150 to 2,255) the prohibition of liquor sales. The state legislature then revised the city charter to incorporate prohibition, to take effect Nov. 1.

Thursday, Oct. 31, the last day of legal liquor, was a wild day in Knoxville. Every saloon in town did a lively business, and liquor sales surpassed all previous one-day records. Remarkably, however, there were only 26 arrests for drunkenness — considerably fewer than on a typical Saturday night, and especially noteworthy considering that it was Halloween, a traditional night of revelry.

As closing time approached, the saloon crowds drifted out and began an informal procession down Gay Street and around Market Square, singing and making merry and saying goodbye to "John Barleycorn."

Morning light on Nov. 1 found the bars locked up tight. The Knoxville Sentinel's headline read "All Over With Saloons in Knoxville." But in reality, of course, it was simply the era of the legal saloon that had ended —the era of the illegal saloon was about to begin.

Nov. 2, 1975

An editorial in The Knoxville News-Sentinel on Nov. 2, 1975, endorsed the reelection bid of Mayor Kyle Testerman.

The endorsement was made with some misgivings, for The News-Sentinel had opposed Testerman four years earlier, and the editorial acknowledged that there were still some "basic philosophical differences" between the newspaper and the mayor. Nevertheless, the editorial pointed to the progress made under Testerman, including the new TVA and City-County buildings and improvements in the zoo and fire and police departments. On the whole, the newspaper decided, Testerman "has been a good mayor for Knoxville."

Most of Knoxville's voters disagreed, however. Many thought Testerman had taken "progress" too far too fast. Some considered him too favorable to businessmen and developers. Others were alienated by his successful advocacy of liquor by the drink.

Testerman's opponent, Randy Tyree, took advantage of this backlash. In the primary election on Nov. 6, he forced Testerman into a runoff. In the runoff election on Nov. 20, Tyree achieved victory — just barely, however, for his majority was a mere 393 votes out of more than 50,000 cast.

Following the election, The News-Sentinel graciously congratulated the winner, commending Tyree's "remarkable grass-roots campaign that lacked the support of any major local political power and (yet) slew Goliath."

Nov. 3, 1818

"Beware of an Imposter," read an announcement in the Knoxville Register on Nov. 3, 1818.

The warning came from the editor of the paper himself, Frederick S. Heiskell, who had just been victimized.

About three months earlier, according to Heiskell, a young man had shown up in Knoxville penniless and ragged. He called himself William J. Martin, and said he had come all the way from New Orleans on foot. Because Martin "appeared to be steady and anxious to get work," Heiskell agreed to co-sign a loan allowing the young man to acquire a set of book-binding tools. Heiskell then set him up with everything else he needed to work and gave him a suit of clothes.

Martin went to work rebinding old books. Meanwhile, he contracted some other debts. Then one day he left his shop, saying he was going to see the blacksmith. But now, Heiskell said ruefully, Martin "has forgot to return."

"He is about 23 years of age, small made, a stoppage in his speech." When he left he was wearing the orange broadcloth coat Heiskell had given him. He had a mother in New York and was probably on his way there. Be on guard, Heiskell warned his readers, "against this petit larceny villain."

Nov. 4, 1945

On Nov. 4, 1945, Knoxville men were experiencing a severe clothing shortage.

World War II had recently ended, and servicemen were coming home, ready to doff their uniforms and slip into some new "civvies." But clothing manufacturers, having sharply reduced their output of men's civilian clothes during the war, had not yet resumed full production.

The result was bare shelves at the men's stores, as reported in a News-Sentinel article on Nov. 4. Shirts, socks, shorts and pajamas were in short supply and winter suits were virtually unobtainable, especially in the smaller sizes that the slimmed-down veterans needed. "We get a few (winter suits) in now and then," one clothing store owner said, "but many are sold before they arrive."

"Most of the Navy boys coming in ask for brown suits while the Army men prefer blue," a salesman noted. "But a number want 'civvies' so badly they will take just about anything." Some were settling for summer suits.

The shortage was actually a boon for some businesses. An ad for Model Laundry and Cleaners told the returning veterans, "Don't get discouraged if you can't buy a new suit. If you can wear your pre-service suit . . . bring it to us! . . .We'll have it ready for wear in short order."

Nov. 5, 1953

Knoxvillians got their first chance to use voting machines on Nov. 5, 1953.

Ninety-five of the new-fangled machines were set up for the city primary election that day. Election clerks were on hand with miniature models of the machines to demonstrate their use to the voters.

On the whole, the public liked the machines, though a few problems arose. Some voters forgot to turn the switch that records the vote and opens the curtain. In one polling place, at a firehall, the election officer could not plug in the machine for lack of an extension cord. Firemen refused to let him borrow the Coke machine extension cord because the Cokes would get warm. The election officer finally had his wife bring a cord from home.

The vote totals were announced just two hours after the polls closed that evening — far sooner than was ever possible when printed ballots were used.

Many hoped that the machines could be used again in the run-off election, though the election commission had already decided against that. A News-Sentinel editorial declared that "there's no point in using machines in the primary and then going back to the old hand ballot system, with all its opportunities for fraud, in the run-off."

Nov. 6, 1860

Nov. 6, 1860, was election day in Knoxville and across the nation. It was perhaps the most important election day in American history, for on that day Abraham Lincoln was elected president.

In Knoxville, the polls opened at 9 a.m. Excited crowds clustered at the city's three polling places (the courthouse, the market house and a site in East Knoxville). The turnout was the heaviest in the city's history up to that time, for the issues were momentous and the election campaign had been an exciting one.

The polls closed at 4 p.m., and the ballots were counted. Lincoln, the Republican candidate, received not a single vote (he was not even on the ballot). Knoxvillians cast the great majority of their votes (737) for John Bell, a Tennessee favorite son and candidate of the Constitutional Union party, whose platform rejected secession. John C. Breckinridge, representing the more radical Southern-rights advocates who had left the national Democratic party, received 303 votes. Stephen A. Douglas, the nominee of the national Democratic party, received 52.

Thus Knoxvillians had taken a conservative stand on the great question of disunion, and they maintained that conservatism even after Lincoln's election was confirmed. But in the deep South plans were already under way to secede.

Nov. 7, 1832

On Nov. 7, 1832, a Knoxville newspaper denounced the president of the United States.

Andrew Jackson had just won a second term as president despite the best efforts of the Knoxville Republican, whose editors (Jacob Harding and J. R. Nelson) despised Jackson. In fact, they had founded their newspaper a year earlier with the expressed intention of supporting the very programs that were anathemas to the state-rights-minded Jackson: a national bank and federal support for internal improvements, manufacturing and education.

Ruefully acknowledging that Jackson had triumphed in the election over his opponent, Henry Clay, the editors of the Republican sarcastically suggested that the pro-Jackson newspapers display this headline: "Glorious Triumph Over Clay and the Constitution!"

The editors then blasted Jackson with the unrestrained prose that their readers had come to expect. No one who really knows Jackson, they said, could "believe the old man capable of administering the government in a manner calculated to benefit the people." Because of the "ignorance and passions" of the president, "the Constitution, laws and treaties of the United States have been trampled under foot, . . . the will of the people has been spurned, and the president, setting himself above all powers on earth . . . threatens, by his acts, to destroy, one by one, our institutions."

Nov. 8, 1928

On Nov. 8, 1928, Knoxville's first traffic lights went into operation.

The new traffic lights — 23 of them, all downtown — were accompanied by new rules. For years downtown traffic had been regulated by hand-operated signals controlled by men in elevated booths at each intersection. Motorists were allowed to turn right and left on red. Pedestrians ignored the signals. But the new rules forbade any turns on red and required pedestrians to obey the signals.

There was some confusion that first day, though policemen were posted at each light to help things along. All day officers were heard to shout, "You are turning on a red light there; you can't do it now!" and, "Come back here; you can't walk across the street any longer when you please!"

That first day's experience taught the authorities some lessons. The timing of the lights was adjusted to allow better traffic flow. The amber light, originally set to flash after both the red and green lights, was reset to flash only after the green.

Once people got used to it, most agreed the new system was an improvement. The News-Sentinel reported that "motorists . . . speeded their cars along in a nimble manner that gave a new traffic atmosphere to Gay Street."

Nov. 9, 1791

On Nov. 9, 1791, a committee of the United States Senate reported favorably on the Treaty of Holston; two days later the full Senate ratified the treaty.

The Treaty of Holston had been signed the previous summer at White's Fort, the future site of Knoxville. Territorial Gov. William Blount, anxious to secure peace between the white settlers and the Cherokee Indians in the region — and hoping to push the Cherokees as far south and west as possible — met with 41 Cherokee chiefs for seven days beginning in late June.

The treaty they all agreed to on July 2 was of considerable importance to the future development of Knoxville. The Cherokees drove a hard bargain. They agreed to cede land as far west as the Clinch River and as far south as Maryville, but no further. This meant that the site Blount preferred for the territorial capital (just below the confluence of the Clinch and Tennessee rivers, site of present-day Kingston) was still in Indian hands. Therefore, Blount had to take his second choice, White's Fort, which he renamed Knoxville in honor of the United States Secretary of War, Henry Knox.

Knoxville served as the territorial capital from 1791 until Tennessee achieved statehood in 1796. Then it served as the state capital until 1812.

Nov. 10, 1908

On Nov. 10, 1908, Knoxville was buzzing with the news of one of the most spectacular murders in Tennessee history.

The victim, Edward Ward Carmack, was editor of the Nashville Tennessean and an outspoken prohibitionist. He had recently lost a bitter fight for the Democratic gubernatorial nomination to the incumbent, Malcolm Patterson, an anti-prohibitionist.

Defeated but not silenced, Carmack continued to attack Patterson and his allies in newspaper editorials. On Nov. 9, Carmack was killed in Nashville in a shoot-out with an associate of Gov. Patterson.

Edward Ward Carmack

Knoxvillians were horrified by the news. Carmack had visited their city often and had many supporters there. The Knoxville Sentinel reported that "seldom have the citizens of Knoxville . . . been shocked as they were by (Carmack's) untimely death." Crowds gathered on the streets and "strong men . . . shed tears." Many were convinced that Carmack had been assassinated by a conspiracy of the "liquor interests."

A Sentinel editorial on Nov. 10 declared that "Carmack may be dead, but the ideas he stood for will, on account of this tragedy, be considered the more surely on their merits. His soul will go marching on."

This prediction proved accurate. Carmack's death was a major factor in turning public opinion in favor of statewide prohibition, which became law in 1909.

Nov. 11, 1918

World War I ended on Nov. 11, 1918, and the whole city of Knoxville celebrated.

Armistice Day was a day of thanksgiving, self-congratulation and joyous merry-making in the city. Knoxvillians were awakened that morning by the ringing of church and school bells and the blowing of factory whistles all over town. The city's fire engines raced through the streets with sirens blaring. Some citizens cheered and fired pistols into the air. Others quietly offered prayers.

Mayor John E. McMillan proclaimed the day an official holiday in Knoxville. "Peace has come!" he announced. "The Allies have won! Autocracy is crushed; Democracy is triumphant!" And he reminded the citizens that in the great Allied victory "Knoxville has had no small part, sending as it has approximately 5,000 of the flower of its young manhood. . . . Let us unite in manifestations of glorious gratitude to God."

Gay Street on Armistice Day, Nov. 11, 1918

All day long and into the night, crowds thronged the streets. A parade on Gay Street was followed by a huge public gathering at the UT athletic field.

"All Knoxville is aroused to the point that all business has been, for the time being, forgotten," The Knoxville Sentinel reported, "and every atom of energy is being devoted to the celebration of the great victory."

Nov. 12, 1930

On Nov. 12, 1930, Knoxville was in the midst of the worst bank panic in the city's history.

On that day the Holston-Union National, Knoxville's biggest bank, went into receivership and closed its doors, never to reopen. Two days earlier it had suffered a disastrous run, during which anxious depositors withdrew $750,000.

The failure of the Holston-Union, in which many Knoxvillians lost their life savings, was one of many bank failures across the nation in that era of the Great Depression. But the Holston-Union's demise was not due to the general economic collapse alone. It was triggered by the shady financial manipulations of Rogers Caldwell, an investment banker who had built a vast financial empire in the South, of which the Holston-Union was a part. Caldwell's empire began tumbling down like a house of cards in early November 1930, and the Holston-Union went down with it.

The closing of the Holston-Union created a panic among the depositors of other Knoxville banks. Despite a reassuring public statement by an association of Knoxville bankers, who insisted that "there is no occasion for alarm on the part of the depositing public," every bank in town suffered a run. Before the Depression ran its course, a number of other banks in Knoxville went the way of the Holston-Union.

Nov. 13, 1833

An editorial in the Knoxville Republican on Nov. 13, 1833, stood up for the rights of native Americans.

The editorial was remarkable, for the Indians had few defenders among whites in that era. It was written in response to a bill then pending in the state legislature that would extend Tennessee law over the Cherokees in the state.

It is wrong, the editor said, to subject any people "to laws written in a language of which they did not understand one word . . . in violation of their just rights, and designed to drive them from the country guaranteed them" by treaty. The proposed law violated the principles of republican government, for the Cherokees "have not entered into the compact under which we choose to live. They have not given their consent that we should make laws for (them). . . And they have had no agency in choosing the law-makers."

The editor also denounced supporters of the bill who argued that even if the Supreme Court struck it down, President Andrew Jackson would ignore the court and support the state (as he had recently done regarding a similar Georgia law). Such a blatant disregard of constitutional proprieties, said the editor, would lead to "the greatest evils."

Nov. 14, 1904

On Nov. 14, 1904, a fire destroyed the Lawson McGhee Library building on the corner of Gay and Vine.

The fire marked not the end of the library, however, but the prelude to an era of remarkable growth. Many of the books were saved, and new quarters were quickly secured in a rented building. The Gay Street structure was rebuilt and leased out, and the income was used to purchase a lot at Market and Commerce.

A new library building opened at that site in 1917. At the same time, Lawson McGhee became a true public library, the city having agreed to take it over and support it (until that time it was privately funded).

Mary U. Rothrock, head librarian from 1916 to 1934, oversaw a great program of expansion. In 1918, a separate library for blacks was opened. That same year, the Lawson McGhee Library assumed operation of the public school libraries, an arrangement that lasted until 1936. In 1921, the library acquired the Calvin McClung historical collection, a major research source. The first branch library opened in 1925 in Park City, and it was soon followed by others. In 1928, Lawson McGhee was opened to all county residents, and the following year a bookmobile program began, providing service to all parts of the county.

Nov. 15, 1958

Six federal agents posing as football bettors raided a Knoxville gambling den on Nov. 15, 1958.

The raid, at Dick Comer's Sport Center on Gay Street, resulted in the arrest of Comer and four others, all charged with accepting football parlay bets without having federal gambling stamps.

The agents, dressed like "sharpies" in pork-pie hats, placed bets and then pulled out their badges. They confiscated a sack full of parlay slips and $30,000 in cash. About 40 patrons were there at the time. All were released.

The Knoxville News-Sentinel had exposed Comer's as a gambling joint two months earlier. Knoxville police investigated, but pronounced the Sport Center "clean as a hound's tooth."

Operators of gambling establishments in Knoxville at that time were caught in a Catch-22 situation. Federal law required them to have a gambling stamp, but a Knoxville city ordinance made possession of such a stamp illegal.

The IRS was not unsympathetic to the Sport Center's patrons, some of whom had placed winning bets but now had no ticket to prove it. Agents announced that winners were welcome to come by the IRS office without fear of being charged as an accessory. "We won't pay anybody," one agent said, "but we'll provide him proof of his claim."

Nov. 16, 1816

On Nov. 16, 1816, the Knoxville Register published the recently revised town ordinance regulating the marketplace.

In those days, local farmers brought their produce into Knoxville to sell directly to the consumer. The town had built a market house for that purpose. Strict rules were needed, however, to keep the market orderly and safe.

The new rules set aside Tuesdays, Thursdays and Saturdays as market days. Produce could be sold only on those days and only in the market house. No produce could be sold before 11 a.m. No one was allowed to buy anything in town for resale at the market, with the exception of garden vegetables grown in town.

Sellers were prohibited from conspiring to set prices and from selling "unsound or unwholesome meats or other articles." The town's high constable was required to be on hand every market day to enforce the rules and to adjudicate disputes between buyers and sellers.

Fines for infractions of these rules ranged from $1 to $5; slaves could be whipped if their fine was not paid. Furthermore, two copies of the ordinance were to be posted at the market house, and a $2 fine would be assessed against anybody "who shall willfuly deface either of said copies."

Nov. 17, 1863

On Nov. 17, 1863, Union troops under Gen. William P. Sanders put up a stout defense just west of Knoxville, which succeeded in delaying the advancing Confederates.

The Confederates were part of a large force under Gen. James Longstreet with orders to recapture Knoxville, which had been occupied by the Union army in September 1863.

In late October, some of the Union troops marched southwest to meet the approaching Confederates. Then they fell back toward Knoxville, using delaying tactics to provide time to strengthen fortifications around the city.

William Pitt Sanders

On Nov. 17 Gen. Sanders halted his troops on a hill (where the Second Presbyterian Church now stands on Kingston Pike) and set up a defensive line. The troops, with little combat experience, hastily put up a barricade of fence rails and repulsed several attacks by Confederate infantry.

Sanders's men held on that day and most of the next before finally being driven back into the defenses of Knoxville. They suffered heavy casualties. Sanders himself was mortally wounded. By order of Union Gen. Ambrose Burnside, one of the forts defending the city was named in Sanders's honor.

Nov. 18, 1960

On Nov. 18, 1960, the UT Board of Trustees voted to integrate all university programs. This action was the culmination of a long process of racial integration, vigorously resisted by UT.

A 1952 federal court decision had forced UT to admit a few blacks to the graduate and law programs, but the university tried to hold the line there. UT administrators pointed to the Tennessee constitution, which forbade integrated education. But public sentiment and the administrators' own conservatism also influenced the university's intransigent policy.

A 1956 Tennessee supreme court ruling that invalidated state segregation laws forced UT to accept more black graduate students and to integrate the extension program. But it took the persistence of a black Austin High School graduate named Theotis Robinson Jr. to end segregation in the undergraduate program. Robinson met with UT President Andy Holt in 1960 and threatened to sue if his application was rejected.

Theotis Robinson Jr.

The state attorney general then advised that segregation could no longer be maintained. Robinson and two other black freshmen entered UT in 1961.

Nov. 19, 1979

A gunman took two hostages in downtown Knoxville on Nov. 19, 1979, and held off police for hours.

The incident generated not only fear but also considerable anger and embarrassment. It was the second time in less than two months that Louis M. Posey had invaded Knoxville Business College with a gun and taken hostages.

In the first incident, on Sept. 27, Posey held a whole class of students hostage and threatened to kill himself. After negotiating with police for three hours, he surrendered and was committed to Lakeshore Mental Health Center.

On Nov. 16, however, Posey was released from Lakeshore on furlough. Three days later, he returned to Knoxville Business College with a gun. He again took hostages (only two this time) and threatened to kill himself. He soon released the hostages, but held the police at bay for 11 hours before surrendering.

Police and college officials were outraged that Posey had been set loose by mental health authorities. Lakeshore officials were embarrassed. State Sen. Victor Ashe demanded that the state Department of Mental Health review its furlough procedures. A spokesman for that agency said that there was no written policy because "it is a clinical judgment. It would be difficult to legislate because there are too many variables."

Nov. 20, 1811

Knoxville's first bank, the Bank of Tennessee, was chartered by the state legislature on Nov. 20, 1811.

Until 1852, there was no general incorporation law for Tennessee banks. Each had to be established by a special legislative act. The act that created Knoxville's Bank of Tennessee stipulated that its stock be sold in shares of $50 each, up to a maximum of $400,000 in capital.

As soon as 500 shares had been sold, the stockholders met and elected the bank officers. Hugh Lawson White, son of Knoxville's founder James White and later a U.S. senator, was named president. The bank occupied a building on the northwest corner of Gay and Main. It opened for business in November 1812 and closed in 1831.

By that time, however, Knoxville had a second bank, a branch of the state bank that was created in 1820 in response to a financial panic then sweeping the state. This bank stood at the corner of Cumberland and Crozier. It ended operations in 1833.

Knoxvillians were not without a bank for long, however, because a branch of the Union Bank opened in town the same year that the state bank closed. At least five more banks appeared in Knoxville before the Civil War, though none survived more than a few years.

Nov. 21, 1864

On Nov. 21, 1864, Knoxville's most outspoken unionist gave a report on conditions in the city — and none of it was pleasant news.

William G. Brownlow was writing to Military Gov. Andrew Johnson in Nashville, who supervised the federal occupation of Tennessee during the Civil War.

Though Knoxville had been in federal hands for more than a year by that time, Brownlow reported that "this town . . . is full of rebels, and rebel sympathizers, who openly rejoice when (our troops) are repulsed, and talk treason openly and notoriously."Among these traitors, said Brownlow, were some of the most prominent men and women of the city.

Furthermore, a number of local people were submitting dishonest claims for compensation for losses due to Union troops. Some were claiming wildly exaggerated losses; others were rebels falsely swearing loyalty to the Union.

The saddest news was that unionist refugees from other parts of East Tennessee were pouring into Knoxville by the hundreds, driven from their homes by vindictive rebels. "It is sickening to the heart," Brownlow wrote, "to stand here and look at . . . men, women, and children, coming in through the mud and rain." Knoxville had become so crowded that there were "no houses, no shanties, no anything else to give them shelter."

Nov. 22, 1926

The first issue of The Knoxville News-Sentinel rolled off the presses on Nov. 22, 1926.

The origin of the newspaper goes back to 1886. That year a Kentucky newspaper publisher, John T. Hearn, came through Knoxville on a visit. Noting that the city had two morning newspapers but none in the afternoon, he perceived a business opportunity. He moved to Knoxville and established The Knoxville Sentinel, the first issue of which appeared in December 1886.

Hearn was a staunch Democrat, and The Sentinel remained a Democratic paper for decades, through various changes of ownership.

In 1921, a rival appeared in the form of The Knoxville News, a politically independent daily established as part of the Scripps (later Scripps Howard) chain. Edward J. Meeman, the editor of The News, quickly gained a reputation as a champion of progressive causes.

In 1926, Scripps Howard bought The Sentinel from its latest owner, Gen. Lawrence D. Tyson, who had used it to further his political career but then lost interest in it.

The News and Sentinel merged that year. The new News-Sentinel absorbed the larger circulation of The Sentinel but retained The News's progressive editor and its political independence.

R RECEIVES THE COMPLETE MULTIPLE WIRE SERVICES OF THE WORLD-WIDE UNITED PRESS A

The Knoxville News
THE KNOXVILLE SENTINEL

VOL. XL., NO. 326. KNOXVILLE, TENNESSEE, MONDAY, NOVEMBER 22, 1926. PRICE FIVE CENTS

L-DOHENY RIAL OPENS IN CAPITAL

r Cabinet Officer Must wer for His Conduct.

ELECTING JURORS

Millionaire Oil Man aces Bar of Justice.

ited Press.
SHINGTON, Nov. 22.— e men, including a negro yer, had been tentatively ked this afternoon for ervice in the conspiracy f former Secretary of In- Fall and the multi-mil- e oil man, E. L. Doheny. h sides had exercised the of peremptory challenge these 12 were in the

ked by a score of attorneys, B. Fall, grizzled ranchman litician, former United States and secretary of the In- from 1921 to 1923, and Ed-

King Benjamin Defends Course

Has Lived the Life of a Celibate For 33 Years, He Says.

"PLOT" DENOUNCED

Declares Money Is Behind the Charges Made Against Him.

By BENJAMIN PURNELL
Copyright, 1926, by International News Service and the Detroit Times

BENTON HARBOR, Mich., Nov. 11.—I have lived the life of a celibate ever since I received this most holy faith, which was approximately 33 years ago. Since that time I have followed religiously the tenets of the faith of which I am the head and not once in that time have I known a single woman, not even my own beloved wife, Mary Purnell.

The stories of these disgruntled ex-members that I attacked them under the guise of a faithful religious rite are falsehoods. Money, the root of all evil, is behind these charges. It is a blackmail, pure and simple.

Diabolical Plot

The plot was hatched within the colony years ago by certain parties. Thwarted in their ambitions to assume a position of power in

Prosecutor George Bookwalter declares that I dare not face Bessie Woodworth in court; that I will exercise all possible legal subterfuges to evade this criminal trial and finally will jump my bonds of $125,000.

Speedy Justice

This otherwise brilliant young man is wrong. I shall demand speedy justice. I shall face Bessie and all my accusers in court as quickly as possible and I certainly shall not fail my bondsmen.

The allegations that I despoiled these former girl members of the colony by telling them it was a holy religious rite whereby I gained more strength and they gained an added star in their crown is bosh.

My faith, based on the Holy Scriptures, opposes even a man and wife living together until after they have reached a stage where they are spiritually above the temptations of the flesh.

COOK SWEARS STEVENS HOME MURDER NIGHT

Friend Testifies He Saw Defendant Going Fishing.

DATE QUESTIONED

Statement Produced Signed By Witness Alleges Uncertainty.

By United Press
COURT ROOM, SOMERVILLE, N. J., Nov. 22.— A succession of witnesses came to court Monday to testify in support of the detailed alibi of Henry Stevens, which forms his defense to the murder charges against him in the Hall-Mills case.

Mrs. Anna Evanson told the jury that on the night Stevens was supposed to have been at New Brunswick while the murders took place, he was at Lavalette, N. J., his home. She cooked his dinner that night, she said.

Weighed Fish

READER, HERE IT IS
Two Papers In One

With this issue the combined Knoxville News and Knoxville Sentinel offer their readers the first number of a newspaper representing the combined strength of two established publications.

The reader will find in this and future issues the best that has heretofore appeared in either paper. The management is no less aware of its obligation than it is of its tremendous responsibility.

The obligation is to justify the consolidation of two large properties by making it equal and if possible surpass both in their former individual capacities.

The responsibility is to provide to the complete satisfaction of the reader a newspaper that will meet every requirement of popular demand. The management will strive to the best of its ability and with every resource at its command to justify the confidence of the public as well as the high hopes and expectations that have been so generously expressed.

It is the aim of the management to print a satisfactory newspaper. It hopes to leave nothing to be desired in the way of a positive and virile expression editorially, a complete cable and telegraph service and finally to give all the local news when it is news.

Going into nearly every home in Knoxville with a city circulation far exceeding that of any paper ever printed in Knoxville, the combined newspaper is sensible of its duty to the readers of every opinion and it purposes to justify its claim on their confidence by presenting to them the largest and best newspaper that the people of Knoxville and the Knoxville territory have ever had presented to them.

A portion of the front page of the first Knoxville News-Sentinel

Nov. 23, 1963

Saturday, Nov. 23, 1963, found the entire city of Knoxville shocked and saddened. The day before, President John F. Kennedy had been assassinated in Dallas.

Mayor John Duncan proclaimed a three-day period of "prayerful mourning" beginning Saturday. Though away from Knoxville at the time, Duncan recorded an official statement and prayer that was broadcast on local radio and television stations.

In his statement the mayor affirmed that "all Knoxvillians are grieved and shocked by the death of our president," and he urged "all religious faiths of our city to hold prayerful services and also ask Divine guidance for President Johnson in the days ahead."

Knoxville's three Catholic churches held special services, as did Knoxville College students and many other Knoxvillians.

Most scheduled public events were cancelled. One exception was Saturday's Tennessee-Kentucky football game, which UT won in Lexington by a score of 19-0.

In a heartfelt editorial, News-Sentinel editor Loye W. Miller wrote that "we weep at the untimely death of a friend whose warm personality had touched all our lives. . . . Though not all of us approved his every act, we noted his courage, his dedication, his manly good looks, his wit, his eloquence. . . . Here was a man who sincerely loved his country."

Nov. 24, 1911

On Nov. 24, 1911, the University of Tennessee board of trustees voted to take control of the Summer School of the South.

Founded by UT President Charles Dabney in 1902, the Summer School of the South was a pioneering effort in summer education. Its goal was professional improvement of the South's public school teachers. Although the Summer School was located on the UT campus and used UT facilities, it was a separate institution until 1911.

Dabney got the Summer School off to a fine start by appointing as its head one of the South's preeminent educators, P. P. Claxton, who worked tirelessly to promote the school. The first session, in 1902, attracted 2,000 registrants. Over the next 16 summers, 30,000 more school teachers came to Knoxville as Summer School students.

The courses they took included "common school" subjects such as arithmetic, high school subjects such as literature, and professional subjects such as school management. Cultural events, including plays and concerts, rounded out the Summer School offerings.

After UT took control in 1911, the Summer School became somewhat mired in the UT bureaucracy, which contributed to its demise in 1918. Other contributing factors included competition from other summer schools and the coming of World War I, which restricted rail travel and diverted public attention from education.

Nov. 25, 1854

Knoxville got some good press in 1854, as the Knoxville Register proudly pointed out on Nov. 25 of that year.

The editor of the Register had come across some travelers' accounts of Knoxville in two out-of-town newspapers, and he reprinted them for his own readers.

The Abingdon Virginian noted that "Knoxville is looking up amazingly, and the people are as busily engaged and are as cheerful and happy as if the angel of death had never flapped his dark wing o'er the city." The town had two new manufacturing shops, "and the hum of machinery and the throes of the engine are now heard where, but a few months before, the silence was only broken by the bark of the watch dog or the song of the school boy."

A writer for the Nashville True Whig also commended Knoxville's booming economy, particularly its lively real estate market. And he described the town's three hotels as first-rate, especially the Coleman House — "without question the finest house this side of the mountains." The town will move "onward to a position of enviable importance," he predicted. "Knoxville is destined to become not only a place of heavy trade, but may, indeed, become one of the principal manufacturing cities of the South."

Nov. 26, 1824

An editorial in the Knoxville Register on Nov. 26, 1824, took exception to the popular practice of "treating" at election time.

In those days it was customary for men running for office to "treat" the voters, i.e., to hand out free whiskey.

This practice, said the editor, has the effect of "increasing the facilities to intoxication, promoting a prostitution of morals, and confirming the most pernicious habits."

Furthermore, he said (reflecting the democratic spirit of that era, which encouraged political participation by the "common man") the practice of treating prevents poor men from winning office, for the rich can afford to treat, but the poor can't. "This will throw legislation into the hands of the rich. . . . Ere long our boasted principles of liberty and republicanism will be corrupted."

The solution, the editor suggested, was for the voters to agree among themselves to refuse to be treated and to vote against any man who insists on treating. By this means "the practice might gradually be brought into discredit and men could then be selected (on the basis of) character and talents. . . But this, we fear, is the promised land of political perfection which, however visible through the telescope of reason, frail humanity must not expect to inhabit."

Nov. 27, 1909

James Agee, one of America's great writers and one of Knoxville's most famous native sons, was born on Nov. 27, 1909.

His parents, Hugh and Laura Agee, lived at 1505 Highland Ave. Hugh died in an automobile accident in 1916. In 1919, Laura moved with her son to Middle Tennessee but returned to Knoxville often to visit her parents.

James Agee's roots were thus firmly set in Knoxville, but he spent most of his life away from there. After graduation from Harvard in 1932, he moved to New York.

Among Agee's better known works are the screenplays for the movies "African Queen" and "Night of the Hunter" and a collaborative work (with the photographer Walker Evans) on the life of southern sharecroppers, entitled "Let Us Now Praise Famous Men."

James Agee in 1932

Agee's major work, however, is an autobiographical novel set in Knoxville. "A Death in the Family" beautifully evokes the city's atmosphere in the early 20th century.

Heart problems and overwork led to Agee's early death, in 1955. His novel was published posthumously and won a Pulitzer Prize.

Nov. 28, 1818

A group of citizens met at the courthouse in Knoxville on Nov. 28, 1818, and put up money for a steamboat company.

The invention of the steamboat in the early 1800s held out the promise that Knoxville could become part of the national economy. The town was difficult to reach by road in those days, and riverboats could only go downstream. Steamboats, however, could travel against the current and thus might bring goods and passengers up the Tennessee River to Knoxville.

In 1818, some Alabama citizens proposed raising $60,000 to build steamboats to operate on the Tennessee, and they asked the people of East Tennessee to kick in half. At the Nov. 28 meeting in Knoxville, the East Tennesseans enthusiastically complied, purchasing 300 shares in the project at $100 each. The Knoxville Register commented after the meeting that "the citizens of this section now appear to be alive to the importance of the navigation of the Tennessee River."

The project proved to be a disappointment, however. No steamboat reached Knoxville until 1828; and, moreover, the direct connection between Knoxville and New Orleans that the investors anticipated never materialized, for the Muscle Shoals posed a difficult obstacle to steamboats. Before long Knoxvillians lost interest in steamboats and began looking to the railroad for their economic salvation.

Nov. 29, 1863

Nov. 29, 1863, was the bloodiest day in Knoxville's history — the day of the battle of Fort Sanders.

Knoxville was under seige at that time by a Confederate force under Gen. James Longstreet. Manning the defensive works that protected the city was a Union force under Gen. Ambrose Burnside.

Rather than wait to starve the defenders out, the Confederates decided to attack. They picked out what looked like a weak spot — Fort Sanders, a large earthwork (at what is now the intersection of Seventeenth and Laurel) held by Union infantry and artillery.

At daybreak on Nov. 29, several thousand Confederate infantrymen assaulted the fort. They immediately encountered some nasty surprises. Wire entanglements in front of the fort tripped up the attackers. Those who reached the fort found a deep ditch around it. Those who tried to go on floundered in the ditch or slipped on the steep, icy embankment. Only a few made it to the top of the parapet.

It was over in 20 minutes. The Confederates were thoroughly defeated, losing 129 men killed, 458 wounded, and 226 captured. The Union defenders inside the fort lost only five killed and eight wounded.

The failure of the attack persuaded Longstreet to give up the seige. Knoxville was never again seriously threatened by the Confederate army.

The battle of Fort Sanders

Nov. 30, 1948

An unusual decision by the Knoxville police on Nov. 30, 1948, allowed local veterans' groups to determine whether three young vandals would be prosecuted.

The three, all students at Central High School, had confessed to throwing yellow paint on a statue on the grounds of Knoxville High School. The statue honored soldiers killed in World War I. The students insisted that their misdeed, which took place on the eve of the Central-Knoxville football game, was merely a prank in retaliation for the painting of Central the previous year.

The police chose to let the local American Legion and Veterans of Foreign Wars (who had jointly offered a reward in the case) decide if the boys should be prosecuted. An editorial in The News-Sentinel protested the police decision, however. "The whole thing is being mishandled," it read. "The police are not judges; nor does the public, we believe, want vigilante government by letting veterans' organizations dispense justice outside the usual channels. Let the boys be brought before a judge."

The boys were brought before a judge the next day, at the behest of the veterans. The judge suspended the boys' drivers' licenses for six months and ordered them to clean the statue. Then he paroled them to their parents.

Dec. 1, 1873

At a public meeting on Dec. 1, 1873, the Knoxville Benevolent Association was founded.

The association was typical of charity organizations established in cities around the nation in that era. It was a time when industrialization and urbanization were creating great extremes of wealth and a destitute underclass. But government had not yet accepted the responsibility of caring for all of society's unfortunates.

Much of the responsibility was therefore assumed by middle-class citizens acting through private voluntary organizations, such as the Knoxville Benevolent Association. The purpose of the association was to help the "worthy" poor. Applicants for charity were carefully screened. As one newspaper put it, no one would get aid just by "put(ting) up a poor mouth and ask(ing) for it. The (association members) will take nothing on trust and they have no notion of encouraging idleness or improvidence."

The Knoxville Benevolent Association was also typical in that it was run by women. In that era, charity work was one of the few activities outside the home that middle-class women were encouraged to pursue. However, the association charter created an "advisory committee" of five men — no doubt reflecting the common assumption in those years that women needed male guidance.

Dec. 2, 1885

"POISONED!" blared the headlines of the Knoxville Chronicle after the discovery of a terrible crime on Dec. 2, 1885.

J. A. Galyon, a North Knoxville grocer, had sat down with his family for breakfast as usual that morning. After eating heartily, however, Galyon and his wife and four children all became violently ill. The family doctor was summoned, and he recognized the symptoms of arsenic poisoning.

After treating his patients, the doctor called in a druggist and the two began investigating. Their attention was drawn to the coffee pot, which they found had been laced with a large quantity of arsenic, easily enough to have killed the whole family. That it did not was attributed to the fact that much of the arsenic had sunk to the bottom of the pot and been trapped by coffee grounds.

Suspicion focused on the family servant, Mary Clayton, especially after one of the children reported that she had argued with Clayton a day or two earlier and that the servant "had been in a bad humor ever since." Clayton protested her innocence but was nevertheless arrested and jailed.

The Galyon family all survived, though Mrs. Galyon and two of the children were in critical condition for some hours.

Dec. 3, 1897

On Dec. 3, 1897, the Tennessee Medical College building in North Knoxville burned to the ground.

The Tennessee Medical College (a private institution not connected with the University of Tennessee) was founded in 1889. Its first building was downtown, at the corner of Gay and Main, and there the first graduates of the school received the degree of doctor of medicine in March 1890.

Soon after, the school's directors purchased a lot at Cleveland and Dameron in North Knoxville and had a four-story building constructed on the site. The college moved to this new building in December 1890. Its destruction by fire seven years later resulted in losses totaling $40,000.

Nevertheless the school survived. Soon after the fire, the directors of the college incorporated, raised capital, rented an unused school building from the city and resumed classes. The Dameron Avenue building was rebuilt, and in 1900 the college moved back into it.

By that time the school had 90 students and a faculty of 20. Women students were accepted beginning about 1904, and at least three were graduated.

In 1909, Lincoln Memorial University bought the Tennessee Medical College for $50,000. The college turned out to be a financial loser, however, and it was closed in 1914. Its building was later used by Knoxville General Hospital.

Dec. 4, 1902

On Dec. 4, 1902, a Knoxville official locked horns with the city hospital administrators.

Knoxville's big new hospital was privately owned, but it received financial support from the city and was required to accept indigent patients referred by the city physician. Hospital officials announced, however, that certain cases would not be accepted, including tuberculosis patients and children under 12.

Alderman Robert McMillan was outraged. "The idea of the board of governors of the hospital outlawing (tuberculosis) like it was leprosy," he said, "is simply preposterous, and if the hospital can't take care of such cases, I will never vote to appropriate another cent to its maintenance."

McMillan renewed his attack the next night at a Board of Aldermen meeting. Why, he asked, could children not be admitted? "If there is anything on earth that will touch a man's heart it is . . . a helpless child. . . . If we can't take care of a poor little boy or girl that happened to get an arm or leg cut off, we had better shut up the doors of the hospital and quit."

In the end the aldermen voted to send a strong message to the hospital board asking that all patients referred by the city physician be accepted regardless of the standing rules.

Dec. 5, 1983

Knoxville Board of Education members wound up with egg on their faces on Dec. 5, 1983, after they tried to change the name of Austin-East High School.

Austin-East was created in 1968 by the merger of all-black Austin High and all-white East. In 1983, some black leaders in Knoxville urged that the name be changed to Austin High. They collected 49 names on a petition and, in November, persuaded the school board to make the change.

The action was ill-considered. Austin-East students, parents, teachers and alumni were outraged. At least 200 of them showed up at the Dec. 5 school board meeting. They wore Austin-East caps and jackets, waved pennants and pompoms and displayed buttons saying, "I love the Roadrunners." And they brought along their own petition, with 700 signatures. They were supported by a contingent of angry East High alumni.

The school board beat a hasty retreat. Board member Sarah Moore Greene apologized, saying she had been misled about the extent of community support for the name change. The board quickly and unanimously passed a motion to rescind the November action.

A News-Sentinel editorial commended the Board for seeing "the error of its ways" and blamed the whole mess on "a few selfish Austin alumni who wanted the school renamed."

Dec. 6, 1960

More than 15 years after atomic bombs were dropped on Japan, the United States government released the first pictures of the devastating weapons on Dec. 6, 1960.

The news was of particular interest to Knoxvillians because the enriched uranium for "Little Boy," dropped Aug. 6, 1945, on Hiroshima, was produced in nearby Oak Ridge as part of the top-secret Manhattan Project.

The News-Sentinel carried front-page photographs of the 9,000-pound "Little Boy," as wells as "Fat Man," the 10,000-pounder dropped on Nagasaki on Aug. 8, 1945.

The two blasts killed an estimated 175,000 persons and probably hastened the end of World War II.

Government officials said pictures of the bombs had been withheld until 1960 "because unfavorable diplomatic results might have been provoked by their release previously." However, the announcement was timed to coincide with the eve of the 19th anniversary of Japan's sneak attack on Pearl Harbor.

A spokesman said the release was "approved reluctantly" by the State Department.

The 15-year ban on photographs of the two bombs contrasted sharply with the military's virtually instant touting of information about high-tech weaponry used during the Desert Storm operation in 1991.

Dec. 7, 1971

Groundbreaking ceremonies for the new terminal at McGhee Tyson Airport were held on Dec. 7, 1971. It was an important step in the evolution of Knoxville's air transportation system.

The earliest pilots simply used any convenient field to land and take off. But in 1927, a local flying enthusiast, Walter Self, established Knoxville's first real airport along Sutherland Avenue. The city bought it two years later and named it McGhee Tyson, in honor of a Knoxville-born World War I flier killed in action in 1918.

By the 1930s, this small airport could no longer handle Knoxville's growing air traffic. In the meantime, however, Tom Kesterson had opened the Island Airport in South Knoxville, and when commercial flights came to Knoxville in 1934, they landed there.

Soon, however, the government decided that Island Airport's runway was too short for the bigger commercial aircraft. City officials in 1935 purchased a site in rural Blount County. Construction then began on the new municipal airport, which kept the name McGhee Tyson. It began operation in 1937. The original terminal building was used until the new one opened in 1974.

The airport terminal under construction

Dec. 8, 1941

On Dec. 8, 1941, one day after the Japanese attack on Pearl Harbor that brought the U.S. into World War II, Knoxville was already mobilizing.

In accordance with standing emergency plans, the 130th Infantry Regiment arrived in Knoxville by truck that day. The commander set up headquarters and began dispatching units throughout East Tennessee to guard dams, bridges and defense plants, including ALCOA and Fulton Sylphon.

The local FBI office began carrying out its orders to keep an eye on potential saboteurs and other dangerous persons, especially enemy aliens. Knoxville's two Japanese were targeted for special observation.

The Selective Service office geared up for the expected flood of volunteers and draftees. The Fire Department began a special training program on incendiary fires. The American Legion announced that its air-raid warning program was set to go.

A News-Sentinel editorial declared that the Japanese attack, despite its tactical success, gave America "something which Japan lacks — something essential to give a peaceful and democratic people the will to fight and the will to win. That essential is clear proof to Americans that their nation is not the aggressor."

Contacted by telephone, Tennessee's great World War I hero Alvin York told a News-Sentinel reporter, "We're going to give Japan a thorough licking."

Dec. 9, 1957

On Dec. 9, 1957, Knoxville's mayor defended the city police against a U.S. senator's charge of laxity in investigating labor violence.

The Senate Rackets Committee, chaired by Sen. John McClellan, was at that time holding hearings in Washington on the Teamsters Union. Among those testifying were a Knoxville grocer whose store had been dynamited during a strike against the local Coca-Cola plant, and a former bookkeeper for Teamsters Local 621 of Knoxville who told of other acts of violence. There had been no arrests or indictments in these cases, which provoked Sen. McClellan to remark that "that is the kind of law enforcement you have down in that community when labor unions are involved."

Knoxville Mayor Jack Dance immediately responded with a telegram to Sen. McClellan. "I must object to the slur against the police department of this city by you," it read. "In cases now before your committee, painstaking investigations were made by our police. If they had been armed with the subpoena power of your committee, their efforts would certainly have elicited the information which you have obtained."

Jack Dance

Dec. 10, 1885

On Dec. 10, 1885, more than 20 years after they laid down their arms and furled their rebel flags, Knoxville's ex-Confederate soldiers met and formed a veterans' organization.

At the meeting that night at Enterprise Hall, the veterans adopted a constitution and bylaws, elected officers, set a time for regular meetings (every other Thursday) and agreed to name their organization in honor of Felix Zollicoffer, a Confederate general from Tennessee who was killed in battle in 1862.

The stated purpose of the organization was "to perpetuate the memories of our fallen comrades, and to minister . . . to the wants of those who were permanently disabled in the service, (and) to maintain that sentiment of fraternity born of the hardships and dangers shared in the march, the bivouac, and the battlefield. It is proposed not to prolong the animosities engendered by the war. . . . We propose to avoid everything which partakes of partisanship in religion and politics."

The local organization of Union veterans sent a resolution of congratulations and good will to the Confederate veterans, and in return the ex-rebels resolved "to promote and perpetuate the kindliest and most harmonious relations between that organization and our own." Then they discussed the possibility of inviting the Union veterans to a party on Washington's birthday.

Dec. 11, 1959

On Dec. 11, 1959, 17 black students filed suit in federal court to force the Knoxville schools to integrate.

Five years earlier, in the famous Brown v. Board of Education of Topeka case, the U.S. Supreme Court had ordered that the South's segregated public schools must be integrated "with all deliberate speed."

Knoxville school authorities were in no hurry to comply, however. When local blacks showed up at city school board meetings in 1959 to urge desegregation, the board members resisted. Late that year, the blacks filed suit.

The case (Josephine Goss, et al., v. Board of Education, City of Knoxville) came up for a hearing in the U.S. district court in February 1960. The court ordered the school board to devise a desegregation plan by April. The board came back with a plan to integrate one grade each year, beginning in September 1960 with the first grade. The district court approved this plan.

An appeals court decided, however, that this plan was too slow, and demanded an accelerated (two grades per year) plan. Various objections kept the case in court for 14 years, by which time the Knoxville public schools (proceeding under the original one-grade-per-year plan) were fully integrated to the satisfaction of the court.

Dec. 12, 1832

On Dec. 12, 1832, the editor of the Knoxville Republican announced plans to establish a second newspaper.

In the Republican of that date, Jacob Harding set forth a proposal for a paper to be called the Western Garland. This would not be a political newspaper, like the Republican and most others in that era, but a literary newspaper, devoted to "poetry, anecdotes, and tales . . . to amuse and instruct. . . . With such a paper many a dull and wearisome hour may be filled up with cheerfulness, and the mind, at the same time, improved with useful knowledge." Moreover, he said, such a paper would "exercise a salutary influence upon the young" by encouraging in them "a fondness for reading."

Harding went on to scold the people of East Tennessee, who he said "have long been dependent upon their brethren of the eastern and northern states for publications of this kind." East Tennessee should have its own literary journals, he said. These would "act as a stimulant to our own literary men" and perhaps uncover hidden talent in the hills of Tennessee.

Apparently Harding failed to persuade his readers that they needed such a paper. There is no evidence that even one issue of the Western Garland ever appeared.

Dec. 13, 1898

The ladies of Knoxville held a gala Christmas bazaar on Dec. 13, 1898, to raise money for a new hospital.

Market Hall was jammed that night with gaily decorated booths representing the states of the union. "All of society appeared to be present," The Knoxville Sentinel reported, "the ladies wearing handsome gowns and the gentlemen with pockets full of money. The different booths were radiant with incandescent lights."

At the Tennessee booth, festooned with red poppies, one could buy dainty girls' dresses, pillow covers and little decorative milkmaid stools. The Virginia booth was made up to resemble a colonial mansion; portraits of Washington and Jefferson adorned it. The Maine booth recreated a snowy scene in the woods, complete with a moose head. The New York booth, which sold lemonade in mugs, represented a traditional Dutch kitchen. The Louisiana booth depicted a bayou scene and sold French coffee and pralines. There was also a gypsy's tent with a costumed fortune teller.

The highlight of the evening was a spelling bee that pitted eight doctors against seven lawyers. As a minister called out words from Webster's speller, the contestants were eliminated one by one. Law triumphed over medicine that evening when lawyer Noble Smithson emerged victorious.

Dec. 14, 1849

On Dec. 14, 1849, Knoxville's aldermen gave the town constable permission to rent an office.

It was one step in the long evolution of the Knoxville police force. Until the 1850s, the whole force consisted of one constable assisted by citizens' patrols. In 1857, the first regular, uniformed police chief was appointed. His name was M. V. Bridwell, and the city provided him with two salaried officers. Two years later, the city doubled the police force, providing for a day chief and a night chief, each with two officers.

Dan Leahy, one of the city's earliest patrolmen

A crime wave during the Civil War necessitated another increase in the force, to 10 officers. By 1885, the force consisted of one chief with two assistants and 14 officers.

Before 1891, the Knoxville police had no paddy wagon. Until then they had to drag drunks and other miscreants to jail, or find an accommodating drayman.

In the late 19th century, the city briefly experimented with mounted police. Four horses were purchased, but the authorities soon decided that the money was better spent on hiring more officers.

The first Knoxville policeman killed in the line of duty was William Dozier, shot through the heart in 1868 while trying to arrest a drunk at the Dew Drop Inn, a Gay Street saloon.

Dec. 15, 1919

On Dec. 15, 1919, Knoxville put out the welcome mat for the commander-to-be of the battleship Tennessee.

The Tennessee, a huge "super-dreadnought," was then under construction in the Brooklyn Navy Yard. The Navy needed 600 recruits to fill up the crew, but enlistment was slow in that post-World War I period.

A 1920 recruiting poster for the Battleship Tennessee

In order to drum up recruits, the Navy undertook a promotional campaign in Tennessee, promising that the whole crew of the new battleship would be composed of Tennesseans and challenging Tennessee's towns to compete against one another in encouraging enlistments.

As part of the campaign the officer chosen to command the Tennessee, Capt. R. H. Leigh, toured the state. He arrived in Knoxville amid great fanfare on Dec. 15. Gov. A. H. Roberts was also on hand.

In a speech at Market Hall that night, Capt. Leigh thrilled the audience with tales of anti-submarine warfare. The recruiting rhetoric was left to Gov. Roberts, who expressed confidence that Knoxville, which had "sent some of the bravest lads that ever shouldered a gun to fight for civilization in the war against Germany," would not fail to do its duty in the current enlistment drive.

The governor's confidence was not misplaced. Of the 600 Tennesseans eventually recruited, 250 were from Knoxville and Knox County.

Dec. 16, 1966

In a scene as dramatic as anything television or the movies could offer, Knoxville police surrounded a house on Dec. 16, 1966, and captured two desperate fugitives.

The two were among four Knox County jail inmates who had carried out a daring escape two days earlier. They overpowered a turnkey, locked him in a cell and stabbed an elevator operator. Then they broke out a window in the jail kitchen, and three of them lowered themselves to the street with a rope made of bedsheets. The fourth cut his way out through a mesh screen in the kitchen's back door.

Two of the escapees were recaptured immediately. The other two were spotted by a deputy, who chased them in his car. But when he caught up with them they overpowered him, took his car keys and drove off in his car.

Two days later, acting on a tip, police surrounded a home on Andes Street where the two fugitives were hiding in the attic. A police captain, using a bullhorn, urged the two to surrender. After waiting and getting no response, the officers fired tear gas into the house. Minutes later the two emerged. "We're not armed!" one shouted. "We're coming out!"

Dec. 17, 1868

A major step in the growth of Knoxville took place on Dec. 17, 1868, when the state legislature approved Knoxville's annexation of East Knoxville.

The area east of First Creek had developed as a suburb of Knoxville in the early decades of the 19th century. By 1856, its population had reached a point that the legislature agreed to incorporate it as a separate town called East Knoxville.

The legislative charter provided that East Knoxville be governed by a mayor and six aldermen, all elected annually. The first town election, in March 1856, put William Swan in the mayor's chair. Among the first aldermen was William G. Brownlow, who later served one term as mayor.

In 1868, East Knoxville's eighth (and last) mayor, S. H. Smith, held a meeting with the aldermen to discuss the consolidation of their town with Knoxville. Mayor M. D. Bearden of Knoxville was also present. A plan of consolidation was agreed upon.

The legislature then abolished the charter of East Knoxville and extended Knoxville's boundaries to include East Knoxville, contingent upon Knoxville's assumption of East Knoxville's debts. That assumption was formalized by the mayor and aldermen of Knoxville on Jan. 9, 1869, and on that day the town of East Knoxville ceased to exist.

Dec. 18, 1962

On Dec. 18, 1962, a Knoxville businessman announced the discovery of an interesting historical relic.

Employees of the Oliver King Sand and Lime Company who were dredging Fort Loudon Lake near First Creek pulled up a 20-foot section of hand-forged chain. Company president C. B. Alexander identified it as a 99-year-old relic of the seige of Knoxville during the Civil War.

C.B. Alexander displays the chain and anchor found in Fort Loudon Lake.

Union forces holding Knoxville in 1863 had built a pontoon bridge across the river near First Creek to maintain communication with the Union forts south of the river. Upon hearing a report that the beseiging Confederates intended to float a log raft down the river to smash the fragile bridge, the Union commander ordered that a long chain be stretched across the river to protect it.

The chain was put in place but was never tested. The Confederates, following their defeat in the battle of Fort Sanders, gave up the seige and departed in December 1863.

The day after Alexander's announcement, workers pulled another section of chain from the lake bottom. Attached to it was a crude, eight-foot-long anchor made from railroad iron.

The chain and anchor were turned over to the East Tennessee Historical Society. Today they are on display at the Confederate Memorial Hall on Kingston Pike.

Dec. 19, 1900

On Dec. 19, 1900, a stolen diamond mysteriously reappeared at a Knoxville jewelry store.

The episode had begun the day before, when jeweler H. W. Curtis charged Mrs. W. J. Williams with stealing a diamond.

According to the jeweler, Mrs. Williams came into his shop and asked to see some unset diamonds. He brought out several. Mrs. Williams picked one up, took it to the door as if to examine it in the light and then returned it to the counter.

The jeweler instantly realized that she had substituted a piece of glass for the diamond. He surmised that she had secreted the diamond in her mouth. He called police right away and had her arrested. Meanwhile, said Mr. Curtis, she swallowed the diamond.

Mrs. Williams vehemently denied the charge, called a lawyer, made bond, and went home.

The next day a man came by the jewelry store and left a diamond with a note that read, "This is the diamond which Mr. Curtis accused poor Mrs. Williams of stealing." The jeweler, noting that "the one returned was the same size and weight of the one I lost and I have every reason to believe it is the same diamond," asked no further questions and dropped charges against Mrs. Williams.

Dec. 20, 1937

On Dec. 20, 1937, Knoxvillians voiced their opinions about a risque radio show.

Some days earlier, the actress Mae West had been a guest on NBC's Charlie McCarthy Show. West, known for her sexually charged persona and suggestive lines, played Eve in a comedy skit about the Garden of Eden. The show caused a minor uproar around the nation, for some thought the skit (or at least West's contribution to it) indecent.

On Dec. 20, The News-Sentinel polled Knoxvillians about their reaction to the skit. Some were outraged. "I think Mae West ought to be kept off the air and the screen," said a minister. "Her sexy kind of stuff is her chief stock in trade and it ought to be outlawed. Such stuff incites . . . the early sex life of juveniles." The president of the Knoxville PTA, who had not heard the radio show, nevertheless denounced Mae West's movies as "below the educational standards we stand for." A school principal declared that "the intonation of Mae West is not suitable to deal with any religious subject."

Others, however, laughed the whole thing off. "It was very clever and I enjoyed it," said one man. "I'm a minister's son-in-law, but I don't think the skit did the young any harm."

Dec. 21, 1842

On Dec. 21, 1842, H. Mercer and Company published an announcement in the Knoxville Register addressed "To the Traveling Public."

Mercer ran a stagecoach line between Knoxville and Nashville, carrying both passengers and mail. According to the announcement, the company was adding a second coach to accommodate those people (especially legislators) who wanted to be on hand for the upcoming General Assembly in Nashville.

"The proprietors of this line," the announcement continued, "are proud to say that their teams (of horses) are fine and able, their coaches new and Troy built, their harnesses entirely new, and that their drivers are scarcely equalled anywhere. . . . The public may therefore rely on getting through on this line without being subject to any of the accidents of running away, breaking down, turning over, failing to get through in proper time, etc., which passengers sometimes . . . apprehend."

A coach would leave Knoxville every Monday, Wednesday and Friday, right after dinner, the company promised. It would proceed to Nashville by way of Sparta. The fare for the 200-mile journey was $15. And — the best news of all — the trip was speedy, requiring only 58 hours.

Not until the railroad came to Knoxville in the 1850s could Knoxvillians expect any faster journey to the state capital by public conveyance.

Dec. 22, 1885

Knoxville's first electric lights lit up on the evening of Dec. 22, 1885.

Knoxville lawyer John C. Houk helped organize the company that brought electric power to the city. In 1885, the company secured a building at 88 Gay Street, installed a generating plant, strung power lines and finally turned on the juice just three days before Christmas.

Knoxville's first lights were all in businesses along Gay Street, except for five street lights. Customers paid a flat rate of $12 per month for power, and the company guaranteed that "there will be no hissing, no flickering" in the lights.

Electric lights were such a novelty that crowds gathered on Gay Street that first evening to marvel at them. "The lamps burn with but little flickering," the Knoxville Chronicle reported, "and the light is very regular."

Because there were no devices besides lights that could use electricity at that time, power was needed only at night. The Knoxville electric company announced that power would be turned on at 4:30 p.m. each day.

The city soon began replacing its gas street lamps with electric lights, though as late as 1892 gas lamps still outnumbered the electric ones by 417 to 114. More and more private customers signed up for electricity, too; by 1892, there were 300.

Dec. 23, 1976

Knoxville police arrested two men just after midnight on Dec. 23, 1976, in connection with the bombing of an adult bookstore.

Less than an hour earlier an explosion had rocked downtown Knoxville. It destroyed the front and much of the interior of the Adult Book Store on Gay Street, which had been the scene of recent picketing by religious groups. The blast was powerful enough to shatter windows for several blocks up and down Gay Street. One patron of a nearby tavern was knocked off her seat. The explosion was heard four miles away.

A witness reported that just before the blast, a black Plymouth Valiant sped down Gay Street and an object was thrown from the car into the doorway of the bookstore.

Minutes later, an off-duty policeman spotted a black Valiant and followed it as it went south on Alcoa Highway. He summoned other officers, who arrested the occupants of the car, two young men. Paraffin tests on the two indicated that they might have handled explosives recently.

At the scene of the bombing investigators found evidence of blasting caps and dynamite. The suspects admitted being on Gay Street that night but denied any connection with the bombing.

Dec. 24, 1889

On Christmas Eve, 1889, one of Knoxville's more unusual churches was founded.

A Knoxville man, A. G. Scott, had long dreamed of an independent Christian church free from any established doctrine. He found a few like-minded people, but met resistance from others — not necessarily because they insisted on a denominational affiliation, but in some cases because they insisted on a sectional affiliation (northern or southern).

In 1889, Scott met the Rev. R. N. Thompson, who was holding a revival. Just before he was to leave town, Thompson toured the new suburb of West Knoxville (now called Fort Sanders), took note of its schools, electric lights and streetcars, and remarked, "I see everything here except something for the Lord." Scott then told Thompson of his dream, and Thompson agreed to stay in West Knoxville to help organize a church.

Ramsey Memorial Church (named for W. B. A. Ramsey, whose daughter donated land for it) was organized on Dec. 24, 1889. Rev. Thompson accepted the call to the pulpit with the understanding that no doctrine would be advocated, only the most basic Christian precepts. The original members of Ramsey Memorial came from seven different Knoxville churches. They erected a building at Highland and Eighth. By 1892, the church had 155 members.

Dec. 25, 1990

The News-Sentinel announced record-breaking contributions to the Empty Stocking Fund on Dec. 25, 1990. As of that day, $137,012.18 had been received for the fund; by the time donations stopped arriving in January, a total of $149,807.76 had been received.

The Empty Stocking Fund was organized in 1912 by a group of charitable citizens who wanted to share Christmas cheer with their needy neighbors. Raleigh Harrison was the first chairman of the ESF committee, and The Sentinel agreed to cooperate with the committee in its campaign for funds. That first year, donations amounted to $162.95.

In its early years, the ESF had the assistance of the Associated Charities in its distribution. More recently, the Knox County General Assistance Office has helped identify those people with the greatest need for assistance.

The proceeds of the fund provide baskets of food and toys that are given away on Christmas Eve. In the early years of the fund, remaining monies were used to buy milk and baby food for the remainder of the year.

With the merging of The Sentinel and The News in 1926, The News-Sentinel became the sponsor of the Empty Stocking Fund. The newspaper requests donations from its readers between Thanksgiving and Christmas each year and is the receiving and disbursing agent.

Dec. 26, 1902

On Friday, Dec. 26, 1902, Sunday school classes all over Knoxville put on their annual Christmas programs.

It was the custom in those days for Sunday schools to hold pageants just after Christmas. These usually featured skits or other presentations by the students, an appearance by Santa Claus and the collection of gifts for the poor.

The Sunday school students at Central Presbyterian Church decorated their stage that year with a large star through which a bright light shone. The students recited lessons and sang songs and then received generous presents from Santa. The Men's Aid Society made a big hit at this pageant, singing "Song of the Sock" (to the tune of "O Tannenbaum") while hanging up stockings.

The program at Epiphany Episcopal opened with devotional exercises conducted by the pastor, then continued with a slide show illustrating Biblical scenes, each explained by students who provided scriptural references.

Other pageants that night included one at First Methodist, which was gaily decorated with evergreen boughs and a beautiful Christmas tree; at Pilgrim's Congregational, which featured a cantata entitled "A Jolly Christmas"; and at Bell Avenue Presbyterian, whose students presented the superintendent with a handsome rocking chair at the end of the program.

Dec. 27, 1922

On Dec. 27, 1922, a speaker reassured the members of the Knoxville Daughters of the American Revolution that the "flapper" was just a fad.

Flappers — young women who flaunted their independence from conventional ideas of a woman's "proper" place by drinking, smoking, wearing short skirts and bobbed hair, riding in jalopies and dancing the Charleston — were a cultural phenomenon of the 1920s. Today historians see them as symbols of an important stage in the liberation of American women. But in their own day, flappers disturbed conservative people, who saw them as a symptom of the breakdown of the traditional way of life.

One of these troubled traditionalists was Mrs. L. S. Gillentine, state regent of the DAR. At a luncheon meeting at the Farragut Hotel on Dec. 27, she criticized not only flappers but the whole modern mentality that encouraged excessive self-gratification. Modern education did not instill character or discipline, she said; and she contrasted contemporary culture with that of the Puritans, who worshipped duty.

The good news, she assured her audience, was that "the flapper is a fashion, not an institution. And the most consoling reflection concerning fashions is that they do change — even though they may leave ugly traces in passing, such as bobbed heads slowly growing bobless."

Dec. 28, 1931

When Knoxville's Holy Ghost Roman Catholic Church was opened on the morning of Dec. 28, 1931, officials were appalled to find that the altar had been desecrated.

It was not the work of cranks or fanatics, however, but of burglars. The thieves had smashed through a marble door in the center of the altar and had removed and carried off a 100-pound safe, presumably believing that it contained marketable valuables. But, as the Rev. Father Cunningham, pastor of the church, explained to a News-Sentinel reporter, the safe contained only articles of the sacrament — precious to the church, but of little material value.

There was good news the very next day, however, when a boy playing in a vacant lot near the church found the safe. It had been forced open but its contents were intact. "I thank God with all my heart," Father Cunningham said. "We consider it wonderful that nothing had been damaged." He also thanked the newspapers, whose front-page stories on the religious significance of the stolen items may have persuaded the thief to abandon the safe. And, with tears in his eyes, he thanked the boy who found the safe and put a $5 bill in his hand.

Dec. 29, 1935

On Dec. 29, 1935, a retiring Knoxville judge offered some thoughts on the criminal justice system.

The News-Sentinel that day published a long, thoughtful article by Robert P. Williams, who was stepping down after 16 years as city judge. In it he set forth his guiding principles. The first was "to establish a court of justice tempered with mercy.

"The average prisoner who gets into a police court," the judge explained, "never has a chance because he belongs to the poorer class of blacks or whites. They have no influential friends to help them. . . . In punishing an offender . . . we do not punish the offender so much as his family at home. Money paid out for bond fees and fines means privations for the wife and babies."

Juvenile delinquency was a particular concern of the judge. "The demand for money for picture shows, gasoline and other such things is causing crime among the youth. Many start out by stealing a radiator cap to get picture show money. . . . As they grow older they become bolder and more desperate."

Mercy, not vengeance, was the answer, according to the judge. "Any youth convicted of his first petty crime should be paroled. Young fellows sent to the pen will return to the pen."

Dec. 30, 1926

On Dec. 30, 1926, University of Tennessee officials spoke out on the issue of college students and automobiles.

The topic was in the news because the University of Illinois had recently banned the use of cars by students. Illinois's dean of Liberal Arts called the automobile "an instrument of distraction . . . an accelerator attachment for social irresponsibilities."

On Dec. 30, The Knoxville News-Sentinel asked UT officials to comment. President Harcourt Morgan replied that "we have escaped the evil here, only a very, very small percentage of our students owning their own automobiles. . . . The small number of students that own cars cannot affect the general scholarship or morals. . . . But it is possible that conditions will make it a problem in a very few years."

Dean J. D. Hoskins was more opinionated. "If student ownership of automobiles were to become a prevalent practice here," he said, "the student grades would certainly show a decided difference, and the problem would have to be faced squarely. The idea that a college student has a real need for a car is simply ridiculous."

Dean Harriet Greve noted a practical problem. A ban on cars, she said, "would be hard to enforce on account of the number of car renting systems close to universities now."

Dec. 31, 1863

Knoxville had a famous visitor on Dec. 31, 1863: Gen. Ulysses S. Grant.

Grant, the commander of Union forces in Tennessee at that time, was on an inspection tour as part of his planning for the upcoming spring campaigns.

He arrived in Knoxville on Dec. 31 and stayed for several days. Then he went on to Cumberland Gap and other points, but made Knoxville his base during the two weeks he was in East Tennessee.

While in Knoxville, Grant stayed at the home of William Henry Sneed on the corner of Market and Cumberland. The Sneed family, prominent southern sympathizers, had been evicted when Union troops occupied Knoxville the previous September. The house became the headquarters of the occupation forces in Knoxville.

Before leaving town, Grant visited Judge Oliver P. Temple, a leading unionist, and discussed military strategy. He also stopped at the home of another well-known unionist, newspaper editor William G. Brownlow.

Ulysses S. Grant, lower left, at Lookout Mountain during his visit to East Tennessee

Index